Psychoanalysis for
Intersectional Humanity

I0095125

Psychoanalysis for Intersectional Humanity considers both the vast realm of sexual diversities emerging under capitalism and outlines what a psychoanalytic clinic that considers these diversities should be like.

Ricardo Espinoza Lolas explores these themes hand in hand with the Marquis de Sade, exploring the monstrous side of our existence – not as a negative aspect of humanity, but as a part of us that strives for a freer and more inclusive life. Espinoza Lolas explores aspects of psychoanalysis, feminism, critical theory, philosophy, history, politics and the arts in considering how human determination can be torn from ego and neurosis. The book concludes with a disarticulation of the categories of neurosis, psychosis and perversion of psychoanalysis and the suggestion of a new clinic and a new politics.

Psychoanalysis for Intersectional Humanity will be of great interest to psychoanalysts in practice and in training, Lacanian clinicians and scholars of psychoanalytic studies, philosophy and critical theory.

Ricardo Espinoza Lolas is an academic, writer, critical theorist and philosopher based in Chile. He is Professor of History of Contemporary Philosophy at the Pontificia Universidad Católica de Valparaíso and a member of the Centre for Philosophy and Critical Thought at Goldsmiths, University of London, UK. His previous books have been published internationally.

The Lines of the Symbolic in Psychoanalysis Series
Series Editor:
Ian Parker, Manchester Psychoanalytic Matrix

Psychoanalytic clinical and theoretical work is always embedded in specific linguistic and cultural contexts and carries their traces, traces which this series attends to in its focus on multiple contradictory and antagonistic 'lines of the Symbolic'. This series takes its cue from Lacan's psychoanalytic work on three registers of human experience, the Symbolic, the Imaginary and the Real, and employs this distinctive understanding of cultural, communication and embodiment to link with other traditions of cultural, clinical and theoretical practice beyond the Lacanian symbolic universe. The Lines of the Symbolic in Psychoanalysis Series provides a reflexive reworking of theoretical and practical issues, translating psychoanalytic writing from different contexts, grounding that work in the specific histories and politics that provide the conditions of possibility for its descriptions and interventions to function. The series makes connections between different cultural and disciplinary sites in which psychoanalysis operates, questioning the idea that there could be one single correct reading and application of Lacan. Its authors trace their own path, their own line through the Symbolic, situating psychoanalysis in relation to debates which intersect with Lacanian work, explicating it, extending it and challenging it.

Psychoanalysis and the New Rhetoric
Freud, Burke, Lacan, and Philosophy's Other Scenes
Daniel Adleman and Chris Vanderwees

Psychoanalysis and the Small Screen
The Year the Cinemas Closed
Edited by Carol Owens and Sarah Meehan O'Callaghan

Speculating on the Edge of Psychoanalysis
Rings and Voids
Pablo Lerner

A Lacanian Conception of Populism
Society Does Not Exist
Timothy Appleton

For more information about the series, please visit: https://www.routledge.com/The-Lines-of-the-Symbolic-in-Psychoanalysis-Series/book-series/KARNLOS

Psychoanalysis for Intersectional Humanity

Sade Reloaded

Ricardo Espinoza Lolas

Routledge
Taylor & Francis Group

LONDON AND NEW YORK

Designed cover image: Herbert Spencer

First published 2024
by Routledge
4 Park Square, Milton Park, Abingdon, Oxon OX14 4RN

and by Routledge
605 Third Avenue, New York, NY 10158

Routledge is an imprint of the Taylor & Francis Group, an informa business

© 2024 Ricardo Espinoza Lolas

The right of Ricardo Espinoza Lolas to be identified as author of this work has been asserted in accordance with sections 77 and 78 of the Copyright, Designs and Patents Act 1988.

All rights reserved. No part of this book may be reprinted or reproduced or utilised in any form or by any electronic, mechanical, or other means, now known or hereafter invented, including photocopying and recording, or in any information storage or retrieval system, without permission in writing from the publishers.

Trademark notice: Product or corporate names may be trademarks or registered trademarks, and are used only for identification and explanation without intent to infringe.

British Library Cataloguing-in-Publication Data
A catalogue record for this book is available from the British Library

Library of Congress Cataloging-in-Publication Data
Names: Espinoza Lolas, Ricardo A., author.
Title: Psychoanalysis for intersectional humanity: Sade reloaded / Ricardo Espinoza Lolas.
Description: Abingdon, Oxon; New York, NY: Routledge, 2024. | Includes bibliographical references and index. |
Identifiers: LCCN 2023014802 (print) | LCCN 2023014803 (ebook) | ISBN 9781032440408 (hardback) | ISBN 9781032440392 (paperback) | ISBN 9781003370116 (ebook)
Subjects: LCSH: Psychoanalysis. | Critical theory. | Sexuality. | Lacan, Jacques, 1901–1981. | Sade, marquis de, 1740–1814.
Classification: LCC BF173 .E675 2024 (print) | LCC BF173 (ebook) | DDC 150.19/5—dc23/eng/20230425
LC record available at https://lccn.loc.gov/2023014802
LC ebook record available at https://lccn.loc.gov/2023014803

ISBN: 978-1-032-44040-8 (hbk)
ISBN: 978-1-032-44039-2 (pbk)
ISBN: 978-1-003-37011-6 (ebk)

DOI: 10.4324/9781003370116

Typeset in Times New Roman
by codeMantra

To Alfredo Aroca, my only therapist... Thank you!

Contents

Series preface

There are many monsters in the labyrinthine structure of psychoanalysis, queer forms that are felt by some to be deep threats, and it is one of the tasks of clinical work to track down these monsters and face them. We need guides and theoretical threads from outside psychoanalysis to detect and weave together a really queer narrative for psychoanalysis in which to contain and frame and then unshackle and free such monsters. They are, this book shows us, cultural-historical forms given a stark socio-political reality for us in the symbolic realm in which we become human, and inhuman, to ourselves and others.

Our "queer human times", as Ricardo Espinoza Lolas describes them in this book, are riven with contradiction, with the accretion of symbolic categories concerning what is monstrous poured into psychoanalysis so that debates about sexuality and freedom inside the discipline are reduced to a constellation of "clinical structures" in which "perversion" has pride of place, and operate as the place of deep fear and shame for practitioners. The Marquis de Sade elaborates what "perversion" looks like, it would seem, but those claims, and what are made of those claims in the psychoanalytic literature, need to be read very carefully, both carefully and provocatively.

You will find provocation aplenty in this book, with exploration of monstrosity and queer potentiality present in a multitude of art forms and theoretical innovations. This is at a time when reactionary forms of argumentation around the supposed underlying nature of sexuality and gender are becoming more apparent inside so many psychoanalytic institutions as well as in the symbolic sphere which sustains them. Here is an argument for turning our attention to culture in order to begin to extricate ourselves from the most miserable and wretched iterations of capitalist logic.

This book shows us that what is most apparently sadistic about psychoanalysis can, in the hands of the master of the dialectic, Hegel, be re-imagined in a labyrinth as a playground, and so there can be some kind of release from the depths of a Dionysian spirit of queer potentiality that redeems our work and forms of psychoanalytic social critique. We imagine such things and suffer them and our fantasies are circumscribed by their presence. The truth of the book, that we all were always queer, is realised again and again in the course of the main text, and then made real in the closing intervention by Jorge Nico Reitter.

Psychoanalytic clinical and theoretical work circulates through multiple inter-secting antagonistic symbolic universes. This series opens connections between different cultural sites in which Lacanian work has developed in distinctive ways, in forms of work that question the idea that there could be single correct reading and application. The Lines of the Symbolic in Psychoanalysis series provides a reflexive reworking of psychoanalysis that transmits Lacanian writing from around the world, steering a course between the temptations of a metalanguage and imagi-nary reduction, between the claim to provide a god's-eye view of psychoanalysis and the idea that psychoanalysis must everywhere be the same. And the elaboration of psychoanalysis in the symbolic here grounds its theory and practice in the his-tory and politics of the work in a variety of interventions that touch the Real.

Ian Parker
Manchester Psychoanalytic Matrix

Introduction

Why a new psychoanalytic clinic and philosophy for queer human times?

The answer to this question can be found in these eight chapters that you will read below and in the epilogue of the prominent queer psychoanalyst Jorge Nico Reitter, author of *Heteronormativity and Psychoanalysis. Oedipus Gay* (Routledge, 2022). And each one of them shows, from a certain perspective, the new human that has emerged in these times, but that has always been present in some way throughout history; and which today will no longer stop its deployment, because it cannot be imprisoned in any labyrinth, because this subjectivity is here to stay. And this human, who we could simply call "queer", needs a philosophical theory that is up to the task of reflecting on what is the real thing that constitutes ones and Others in the midst of things; and, at the same time, for a clinical practice that can support us and, in doing so, cures the pain that in these times of brutal Capitalism doesn't let us live and plunges us into depression and the accelerated immediacy of the logic of capital itself.

This book's chapters progress holding the hand of the mythical Marquis de Sade, as a fundamental character, because the Marquis allows us to rethink what is human beyond empty and stale definitions that are currently not enough, quite the contrary, they only cover up human beings and try to classify them in order to dominate them in the very machinery of capital and its collateral expressions such as colonialism and patriarchy. Sade is always present in the book, moving in and out of it, and in this the psychoanalysts "feared and cursed" perversion is updated in another way, breaking psychoanalysis from the inside from its beginnings with Freud (and shows us the importance of Klein and Winnicott and, especially, of the second Lacan, the one of the Real); and, at the same time, it requires philosophy to reflect, in our material history, on the very freedom that constitutes us, even if it is painful and causes panic to the human animal, but only from freedom is the Real shown in what it is, its radical contingency, finiteness and meaninglessness. And thus, with freedom, we can deal in a more radical way with what we are as humans, with what we should be as such and with how we could articulate ourselves socially and politically.

Sade operates in the book as the one who makes explicit the logics that work in psychoanalysis and philosophy (also in feminism of identity and essence); and, for the same reason, Sade is the one who can take us to the depths of what we are at

DOI: 10.4324/9781003370116-1

a material historical level: from the old god Dionysus to the present Žižek, Butler, Preciado, taking in giants like Hegel and Nietzsche in deep dialogue with Freud and Lacan, without neglecting Klein and Winnicott and their shift in the clinical practice itself, namely, from a neurosis clinic established by Freud to Winnicott's clinic of psychosis. And what I propose is that clinical practice itself must transition today to a more radical version; that is, a clinical practice of "monsters", of differentials, of "perverts", of those who transit, of those who mix, of "queers" in these current times. And to analyze this new clinical practice and philosophy of how we happen to be "monsters", as said since ancient times, or "perverse" in classical psychoanalysis or "queer" using the terminology of Anzaldúa, Butler and other feminists, we expose what we are radically working in each chapter of the book with different aesthetic and thinking supports: from Sarah Kane's theatre, Bowie's songs, Goya's engravings, Sophocles' tragedies, Sacher-Masoch's books, Buñuel's, Wenders' and Haneke's films, the texts of Shelley, Artaud and Büchner, Hölderlin's poems, Ligeti's music, Winnicott's psychoanalysis of Margaret Liddell, Walter Otto's philology, the analysis of the human from the Slovenian School, Deleuze's interpretive nuances, Iwan Bloch's sexology, the Lacanian Real, etc. And so, through these supports, we are pointing to the queer in us which can never be categorized, because it would mean to stop thinking and experiencing our own contingency, and, furthermore, this is so because we are inherently prior to a definition that encloses us in an epistemological and ontological totality.

The first chapter immerses us in that monstrous quality, that queer thing, which we are and that psychoanalysis still doesn't know how to face even in our times; it is enough to think about everything that Jacques-Alain Miller points out in these times against queer theory and, especially, against Butler. And for this reason, we dive radically into psychoanalysis and how it structures the psychic apparatus, which has been promoted since Freud, as neurosis, psychosis and perversion. And then this structure is dismantled thanks to the light shed by Preciado, Deleuze, Hegel and, especially, with the great English playwright Sarah Kane and her *In-Yer-Face* theatre. And from there we can see the "monster" that we really are and we no longer allow ourselves to be trapped by the naturalized representation of the human that is simply just not enough. And which causes so much discomfort and disease and that also leaves us submerged, living in a labyrinth of violence among ourselves.

The second chapter is a text written with great subtlety and intimacy; and exposes a fundamental human temperament, namely, our ability to wait: waiting as a name that expresses what is most characteristic of each one of us. And this waiting condition has radically accelerated with the COVID-19 pandemic. And, now, we see much more radical humans than classic neurotics, they rather cross the limit of neurosis and thus the wait for psychosis is produced, a wait against the Real itself. And so, with Wenders and his marvellous film *Paris, Texas* (1984) we try to understand that psychotic waiting and, in this way, we talk about an operative psychosis that allows us to transgress what has been imposed on us as the obvious and in a thoughtless way, ahistorical and without any materiality. And if we keep waiting, it is possible that the necessary changes will take place in each individual and thus, in society itself. Only in an expectation that is maintained as such, can we cope with this neurotic life in which we live all day in the immediacy of the symbolic, that is, Capitalism. And only in this waiting can the naturalized limit of one and all be perverted: it is the Real itself that makes its arrival in us. And there, in this game with the Real, another symbolization opens up giving us a more pleasant way of life with the Other.

In the third chapter, through the mythical song of the 1960s, entitled *Space Oddity* (1969) and written by David Bowie for the Apollo XI moon landing (1969), and in light of Kubrick and his great metaphysical work of *2001: A Space Odyssey* (1968), I show how art allows us to understand what is human in the midst of a certain era and how it expresses what we are, that is, delirious people who do not want to be locked up in current Capitalism, nor in the factory of success and recognition in the market, but that what we seek is simply to be free and creators of our own values. And in this way, love ourselves and connect with other bodies. Bowie's song expresses what we were living 50 years ago and there is no ideology that can silence us; it's about releasing ourselves of every foundation that wants to tie us to some "control center" and that means to determine our lives. Bowie expresses us, that Dionysian trait, of being walkers, dancers and stepping out of every comfort zone and living without any anchor point, neither of the self, even less from the state or nation, or anything related to genre. Through Bowie we pervert all the limits that have been imposed on us and so freedom happens to us in the midst of the very materiality of life and despite Capitalism itself.

In the fourth chapter, through Sophocles and his *Antigone* (5th century BC), I delve into ancient Greece, before Plato and Aristotle, and from it arises a great vision of the deinón as an expression not only of the human but also of the drunk dancing god, that is, of Dionysus: an initial way of naming the Real. And through this we can understand, from our times, that the Dionysian vision of the world expressed a "queer" vision of the Greek world, one which is later radicalized by Euripides in his *Bacchae*. And this has not been remarked upon by scholars of Greek antiquity: philologists, philosophers, historians, aesthetes, etc. For the Greeks, both the Real and the human are not trapped by the essentialist signifier of gender, and even less so by the masculine gender: the gods were not masculine, but merely feminine, in the sense that is, that they were open in themselves. The gods as well as the Real express that Dionysian life-death tension that is the very differential of the human in the midst of the world, that is deinón and how the Real is understood. And then we can see that it is Aristotle himself who, unable to understand this movement of things, of the vegetative, of the animal, of the human, of the gods, calls "monster" what is not in what it should be. "Monster" is the negative Aristotelian name for what is positively queer today, namely, that very movement of all things making them transit and in which their life-death takes place.

The fifth chapter points out how the Slovenian or Ljubljana School is today the heir to the best of Hegel's thought, it has passed through Lacan's psychoanalysis, and allows us to understand a human up for the challenge; very different from other schools of thought such as those of Essex or Frankfurt where sexuation and with it a theory of the Real is not developed from the contingent itself. And so we encounter its great thinkers such as Žižek, Zupančič, Dolar and others, reflecting the human from Lacan's own formulas of sexuation (*On Feminine Sexuality, the Limits of Love and Knowledge: The Seminar of Jacques Lacan*, Book XX, Encore, 1972–1973), however, the work by the Slovenians, although very novel, always starts from a certain structural and, at the same time, Kantian trait (a Real with something of the "thing in itself"), which keeps the richness of Hegel's own thought hidden, a line of thought with a plasticity that makes us understand this Dionysian human at the same time as: gay, trans, abject, monstrous, mestizo, emancipator, in a word, queer. And that is why Žižek is permanently attempting to find that human that escapes him, because his theoretical starting point prevents him from doing so and he is always late to find the monstrous queer.

The sixth chapter is focused on the analysis of Lacan's Real and we examine the last teaching of the French thinker-psychoanalyst and in it his departure from the symbolic (because the symbolic is no longer enough for the challenges of the times) and this results in Lacan's radical deepening of the feminine; and from this we can outline a certain interpretation of trans, of queer, of the human in present times in this last thought. However, this Lacanian Real always carries within itself something of a "rock", something Kantian, which doesn't allow us to free ourselves from everything that torments us and causes so much pain to us queers and to all of us in these times of Capitalism. Lacanian theory (Lacan died in 1981 leaving everything unfinished), and so his clinic approach can't express the singularities, the human monstrosities we are. That is to say, it can't listen to that other as an Other who perverts all limits and transgresses them. This is why this chapter is a reckoning with the best of Lacan and, at the same time, it shows what his thinking makes possible in the current debate. And, for this reason, it is essential to immerse ourselves in what he understood as the Real to accommodate the sexual, mortal and historical that we are along with the Others that constitute us.

The seventh chapter is a crucial text for the current debate on the human, because I point out how Butler and Žižek, the great thinkers of the human of these times, are two unilateral faces of Hegel; and for this very reason they are faces that cannot give a full account of what happens to each one of us, since their one-sidedness prevents them from giving a more complete answer. It is not that the human, as Butler thinks, in light of the *Phenomenology of Spirit*, is an expression of history, but neither is the human a structuring, as Žižek thinks, that from the science of logic can make us understand our present, for example, as queer. We are rather differential structures, that is, dynamic, sexual, finite, and historical structures articulated among themselves and along the Other par excellence, that is, our own void of material meaning which constitutes our own bodies, but always at a radical distance from the Other in order to be, necessarily, with the Other.

And finally, in the eighth and final chapter of the book, also its conclusion, although a conclusion that wants to conclude and close something of the human is impossible. And here the psychoanalytic categories of neurosis, psychosis and perversion, which have been present throughout the book, are exposed again, and they are dismantled by both Goya's engravings and a Hegel more radical than Sade himself. And here we find a Hegel that allows us to read the queer, how monstrous we are, in a radical way; and Sade himself now appears as an aged writer unable to give an account of ourselves. Sade turned into a rationalist child who liked to play, to scare the bourgeoisie of his time. And it makes clear that the human is, in itself, dynamic and that is how it is structured in a precarious and contingent way; and if a psychoanalytic category had to be chosen as the most human, it would be that of perversion. This is what Hegel radically proposes and, because of that, he is the true Sade, it expresses an emancipation of the human that allows us to understand our present hand in hand, for example, with Anzaldúa and the intersection, of a new clinical practice closer to Winnicott and a policy of "loving" beyond the neurotic as in Haneke.

The Epilogue by Jorge Nico Reitter is a beautiful climax because it confronts the criticism made in the book to the core of psychoanalysis and tries to show that a new type of clinical practice is possible: one of monsters, that is, of queers. And it is what he himself does at the level of praxis as well as in the theoretical level with his books and writings. And in this he points out that queer, as a constituent of the human, indicates something more radical and that "bourgeois" psychoanalysis (as Reitter calls it), which is criticized in the book, is a psychoanalysis that not only arrives late to the cure, but cannot find the Dionysian psychoanalysis that is proposed. And this current psychoanalysis resists the Dionysian. And it is so, because what is proposed in the book is a cure without a neurotic device, that is, without any Christianity and it no longer operates with anything associated with a fault or a debt, but here a Dionysian healing device is shown that is good for the Other and it invites him to dance and to come out of that neurosis that has made him sick by escaping the labyrinth that has enclosed him. And, finally, Reitter realizes that the ancient Greek term deinón is nothing less than a name for the Real that becomes very important for what happens to us today and expresses the freedom in which we live in the very finiteness of our existence.

This book, in short, is an invitation to rethink what we are in a critical dialogue with psychoanalysis, critical theory, feminism, philosophy and contemporary aesthetics. And, thus, to be able to build a clinical theory for these times that soothes the pain in each one of us and which is able to show a theory of the Real that accounts for the human, the political, and how today we can love each other in times of so much capitalist stupidity that sometimes we get lost in the labyrinth of ourselves and our most primeval fears, that is, our mortality.

1

The roaring monster is hunting us down to disturb us

After having intense sex for hours in the night with the woman I love, I fell asleep, when I woke up I started thinking, as I'm not a smoker, I think obsessively... and I feel somewhat ill at ease about what's happened, but it gives me pleasure, it's as if during the night I crossed the line... or was it she who made me cross it?... or was it me who willingly crossed it as I submitted to her will?... or did she cross it with me?... or was it the two of us who crossed it together?... I don't know; I doubt, I despair, I worry... am I becoming perverse?... was it love or an "unconscious" pact of submission between us two?... or is that today also part of love?... or has it always been?... It is interesting to remember what young Hegel called love between an individual and another in Frankfurt (1797/1798)[1] later, much older, he calls it in Jena (1807): the struggle for life or death between, precisely, one individual and another, between both...

But the monster is always silent and lies in wait for us; it hunts us down through day and night, there is no sea, mountain range or mass of ice that can stop it; he drives us and befalls us. A nameless monster who is later given the name of its own creator father, as it happens with every son, that is, a parricide: every son kills his father and takes his name: Frankenstein. And the monster finally spoke:

> But it is true that I am a wretch. I have murdered the lovely and the helpless; I have strangled the innocents as they slept and grasped to death his throat who never injured me or any other living thing. I have devoted my creator, the select specimen of all that is worthy of love and admiration among men, to misery; I have pursued him even to that irremediable ruin. There he lies, white and cold in death.[2]

Psychoanalysis was born, explicitly, between 1894 and 1900, as a "psychic analysis",[3] as a necessity of doctors themselves, in a European Victorian capitalist world, a sort of totality that structured it in a radical way, like all totality by the way, and not to mention the totality of our present; that totality of the European 19th century of the Germanic world weighs on the human, crushes it, traumatically structures it in its singularity in a pain that won't abandon it; the human condition can't bear anymore its anguish, in its inhibition, in its symptom and which literally caused

DOI: 10.4324/9781003370116-2

illness not only on the bourgeoisie, but on everyone (especially the most deprived, the proletariat, to put in Marxist language): although the bourgeoisie has greater access to psychoanalysis and this is evident today, either because of the high cost of the session, or because of the very methodology of the couch and the listening-speaking, although now, thanks to the pandemic, clinical practice is being democratized via the virtual medium. And this "disease", calling it by the brutal name common at the time[4] (but Lacan in the full swing of the 1970s was still treating neurotics as ill individuals), manifested itself not only as the simple disturbing dream of a daughter who dreams she symbolically has sexual relations with her father to the point of tremendous physical and melancholic pain that can lead her to suicide or even make her hallucinate like a schizophrenic and attack herself or others; this disease, which was apparently new at the end of the 19th century, could be literally disabling to live with, that is, waking up in the morning and not having the will to live, that is, to work and love, as Freud would say (as a good European) in 1898:

> It is quite true that anyone who, owing to sexual noxae, has made himself disposed to neurasthenia, tolerates intellectual work and psychical exigencies of life badly, but no one ever becomes neurotic through work or excitement alone (…) they have fallen ill not because they have tried to carry out duties which are in fact easily performed by a civilized brain, but because all the while, they have been grossly neglecting and damaging their sexual life.[5]

This new disease was called neurosis and, in particular, it was a radical type of disease, which had been named for years, unfairly, from the feminine as: hysteria (from the Greek *histeron*: uterus), because sexual desire in women looked horrendous and that was condemned for centuries (even now);[6] that's why, among other reasons, young Freud (1896)[7] in order to annoy the medical scientific community presents the case of the hysterical man (before the Vienna Medical Society), a kind of monster, and he breaks from the outset a sort of erroneous and horrific naturalization of woman (and, therefore, of man):

> Gentlemen, when on October 15, I had the honor of claiming your attention to a short report on Charcot's recent work in the field of male hysteria, I was challenged by my respected teacher, Hofrat Professor Meynert, to present before the society some cases in which the somatic indications – the 'hysterical stigmata' by which Charcot characterizes this neurosis (...) Before beginning my demonstration, I will merely remark that I am far from thinking that what I am showing you is a rare or peculiar case. On the contrary, I regard as a very ordinary case of frequent occurrence, though one which may often be overlooked.[8]

Psychoanalysis dealt in general with neurosis, and with hysteria in particular, since it took charge of the ancient women who became "witches"[9] by letting the "demon" inside their bodies (although it has always been present in psychoanalysis: obsession, the older Lacan dealt with it in a very novel way, because he was obsessive);[10]

and very little about psychosis (Freud did not formally treat it; he did it as a young doctor, but not as a psychoanalyst), even less perversion, although it was Freud who sketched its key concepts in an attempt to respond to narcissism in his early *Three Essays on the Theory of Sexuality* of 1905, especially in Essay I: "Sexual aberrations".[11] And today, in full swing of the 21st century, we no longer live in the times of that Victorian bourgeois Capitalism (Marx radically fought against that form of Capitalism and hence the problem of human alienation),[12] instead we live in a radically voracious one that I call messed up militarized landed Capitalism which can be considered as the Labyrinth of Capitalism (which is no longer about an alienation from the true human being, Aristotle again, in the 19th century, but about a global human being as the creator of capital, at its service and happily enjoying it without limits);[13] and it is a Capitalism that occurs everywhere and, in some way, structures everyone's unconscious.

The unconscious (*Das Unwebusste*), if there is one, is not something that is underneath something, nor is it hidden, neither behind or above, it has nothing substantial (all that epistemology and ontology of the unconscious is fundamentally wrong; and that is why it must be abandoned, and soon); the unconscious is not objectlike. The unconscious is our own physical driven body of a non-specific nature open in the midst of the materiality of things; and especially always keeping up with the times. The older Lacan says categorically, in *Seminar 23: the sinthome* (1975–1976), that the drive is: "the echo in the body of the fact that there is a saying"[14] The range of the Real is expressed in that echo (Freud and Lacan go hand in hand). If it is so, the unconscious does not work as a vessel for anything, it is not a container, but rather is itself sexualized because we move in and by that drive; it is the human essence (this was very clear to Iwan Bloch, the sexologist who edited Sade, as we will see, from whom Freud learned very much). And Freud can build, from this structural fact that structures the unconscious, his way of seeing aberrations in the human: "The fact of the existence of sexual needs in human beings and animals is expressed in biology by the assumption of a 'sexual instinct', on the analogy of the instinct of nutrition, that is of hunger.";[15] evidently it's an aberration with respect to a first analogy, namely, the idealised human from the Victorian European (that human like Da Vinci, city of Urbino, that Greek world from Winckelmann, etc.); it is a "deformation" of that idealized-historical form. In his essay on aberrations, Freud as a new Sade, just as rationalist as the French and Aristotelian (both faithful to the adaptation of shape with matter starting from the shape):

> The popular view of the sexual instinct is beautifully reflected in the poetic fable which tells how the original human beings -man and woman- and how these are always striving to unite again in love. It comes as a great surprise therefore to learn that there are men whose sexual object is a man and not a woman, and women whose sexual object is a woman and not a man. People of this kind are described as having 'contrary sexual feelings', or better, as being 'inverts', and the fact is described as 'inversion'. The number of such people is very considerable, though there are difficulties in establishing it precisely.[16]

And Freud behaves like the later Aristotle of the *Reproduction of Animals* that we will examine later; it is the old *homoisis* of Aristotle, the *adequatio* of Saint Thomas, the *Richtigkeit* of Leibniz, etc., which is updated at the beginning of the 20th century. One could say where Aristotle sees "monsters" Freud will see "inverts" (the perverse). That *Essay I*, which is divided into seven parts, will provide enough of the future taxonomy to create the personality structure called perversion. And it is important to note that Freud used the "conservative manual" of the physician Richard von Krafft-Ebing titled *Psychopathy Sexualis* of 1869; a text that became a classic. From that book come such terms, as viewed from the perverse action: sadism, masochism, fetishism, exhibitionism; and of perversion viewed from its object: homosexuality, pedophilia, gerontophilia, bestiality and autoeroticism. And Freud clearly follows it.

And what if that binary structure of the psychic apparatus was not so, in order for the neurotic to function, for it not to get sick or become abject or insane? And what if the material is something that in itself carries a dynamic differential inside (Heraclitus, Hegel, Marx, Nietzsche, Klein, etc.). And if to that sexualization of the unconscious, namely, in the formal and structural aspects of oneself, we add its own mortality, its expiry time, its finitude, namely, the unconscious is structurally dynamic, that is, sexed-mortal. The unconscious is mortally sexualized, as, in general, all things seem to be (everything is constituted from *the deinon,* as Sophocles would say, that is, Dionysian, tense, dialectical, contradictory, pulsional). And finally, that mortally sexualized unconscious always operates keeping abreast of the times, because it cannot be any other way. The unconscious is a dynamic structure that in turn recreates itself and is constituted in a non-specific way through time. It is, therefore, a sexualized, mortal and epochal unconscious. Put in another philosophical language, the unconscious is real and it is in time (perhaps the old categories of reality, being and time help us to understand the Lacanian ones of the Real, the Symbolic, the Imaginary). And it is in that epochal Imaginary, where we temporalize ourselves as real beings and open from the outset, this is "monstrous", perverse or whatever we are called. And that temporality of the sexual and mortal unconscious, due to its epochal character, is nurtured and performatively fed by discourse; and today that hegemonic discourse is Capitalism. And that discourse points out that it symbolizes, subjectifies and ideologizes us, it operates immediately as the Real (paraphrasing Nietzsche, it is the last Real, an "as if" of the Real), that life is this and not something else; it is a Real with no deepness and it connects and fuses us, in its first opportunity (which is never the first), with the matrix of mortal sexuality through the logics of power and in there the human today moves between perversion and psychosis in order to energize our complicit neurosis and move it, scratch it, brush it from within (just as Bacon worked with his anti-face skull-heads). Ricardo Saiegh, psychoanalyst, says it very clearly in the Seminar titled *Existential Weaving* and he says it about the Nazis, Hitler, the concentration camps:

> the breeding ground for these monstrosities is not necessarily perversion, which is the most comfortable to suppose, a pervert becomes more perverse

and becomes a murderer, strictly when Hannah Arendt analyzes the characteristics of these people she sees that they have many traits of being miserable, mean, cowardly, mediocre; it means that what happens in this oedipal plot, if the son hates lies, hypocrisy, cynicism in the oedipal bond, that is not without consequences, it is what Freud calls in *Unglauben*, not believing it, that's when a breakdown occurs in the generational transmission because someone could hardly want to transmit to their children what they think has been the lie in their parents' relationship, so it is interesting to see that the breeding ground has to do with cowardice, with the direction of the neurotics, which is the general thing, what abounds on the market... that Hitler had the stupidities of a narcissistic neurotic, that things hadn't gone well for him: nor as a student, or as an athlete, nor as anything... and one says my God that can justify... yes, justify those monstrosities.[17]

And psychosis tries to get us out of neurosis (and the complicit evils of the horror of being in this Capitalism) and perversion to challenge and transgress it. And in this game of our lives, the present is no longer that of neurosis, but rather it collapsed and became a past that should be overcome. And so, perversion takes action on the matters of today.

Let's not forget that the unconscious is written in German as *das Unbewusste* (a term already used before Freud,[18] for example, by Schelling and his brilliant book *Philosophical Investigations into the Essence of Human Freedom* from 1809 (a book that Freud surely did not read and that would have been useful to him and that traces its roots back to Jakob Böhme)[19] and in a "similar" way to that of Freud, but with a philosophical vision that indicates a reality's certain way of being. What's interesting about the term is that it has nothing to do with consciousness (*cum-scientia* from the Latin) because it does not indicate any knowledge that is articulated from a totality, it is not a unity in the whole, least of all in God (which was so typical in the Middle Ages). In the German term you hear and see literally *wissen*, that is, knowledge. A knowledge that indicates a point of view and a way of living, very similar to the *sophía* of the Greeks (Heraclitus and Aristotle are essential to understand *sophía*). It is a living being, I would say, that illuminates, radiates, that is open, but that here is built with the past *wusst*, that is, it indicates a sort of interior time and one of the past that constitutes us, our present. And that *wusst* is built with that particle *be*, that is, outside, it comes out, it becomes accusative, they are in the middle of the world, of things illuminating (by the way, because things are in it). And that *Bewusste* (which is not yet *Bewusstsein* to really be something, but is its own hole of drive) is structured with that radical *Un*. And, to further annoyance, it could be said that the conscious does not exist, it is not symbolizable, logifiable. The conscious has no way to signify in a complete way, because obviously it is a perforation in itself. We are that perforation, that hole, that hole that we illuminate in our temporal mortal finitude. That *Un* indicates the very non-specificity of our own body in the midst of the materiality of things and keeping up with our history.

Cleansed[20] by Sarah Kane expresses what the mature Hegel of 1807 does not make entirely clear, that which showed itself as love when he was young in Frankfurt and then over the years turns, in Jena, into a struggle of life or death: "...The relation of both self-consciousnesses is in this way so constituted that they prove themselves and each other through a life-and-death struggle."[21] When this third play by Kane premiered (April 30, 1998) at the *Royal Court Downstairs Theater* in London it was again a scandal (critics said it felt like a "punch in the stomach"), as it usually happened with the plays of this brilliant young English playwright, one who had a unique and beautiful use of English together with a staging of millimetric precision that jumps out at you and explodes in your own eyes, namely *In-Yer-Face* as coined by Aleks Sierz in 2001.[22] She tells us, through her free verse, the fragmented, mutilated text (provoking an effect of exploding violence), in a non-story, because there are no longer great stories (the story does not exist), of a non-human (several non-humans that do not exist either, the human does not exist, it is an impossible in the middle of an impossible) that as a non-human, a monster, it is shown in its time in relationships of love and destruction; and the same thing happens in a play that is performed not only before oneself, but the play happens "in" oneself beyond all representation; that explains the radicalness of that staging and the behaviour of these actors. Sierz himself describes it like this: "were skeptical of easy solutions to complex problems, refrained from telling people what to do and were aware that ideological plays with big messages were old-fashioned".[23] It is not possible to say what happens to us (it is no longer a great idealized story) but the way in which representation must be avoided in order to not be complicit in it. In the harsh times of the Balkan War, of job insecurity, of human pain and depression, of anarchic resistance via punks and drugs and alcohol, of the daily effects of Thatcherism, etc. And in that harsh world, love is what remains, but at the same time it is what subjects us to that horror, because in that pain we can show how Capitalism beats the shit out of us and at the same time allows us a certain redemption in a radical way. Amelia Howe Kritzer puts it this way: "These works pay special attention to the elements of society usually hidden from public view – unemployed young people, mental patients, drug addicts, homeless vagrants - absent in commercial theatre"[24] In her monstrous way of manifesting what happens through her dramaturgy, Kane allows us to see and feel the horror (love) and take a step in it, but we do not know precisely where, however, we inexorably take a step. *The Guardian* describes it in a radical way: "Kane wrote simply and starkly about the world she saw around her, a world in which violence and love were profoundly entwined, and hope and despair were mirror pictures of each other"[25] Kane, as Mark Fisher did later and Sade himself before him, explicitly exposes the monster we are today and describes it in the midst of the most brutal Capitalism that has ever occurred. We have open wounds in our body and they bleed; and only by scraping that capitalized body, perhaps it is possible to affirm life in some way. It's a "sado-masochistic" love that attacks you in order to heal and redeem you. This is brilliantly displayed by Kane in the 11-minute 1995 short film *Skin* directed by Vincent O'Connell (and it needn't be any minutes longer).[26]

Her work, like that of Büchner, Beckett, Pasolini, Lars von Trier, David Bowie, Nick Cave breaks representation from within, that is, Hegel's mortal enemy: the immediate (so loved by Kant). How did the *Phenomenology of Spirit* and the *Science of Logic* begin their journey? A beginning (*Anfang*) in movement, in a life that tells us that there is no beginning (*Ursprung*) possible, that the representation is a game of the beginning, a false movement, but necessary to see the very operation of movement in movement. "Es ist eine natürliche Vorstellung dass".[27] The problem of representation is its own nature of being the most immediate. It is thinking that things, whatever they are (sexual difference, neurosis, the symbolic, etc.), are like this and not otherwise because they are precisely like that, namely, a natural representation; that which presents itself presents itself reduplicatively, as being all that it is in its mere presentation. In the *Science of Logic* the "Doctrine of Being" begins like this: "Das Seyn ist das unbestimme Unmitellbare."[28]

The being, the famous being, is nothing more than the indeterminate immediate, that is, an initial immediacy, but one that is mediated and that does not know of its own mediation that is operating in its immediacy (it is unconscious to consciousness); and it sees in this a superb beginning,[29] "its absolute beginning". That was the love of young Hegel that later showed its inner truth, that is, a fight for life or death: *Cleansed*: "Voices: Dead, slag / She was having it off with her brother / Weren't he to bender? / fucking user / All cracked up / Shit no / Shit yes / Crack Crack Crack."[30]

Kane at the end of the 20th century points us to what was already present since the beginning of the 19th century, that human beings, sexual relationships, love are and operate as in a concentration camp, in a prison, a bad plot of land, next to the territory of certain confidence as Barthes said: "On Love, the *doxa* produces a structural commitment: it recognizes Love as a good territory, but in this territory there is a bad plot, an abscess of fixation."[31]

There is always the tension of one with another that won't let itself be dominated by a rigid or epochal formulation, it is only a moment of a possibility of determination, but deep down it is not, and history prevails. Hegel is just as brutal as Kane in showing the human in the midst of and "despite" (*trotzdem*, as Nietzsche would say), in his works he never tires of saying it in our eyes, breaking any natural representational game. That natural quality is diluted against the passage of history like the brutality of a staging that places us in the middle of the field of war, the slaughterhouse of life. Hegel called history *Schlachtbank*: the slaughterhouse bank, we will examine it at the end of this book. And that happens because we don't learn anything from history as Žižek would say,[32] following Hegel; only a repetition of the worst happens.[33] And today, in the midst of the 21st century pandemic, the thing explodes in our heads and neurosis no longer accounts for anything, but is part of the capitalist discourse that structures us symbolically, which is a natural representation. What can be done? Lenin asked himself. The question, "what can be done?" has been raised with particular insistence in recent years by the Russian Social Democrats. It is not about choosing a... but about knowing what practical steps we must take on a certain path and how we must take them. It is a system and a plan of practical activity. And it must be admitted that, between us, this problem of character and methods of struggle – fundamental for a practical party – is still unresolved; continues to arouse serious divergence, thereby revealing a regrettable instability and vacillation of ideas.[34] The revolutionary was at stake there: more of the same or transgression, because the other alternative was death, leaving and canceling oneself from this world, or death in life (like a zombie, so typical of today's neurotics),[35] being part of the Labyrinth of Capitalism. Where to start the revolutionary movement? Well, we must transgress what we are told is so and does not change in order to overcome the "Gatopardism" of capitalist subjectivity.

And a certain psychoanalyst, not only heterosexual, patriarchal, neutral, but especially capitalist and neurotic, doesn't know very well what to do with today's human, if he never knew about love before because he denies it (from his model closed on the self, there is no Other that constitutes you) and, furthermore, he must not tell that truth, the impossibility of love, of the sexual act, of the sexual relationship, etc. to his analysand, because that leads him, to put it ironically, to an annoying problem beyond the patient: the analytic clinic itself can fail and that the analysand doesn't get access to the analysis (if it is impossible, why go to the analyst?). Lacan already said it this way to his analysts in the unpublished *Seminar 14: The Logic of the Ghost* (1966–1967):

> I would efface what I said about the "great secret" as being that there is no sexual act, precisely by the fact, that it is not a great secret! That it is obvious, that the unconscious ceaselessly cries it at the top of its voice and that this indeed is why psychoanalysts say: "Let us close its mouth when it says that, because if we repeat it along with it, people will no longer seek us out![36]

And why does he have to go to that meeting? Why this dogmatic truth? Why analysis? Why analysts in times of Capitalism? And why analysts and analysis if we are transgressors? And what if we all are and live and realize that impossibility in what is impossible under that categorical structure? And what if we are monsters, nothing more than monsters and, therefore, we love? Lacan already realized in that same *Seminar 14* that perversion does not comply with that "truth":

> This is well designed to make us say that, as regards the way in which it emerged in our experience, the phantasy has the characteristics of the experimental aspect, of a foreign body (...) That we should have been lead – this by reason of a veritable theoretical bridge in Freud – to sense this firm meaning, is related to something else, much more developable, much richer in virtualities, which is called properly speaking perversion. Perversion, then, I said, is something which is articulated, is presented, as a proper way into the difficulty which is generated, let us say: by the project – and you should put this word in inverted commas, namely, that it is only analogical here; I am bringing it in as a reference to a discourse other than my own – the putting in question, to be more exact, which is situated in the angle between these two terms. There is no..., there is only... something of the sexual act, ... the sexual act (il n''y a pas..., il n''y a que..., d''acte sexuel... l''acte sexuel)".[37]

The famous "scar" of *A Child is being Beaten* of 1919 that Freud[38] sees in the Oedipus complex, makes Lacan think of perversion as an exit or I would say as something prior to neurosis, inscribed into the Oedipus itself and which will not leave it alone.

But the analyst now, too, does not know how to carry out his practice without selling himself, as merchandise, to the normalizing capitalist market of the usual neurotic (that accomplice of the system who is always against the perverse and psychotic; said in that old homogeneous language). And besides, he doesn't know what to do with the Other that structures the human, another way for its jouissance and thus in its own position in life (for example, beyond the sexual difference so dear to Oedipus). The analyst, in general, as a good omnipresent obsessive neurotic thinks he is Superman and seeks to "listen" to the Other under his own patriarchal and capitalist neurotic structuring, therefore, the psychoanalyst doesn't listen, because the singularity of the Other does not happen to him. And it doesn't happen to him because he can't hear it (Lacan tried to rethink this at the end of his life through the Borromean Knot, RSI).[39] And if we continue ironizing, it is most likely that listening does not exist. Listening does not exist! And the truth of the transfer, and the transfer itself, sinks in the midst of the Labyrinth of Capitalism. It is strange, sometimes transference is defended so strongly by the analyst that one might think that it is the only possible way of love for the analyst himself; it is a perverse way of loving one and the Other in this life and death struggle between analyst and analysand (patient). It's the perverse exit of the analysis itself.

In any case, it is so annoying to talk about perversion (it has bad press, it is the fault of the neurotic capitalists and the Sade legend), even today, that some resource must be used so that it does not bother the reader and we can see how it operates in the midst of WeOthers the "monsters". Judith Butler (since 1990 and her book *Gender Trouble* that became a success)[40] has helped us a lot by making perversion visible in a more "friendly" way in these times with the term Queer ("twisted", "rare") which Gloria Anzaldúa had already used in 1987 in her brilliant *Borderlans / La Frontera*. Teresa de Lauretis, the Italian thinker, already said it a long time ago in 1988 in her work *Sexual Difference and Indifference*[41]

> …in spite of everything, it is true, as Rubin observes, that 'lesbians are also oppressed because they are considered queer and perverted', and not just because they're female. It is equally true that some lesbians are oppressed not only because they are considered *queer* and perverted but also because their skin is of a different color.[42]

It is a text that clearly shows the use of queer for weird along with the idea of perverse, in a brilliant critique of Lauretis from Rubin. It also shows the Intersectional of feminism, which Gloria Anzaldúa was working on at that time. And, furthermore, with the entire movement, already on a global level, LGBTIQ+ gradually perforates what seemed symbolically structured and impossible to de-structure, including psychoanalysis.[43] And Butler makes it very clear in 1993 in her other great book *Bodies that Matter*: "Indeed, it may be precisely through practices which underscore disidentification with those regulatory norms by which sexual differ-ence is materialized that both feminist and queer politics are mobilized."[44] And what seems an immovable beginning, what sets everything in motion, then becomes a mere beginning in the movement (as was always everything originary that dresses up as "in itself"). And what is traditional opens and mutates within itself. The French quartet of the 1960s: Barthes, Derrida, Foucault and Deleuze generated all kinds of transgression, they were perverse boys, who were dismantling the French institution and later the European one. And the unity with Lacanian psychoanalysis was destroyed in May 1968. Their discourse was perverse, they sought a way of writing that in itself would generate a mutation, a revolt in what was established as originary. Deleuze himself gave it a lot of thought in the 1960s and 1970s, but in another way, from a way of writing, of inscribing the text, an anti-institutional way of thinking-writing and, mainly, of living. In July 1972, he presented his classic: "Nomad Thought", in the colloquium: ¿Nietzsche aujourd'hui? It was held in July 1972 at the Cerisy-la-Salle International Cultural Center. And what he does there is to be "against" the institutional, which is typical of the defiant way of harassing the monster in the establishment itself, which is a manifestation of the Law which operates as a sovereign that constitutes us (let's not forget the speech of November 17, 2019 by Paul B. Preciado before the École de la Cause freudianne of France, because it is a worthy example of what it is to be a monster and behave as such: I am the monster that speaks to you. And what happens with nomadic thinking is that Deleuze is against the psychoanalytic institution centered on Lacan and his Oedipi-fication, against the philosophical institution centered on Heidegger and his French sons and their ontologization, against himself and his book Nietzsche and Philoso-phy (1962) centered on the institution of the book The Will of Power (about the horrific spawn of Elizabeth, Nietzsche's sister) and his own way of philosophizing through content, against Colli and Montinari and the institution of the archive and its control over what is true and what is not, etc. In Deleuze, faced with so many famous Nietzschean "friends", he tries to show the perverse gesture of Nietzsche's writing and finally of his Zarathustra; and of the human in its Nuance of the Sub-tle,[45] in that initial differential that never lets itself be tamed, but always updates itself and returns (it repeats, par excellence, like the sexual act).[46] Deleuze rethinks perversion as the outside of every institution insofar as it transgresses it from within and tenses it: he dynamites it internally (as was Bacon's operation when painting, yet another "monster"; an infamous visual artist); and for this reason Deleuze even goes against the institution of reading (and this is very important in France). And so the French philosopher makes that perverse outside function as something singular, not as the strictly rigid, repetitive and perfectionist scene of Sade's rationality; who wrote the same story over and over again, for example, that of Justine or the Mis-fortunes of Virtue (1791),[47] in its first redaction The Misfortunes of Virtue (1787) has many archetypal rigid scenes of transgression:

The charitable priest clapped an inquisitive eye upon Justine, and made her answer, saying that the parish was heavily loaded; that it could not easily take new charges unto its bosom, but that if Justine wished to serve him, if she were prepared for hard toil, there would always be a crust of bread in his kitchen for her. And as he uttered those words, the gods' interpreter chuck'ed her under the chin; the kiss he gave her bespoke rather too much worldliness for a man of the church, and Justine, who had understood only too well, thrust him away.[48]

Sade's caricature characters in this perversion are playful, schematic, of a childish dialectic against authority and the empty God of universal reason (the French philosophers of the 20th century, such as Bataille, were aware of how Sade operated),[49] of the 18th century; his texts are never pornographic, not even the most radical like *The 120 Days of Sodom*; they are not even sensual: there are brutal and violent days, like those in February, but in addition to not being described, they are like horror caricatures to annoy the reader. Something similar is seen in the film *Nymphomania: Part One* by Lars von Trier (2013). It is a film that repeats Sade in his rationality keeping up at the level of this Capitalism; hence the film fails (it is neither pornographic, nor sensual, nor perverse; it is a schematic game of transgression). Very different from the film *Love* by Michael Haneke (2012); where the idea of transgressing is developed in detail in a narrative and formal way that provokes and internalizes us. This is what Deleuze talks about in 1972, namely, this other way of immersing ourselves in the experience of one another; but an experience that operates in the experience itself and not in a papier-mâché experimentation.

In these times we are faced with how human each of WeOthers are; and in those singularities: exteriorities without interior, such as Klein's Bottle, Escher's Drawing Hands, Moebius' Strip, Menger's Sponge, Winnicott's Holding, Lacan's Borromean Knot, Hegel's Circle of Circles, Nietzsche's Ring of Return, Roy Andersson's films, Nick Cave's songs, Sarah Kane's texts, Sade's stories, Goya's engravings, etc. And so, what we are is understood in another way and our enjoyment opens up like a Yes in the middle of the No of the Labyrinth of Capitalism that tries to imprison us under categories that have exhausted themselves.

In this way, Deleuze expresses the nomadic doing characteristic of WeOthers the monsters; of how a contraption operates against the patriarchal normativity that seeks to determine us; multiple modes of perversion that open up the Labyrinth for us and we can partially dissolve it: Nietzsche, for his part, wants to be or sees himself as Polish with respect to German. He seizes on German to build a war-machine which will get something through that will be uncodable in German. That's what style as politics means. More generally, how do we characterize such thought, which claims to get its flows through, underneath the laws by challenging them, and underneath contractual relations by contradicting them, and underneath institutions by parodying them? Let me come back quickly to the example of psychoanalysis. In what respect does a psychoanalyst as original as Melanie Klein still remain within the psychoanalytic system? She explains it herself quite well: the partial objects that she tells us about, with their explosions, their flows, etc., are only fantasy. The patients bring lived experiences, intensely lived experiences, to Melanie Klein and she translates them into fantasy. There you have a contract, specifically a contract: give me your lived experiences, and I will give you fantasies. And the contract implies an exchange, an exchange of money and words. In this respect, a psychoanalyst like Winnicott truly occupies the limit of psychoanalysis, because he feels that this procedure is no longer appropriate after a certain point. There comes a point where it is no longer about translating, or interpreting, translating into fantasies, interpreting into signifiers and signifieds – no, not in the least. There comes a point where you will have to share, have to put yourself in the patient's shoes, go all the way, and share his experience. Is it about a kind of sympathy, or empathy, or identification? But surely, it's more complicated than that. What we feel is, rather, the necessity of a relation that would be neither legal, nor contractual, nor institutional. That's how it is with Nietzsche. We read an aphorism or a poem from *Thus Spoke Zarathustra*. But materially and formally, texts like that cannot be understood by the establishment or the application of a law, or by the offer of a contractual relation, or by the foundation of an institution. Perhaps the only conceivable equivalent is something like "being in the same boat".[50] That is what being human is about, an experience of "being in the same boat". Nietzsche puts it in a unique way in his *Zarathustra*: "There standeth the boat—thither goeth it over, perhaps into vast nothingness—but who willeth to enter into this 'Perhaps'"?[51] And as we know Nietzsche talks about the boat of Dionysos and Ariadne which sails above death (which can be seen literally in many ancient Greek objects). That boat is life in the midst of death (empty and meaningless), of our life with Others, of love, of the struggle for life or death, of sexual intercourse, of the child-mother bond, of transference, of breaking with the natural representation that has built us as neurotics at the service of the Symbolic: the Capitalism of the contract par excellence that is the Law of the Father that regulates us. And sometimes it remains unsaid, but Deleuze points it out, provoking the French themselves, that Winnicott was the analyst who did the impossible for the Other.

Let us not forget the analysis reported by Margaret Little (between 1949 and 1955, 1957) after two failed analyses (with a Jungian and then with a strict Freudian). She is a psychotic analyst and Winnicott gave everything for her, working at the level of regression, countertransference, etc. The analysis is really surprising, among other things so that she did not commit suicide.[52] DW Winnicott in a 1965 lecture for the British Psychoanalytic Society shows how analysis works radically and this is what Deleuze sees in an exceptional way, unlike French analysis:

Naturally there are very great difficulties when a patient attempts to relive madness, and one of the big difficulties is to find an analyst who will understand what is taking place. It is quite difficult in the present state of our knowledge for the analyst to remember in this kind of experience, that it is the aim of the patient to reach the madness, i.e. to be mad in the analytic setting, the nearest that the patient can ever do to remembering. In order to organize the setting for this the patient has to be mad in a more superficial way, i.e. has to organise what Dr. Little calls a 'delusional transference', and the analyst has to take the delusional transference, accept it and understand its performance.[53]

And Winnicott was in the same boat with his patient, on a boat above death itself; and from there he tried to work with his patients, but he had yet to make the leap to the complete experience of articulation of one with the Other, but he radically advanced in that step. Here is the basis for love, which is so difficult for Lacan (and also for Freud), namely, to love the madness of the Other.

The nomad quality of an inscription (the scar that Freud spoke of in *A Child is Beaten* in 1919), whichever it is, in the inscription itself transgresses, transvalues what is inscribed and naturalized (the Oedipus too) and that natural representation gives way to something else. And so, we can live and continue without the need to psychotize ourselves like Major Tom, the new man presented by the young Bowie in 1969. Hence the demand for analysis that meets the expectations of the times that Preciado claims, a monster who radically tells psychoanalysts, philosophers, intellectuals and each one of WeOthers not to understand as a mere "we" normalized from the Name of the Father (even though Miller is horrified by this and, perhaps, a certain conservative Žižek too), that contract cannot can be accepted: "Psychoanalysis needs to enter into a critical *feedback* of the traditions of transfeminist political resistance if it wants to stop being a technology of heteropatriarchal normalization, and become a technology of invention of dissident subjectivities against the norm."[54] By means of the partial objects, the perversions point out the monster that we are and that persecutes us, on the one hand, from within; and, on the other hand, from outside, from the law, the norm, the father: Oedipus. And Melanie Klein herself (also loved by Deleuze) knew it so long ago, we are that:

> But when this happens its sadistic phantasies and feelings, especially its cannibalistic ones, are at their height. At the same time it now experiences a change in its emotional attitude towards its mother. The child's libidinal fixation to the breast is develops into feeling towards her as a person. Thus feelings both of a destructive and loving nature are experienced towards one and the same object, and this gives rise to deep and disturbing conflicts in the child's mind.[55]

That is why some say, if Freud discovered the psychic apparatus, the unconscious, namely, Greece, it was Melanie Klein with her work with children who discovered none other than Mycenae: before Oedipus (and castration: two faces of the same, that is, a heteronormative device) we have the whole child-mother bond as a fused unit. In this unit "the child does not exist" (which is why Winnicott says that the current question is no longer "Are all babies neurotic?", but "Is every infant mad?").[56] But Melanie Klein, in this she was Freud's daughter, took this treatment of the child as an object with his mother as a fantasy (this is subjective), as others consider it Symbolic, so as to avoid ceasing to operate with the contract in the capitalist way. And in that case, there is no possible transference, because what was alive in the experience of an analysand's consciousness becomes dead in the analyst's science, although Klein was revolutionary and later very much hated by all patriarchal psychoanalysis, especially by Anna Freud. And the interesting thing is to observe that doubly destructive and affirming moment of the partial object and the total object by the child. Here are the bases for the perversion which is then tried to normalize, by oedipification and castration, to make the neurotic work in the institutional system of capitalist contracts. However, we have resisted that.

Hegel himself, once again, originally called his *Phenomenology of Spirit*: *Wissenschat der Erfahrung des Bewusstseins* (*Science of the Experience of Consciousness*, translated into English, but the verb *Wissen* is lost; to know in the full sense, both objective and subjective; as in Heraclitus). That is the internal name of the Book, its truth (and not a mere Introduction). The *Bewusstsein* experiences the knowledge that constitutes it, and this knowledge experiences the *Bewustsein* that constitutes it. Those double genitives (objective-subjective) indicate the double movement of life from life itself, the radical transference. It is an "experiencing" Science (knowledge) and an "experiencing" Consciousness (being known). And in that co-actualization life itself happens and the natural representation that arrogantly appeared as something different and independent is eliminated, one is performed with the other and the other with the one and it is realized. "In the same boat", even the boat of madness that Winnicott spoke of (and Bosch knew very well about this boat),[57] the boat of struggle, the boat of love is "Science of the experience of consciousness". And it is how today we must "experience" each other: We-Others. It is what I would call a materialist clinic, since it carries the object-subject contradiction within itself and it is resolved in transference. And transference, that love, is nothing outside the transference itself, but it happens in that double moment that constitutes it. The transference, if it happens, is revolutionary and it could not be otherwise.

Although my relationship with psychoanalysis is, as it is known, tense (although I myself have undergone analysis three times a week for many months), because sometimes I cannot find what is human today, nor with myself as a human, because as Kant said in the *Critique of Pure Reason*: "Thoughts without content are empty; intuitions without concepts are blind."[58] That is, theorists without clinics are empty (Lacanians) and clinicians without theories are blind (Winnicottians). A clinic has to be absolute, materialistic, that is, to carry out in its transference an experience in the same boat as the patient. And stop being submerged in the desert of Capitalism, and thus become an accomplice of its contractual symbolization that rules us from a father. And if love does not exist because they make us see that it does not exist because they are already trapped in their old categories in their élite clinic, because they cannot listen to the experience that dissolves the natural representation of those categories by the very demand of the analysand. The prohibition that operates in love because the incestuousness of the initial bond is feared and dismantles neurosis (which is always phallic: castration and Oedipus), and Capitalism, is a spent fear and does not have much support today, because the human is human beyond the phallic and castration and oedipification. That subject of the self must disappear and with it a WeOthers must appear that updates the bond for us keeping up with the event, which, moreover, has always been present in some way, for example, in the family, ultimately, in love. It is about thinking and putting that self, that subject, at risk, putting in crisis what in itself puts us in crisis for a long time and that today becomes sick. Neurosis is the disease because the ego is the disease, the neurosis was a mere symptom of the self and the perversion its way out, that is, becoming healthy. The very epistemology and ontology of the subject, so close to Kant and the multiple Kantian heads such as Miller's, and in a certain way to Lacan himself and part of philosophy, is the problem: not the human.

The drive, the Real (the logical would say Hegel, the Dionysian Nietzsche) from Freud to Jorge Nico Reitter himself, has been rethought over and over again; and sometimes Lacan illuminates, like Winnicott and Bion in the past or Miller in a certain present, but what is clear is that it is not enough; because dimensions that are updated of the human are opened up to us according to these times and in the midst of Capitalism. For the same reason, clinical practice, philosophy, feminism, literature, cinema, theater, Slovenian critical theory, music, etc. can be articulated "In the same boat"; and thus, is able to express not the monster that is alien to us, but the monster that I am myself as in WeOthers. Writing itself must be perverted in order to give expression to the Frankenstein that we are, but as a Frankenstein of writing. Because it is not only about perverting the clinic, philosophy, but Capitalism and in it our own subjectivity. And today Butler shakes hands with Žižek, Foucault with Deleuze, Lacan with Hegel, analysts with philosophers, writers with politicians, Sade with each of WeOthers: that which we call human with itself beyond men and women. As Butler says, there is a certain melancholy of gender that connects us with each other and creates community in the differential, without going entirely through the neurotic rigidity of the obsessed analyst, philosopher, legislator:

> Heterosexuality is cultivated through prohibitions, where these prohibitions take as one of their objects homosexual attachments, thereby forcing the loss (…) When the prohibition against homosexuality is culturally pervasive, then the 'loss' of homosexual love is precipitated through a prohibition that is repeated and ritualized throughout the culture. What ensues is a culture of gender melancholy in which masculinity and femininity emerge as the traces of an ungrieved and ungrievable love.[59]

Today breaks with certain prohibitions and limits; and it is articulated with Enjoyment and multiple enjoyments, sexual diversities, because what I call the logics of the world and of the State have changed. Jorge Nico Reitter says it this way, and as a clinician he knows it from the inside on a day-to-day basis; it is not only about a desire of this or that human, but rather we are in the "Hegelian" dimension of the matter, namely, of logics of power that allow or do not allow the performative and in this to talk about that diversity and to feel accepted as such:

> If everything could be reduced to issues related to the subject, to his desire, to a subject that is thus reduced to the individual, if it were enough to approach it based on the 'case by case', as if each one could do whatever they want in absolute (undetermined) terms, why did no one speak for such a long period of time

and then the voices rapidly multiplied? It is evident that a change in historical circumstances (read, in power relations) made it possible to speak.[60]

And the human is modulated and loves and suffers today (as it always has), no longer as only neurotics, but as humans who, in what we feel today, seek to dance in another way with the Other. I would say mythically how Ariadne dances with Dionysos, despite so much pain and division, to put our body, in the flat and immediate Capitalism that devours us, crushes us, inhibits us (Capitalism is resisted by letting out the monster that we are).

While I feel that love is "in spite of" so much conceptual theorizing and aestheticizing of a predetermined and primary scene that has been naturalized and operates as the Real (with a Kantian smell) that seeks to be symbolized and recognized as true over and over again by everyone, love shows itself in a certain unconditionality, in a transfinite instant (namely, always in struggle, with its obstacles), which happens, for example, when we wait for anything, from Godot to a son, whom we love; when we have a child, and not only blood related, there are many ways to be a father and mother; we feel that he is an Other whom we cannot and do not want to determine and who is never attacked or punished and that we always accompany by his side with all the difference that this has: always, without suffocating him, so that in this way our child occurs in all his finite and mortal expression and in turn the child itself can love. And that the traumatic "was" of the past (*wusst*) that determines us, apparently, turns into a "perhaps" (and I am referring to the dogma of castration). There is no more life than this, let's not forget, dear readers, we are "less than nothing" as Žižek says, because, if we were nothing, we would be under the yoke of *Creatio ex nihilo* that constitutes our theological ontology, even if we do not believe and consider ourselves atheists. And of that: no more! And what happens is that in our material character without any meaning, we are; in that hole that we are: we are! And the Other constitutes us and makes us be, in the middle of that hole, affirming this miserable existence that makes us suffer and frightens us; makes us melancholic. In this productive melancholy Love occurs, which always happens as a bodily physical gratitude of one in the Other, carrying within itself its own incompleteness (who said that the system should be closed in discourse). The WeOthers is eminently the sexual act, although it does not exist because it is not performed, and it is incomplete, because it cannot be complete by itself due to the very lack of being what we are, that act and that is why one becomes TWO (we merge into the very difference that never was) and Zarathustra-Dionysos passes us by and touches us as Nietzsche said in *Beyond Good and Evil* (1886):

This song has ended, — the longing for the sweet cry / dies between the lips : / It was the magician, a friend of good timetables, / the friend of midday —shut up! don't ask who he is— / it was at noon that one became two (…) Now we celebrate, sure of our victory, / the festival of festivals: / friend Zarathustra came, guest of guests! / Now the world laughs, the gray curtain rises, / light and darkness swearing love…[61]

And so, Ariadne's Labyrinth in Crete dissolves and no longer operates to cover up the pain of life and thus deceitful Capitalism partly dissolves. And in this way Ariadne's Lament on Naxos,[62] then, allows us to dance without fear above death being mortal, knowing that we die and that we are sick and our bodies wear out day by day. And that we are, as Silenus said to Midas: "A miserable race of a day, children of chance and fatigue…"[63]

We are a depth in our surface being, being skin, being Baubo,[64] an open and humid mask that manifests what is proper to the unconscious; and that is shown in love. That indication of love in Joviality, in Ariadne's Lament, because her labyrinthine scene, apparently original, has fallen and it is then possible to harbor Love if we go through the Lament; but if you don't want to suffer, that is, if you want to continue in the deception of denying and rejecting and refuting that analysis points to, your own epochal finitude: you will never love! That is why the Preciado monster is so right when he indicates and shouts at the analyst that: "From here I make a call for the mutation of psychoanalysis, for the appearance of a mutant psychoanalysis, that keeps up with the historical challenge and the paradigm shift that we are experiencing."[65]

References

Barthes, R., *The Loving Speech*, Paidós, Madrid, 2011.

Bataille. G., "Sade and morality", in *Marqués de Sade. Obras Selectas*, C. S. Ediciones, Buenos Aires, 2005.

Bourlez, F., *Queer psychanalyse. Clinique mineur et déconstructions du genre*, Ed. Hermann, Paris, 2018.

Butler, J., *Bodies that matter*: https://warwick.ac.uk/fac/arts/english/currentstudents/postgraduate/masters/modules/femlit/bodies-that-matter.pdf

Butler, J. Melancholy Gender / Refused Identification: https://web-facstaff.sas.upenn.edu/~cavitch/pdf-library/Butler_MelancholyGender.pdf

De Lauretis, T., "Sexual Indifference and Lesbian Representation", in *Theater Journal*, Vol. 40, 2 (May, 1988).

De Lauretis, T., *Differenza e Indifferenza Sexy. Per / elaborazione di tm pensiero lesbico*, Festro Strumenti, Florence, 1989.

De Lauretis, T., *Differences. Stages of a Path through Feminism*, Hours and Hours, Madrid, 2000.

Deleuze, G., *The Desert Island and Other Texts*: https://monoskop.org/images/2/23/Deleuze_Gilles_Desert_Islands_and_Other_Texts_1953-1974.pdf

Espinoza, R., *Capitalism and Business. Towards a Revolution of NosOtros*, Libros Pascal, Santiago, 2018.

Espinoza, R., *Nietzsche. Pagan Ideology*, Akal, Madrid, 2023 (in press).

Espinoza, R., *NosOtros. Manual to Dissolve Capitalism*, Morata, Madrid, 2019.

Espinoza, R., *NosOtros. Manuale per dissolvere il capitalismo*, Mimesis, Milan, 2023 (updated and expanded version).

Freud, S., *The Standard Edition of the Complete Psychological Works of Sigmund Freud*, Volume I, Vintage Books, London, 2001.

Freud, S., *The Standard Edition of the Complete Psychological Works of Sigmund Freud*, Volume II, Vintage Books, London, 2001.

Freud, S., *The Standard Edition of the Complete Psychological Works of Sigmund Freud*, Volume III, Vintage Books, London, 2001.

Freud, S., *The Standard Edition of the Complete Psychological Works of Sigmund Freud*, Volume VII, Vintage Books, London, 2001.

Freud, S., *The Standard Edition of the Complete Psychological Works of Sigmund Freud*, Volume XVII, Vintage Books, London, 2001.

Hegel, G.W.F., The Phenomenology of Spirit, https://www.marxists.org/reference/archive/hegel/works/ph/phba.htm

Hegel, G.W.F., Science of Logic, https://www.marxists.org/reference/archive/hegel/works/hl/hlintro.htm p.50

Hegel, G.W.F., *Philosophy of History*, Dover Publications Inc., Mineola, 2004.

Kane, S., *Skin*, played by Ewen Bremner and Marcia Rose. Produced by Tapson/Steel Films for British Screen and Channel 4 Films, it was filmed in September 1995 and directed by Vincent O'Connell: https://www.youtube.com/watch?v=G2ZjplLullc

Kane, S., *Cleansed*, Methuen Random House, London, 1998: https://kupdf.net/download/sarah-kane-cleansed-2000-pdf_58a3c01e6454a7df31b1e9cf_pdf

Kant, I., *Critique of Pure Reason*: http://files.libertyfund.org/files/1442/0330_Bk.pdf

Klein, M., *A* "Contribution to the Psychogenesis of Manic-Depressive States", *Int. J. Psychoanal.*, (16), 1935, pp. 145–174.

Kritzer, A.H., *Political Theater in Post-Thatcher Britain. New Writing: 1995–2005*, Palgrave Macmillan, Basingstoke, 2008, p. 25.

Lacan, J., *Jacques Lacan Seminar. Book XXIV: L'insu que sait de l'une-bévue s'aile à mourre*, (unpublished). This Seminar is between 1976 and 1977. The Class is from 17 May, 1977.

Lacan, J., *The Seminar of Jacques Lacan, Book XIV. The Logic of Phantasy*. Translated by Cormac Gallagher from unedited French manuscripts, Karnac, London, 2002.

Lacan, J., *The Sinthome: The Seminar of Jacques Lacan*, Book XXIII, 1975–1976. Edited by J-A. Miller. Translated by A.R. Price, Polity Press, Cambridge, 2016.

Lenin, V.I., "Where to begin?", in *Complete Works*. Volume 5, Akal, Madrid, 1976.

Little, M., *Psychotic Anxieties and Containment. To Personal Record of an Analysis with Winnicott*, Jason Aronson Inc., London, 2000.

Marquis de Sade: https://altexploit.files.wordpress.com/2017/07/4322115-marquis-de-sade-justine-in-english-translation.pdf

Marx, K., *Fundamental Elements for the Critique of Political Economy (Grundrisse) 1857–1858*. Volume 2, Siglo XXI, Mexico, 1997.

Mayer, H., *Hysteria*, Paidós, Buenos Aires, 1990.

Michelet, J., *The Witch of the Middle Ages*: https://www.gutenberg.org/files/31420/31420-h/31420-h.htm#CHAPTER_VI

Milner, J.C., *The Clear Work. Lacan, Science, Philosophy*, Manantial, Buenos Aires, 1996.

Nicolás Román, S., "Entre el amor y la torutura: Cleansed de Sarah Kane", University of Almería: https://webs.ucm.es/info/especulo/numero44/cleansed.html

Nietzsche, F., *So Spoke Zarathustra*: https://www.logoslibrary.org/nietzsche/zarathustra/56.html

Nietzsche, F., "Beyond Good and Evil", in *Friedrich Nietzsche. Complete Works*. Volume IV. *Work of Maturity II*, Tecnos, Madrid, 2017.

Nietzsche, F., *The Birth of Tragedy*: https://www.gutenberg.org/files/51356/51356-h/51356-h.htm#THE_BIRTH_OF_TRAGEDY

Nietzsche, F. *Nietzsche contra Wagner:* https://www.gutenberg.org/files/25012/25012-pdf.pdf

Preciado, P.B., *Can the Monster Speak?*, Anagrama, Barcelona, 2020.

Reitter, J.N., *Oedipus Gay: Heteronormativity and Psychoanalysis* (Second Edition), Letra Viva, Buenos Aires, 2019.

Saiegh, R.: https://www.youtube.com/watch?v=dtOhhUm8Z2g (Madrid, January 25, 2014).

Schelling, J.W.F., *Philosophical Investigations into the Essence of Human Freedom*, State University of New York Press, Albany, 2006.

Schopenhauer, A., *The World as Will and Representation.* Volume I, Dover Publications, Inc, New York, 1966.

Schopenhauer, A., *The World as Will and Representation.* Volume II, Dover Publications Inc., New York, 1966.

Shelley, M., *Frankenstein or the Modern Prometheus*, The Project Gutenberg eBook of Frankenstein.

Sierz, A., *In-Yer-Face Theatre. British Drama Today*, Faber and Faber, London, 2001.

Vieites, M.F., "Dramaturgies of Pain and Barbarism in the Face of 'Spectacle'", in First Act II, N°, 293, 2002.

Winnicott, D.W., *Psychoanalytic Explorations*, H. Karnac (Books) London, 1989.

Žižek, S., *Pandemic. COVID-19 Shakes the World*, OR Books New York and London, 2020.

2

The wait

It drives us crazy

When waiting sometimes we do not realize that we are also drilling into that familiar thing that appears naturalized to us, because "it is a natural representation", that is, that representation is immediate, seeing it without any mediation, and thinking that this is so and not in another way, or that it could be otherwise. And so, we operate immediately from a thinking belief, but waiting disturbs us, drives us crazy, unsettles the familiar, it becomes sinister, but allows us to see, as in dreams, what sometimes cannot be seen in the familiar, which is also always ideologized: the ominous, the sinister, the terrifying (*das unheimlich*). And, as Freud puts it in his profound study in 1919:

> It may be true that the uncanny {*unheimlich*} is something which is secretly familiar {*heimlich-heimisch*}, which has undergone repression and then returned from it, and that everything that is uncanny fulfils this condition (…) The condition under which the feeling of uncanniness arises here is unmistakable. We- or our primitive forefathers- once believed that these possibilities were realities, and were convinced that they actually happened. Nowadays we no longer believe in them, we have *surmounted* these modes of thought; but we do not feel quite sure of our new beliefs, and the old ones still exist within us ready to seize upon any confirmation.[66]

That repetition that returns not as the eternal return of Nietzsche (the giver of life because in it the free and differential occur) but as a repetition of the repressed familiar that bothers us because it has been lost and will no longer return; and what comes back is not what it was. In this movement that worries us and imposes itself on us, perhaps it is not simply that something is repressed, but rather that something that appears to us and stresses us out is what is human, namely, something that surpasses us; our own differential, open and empty of meaning (our "scar" that pierces Oedipus).

At the start of *Paris, Texas*, by Wim Wenders (1984), Travis is seen, with a jacket, yellow tie and red hat, walking erratically in the middle of the Colorado Canyon in the USA and walking under a tremendously hot and crushing sun; and he is tormented and about to faint. Travis waits and hopes to be reunited with Jane,

DOI: 10.4324/9781003370116-3

a woman who is totally blurred in his life, but who is still there in that blur constituting it day by day, second by second. He waits for her, she is his desire, she is his love; an already psychotic love that went through the perversion of the fusion of bodies before the collapse of everything symbolic caused by the wildest American Capitalism, not only imperial, but especially local, for Americans themselves. Travis and Jane left their usual neurosis, their obsession and transgressed everything to the limit of the Symbolic and jumped into the madness of psychosis. It is the wait in these radical times, but is it the only possible wait? Is waiting in times of Capitalism to become psychotic ourselves? Perhaps we see in it a way out of the waiting, but with radical consequences.

The COVID-19 pandemic has left us radically alone with our own existence, because, regardless of where we are and what we are in, "we are" radically alone with ourselves WeOthers; and the Other pierces us. What is that Other? We'll see…

The pandemic has made visible, without the permanent daily noise of the Labyrinth of Capitalism, what we simply are. And what are we? Apparently "less than nothing", namely, without any resource to an ontology of *Creatio ex Nihilo* (regardless of whether or not we believe in any god), namely, an ontology that founds us from nothing, and from there all our ways of thinking and living under the game-yoke that we are "something" determined and, therefore, with some purpose, with a meaning, with an "alpha and an omega", a "yes and an amen" (that is, a patient of Freud, a character of Sade); however, we are simply like "chunks" of matter where we do not have a nihilistic horizon that lifts us from that nothingness; neither God, nor any will, nor scientific algorithm, nor botched magic, etc., nor anything performs the game of placing in front "of" (some horizon) ourselves as the mere matter that we are, that is, without any meaning. And if there isn't, what can we wait for?

What can we expect from each of WeOthers? The pandemic has shown something very sad: despair, as Hegel would say (*Verweifung*). It has been so radical to be in the wilderness of Capitalism and, especially, in the very wilderness of our existence, that what has happened has been an almost "natural" response, immediate, of being desperate in the very wait of our emptiness that constitutes us and that feeds and encloses Capitalism as a Labyrinth; our emptiness is subdued and crystallized like a Minotaur within Capitalism. And that monster is going to come out and it will make us explode, like a son who looks for his father so that he can name him and thereby introduce him symbolically to the culture, that monstrous human in his singularity is also accepted (because we are all those monstrous children born of monstrous parents). And if we use the old categories of the human by Freud and Lacan to give them a twist of what we are as an abyss, for example, the repression (*Verdrängung*) of the neurotics, the denial (*Verleugnung*) of the perverse and the rejection (*Verwerfung*) of psychotics, that is, what we are in these three traits is imposed on us in the pandemic in the midst of this brutal Capitalism (they are traits, not "essences"); and right there we psychotize, everything has been emptied of meaning, like Travis walking in that same "desert of the Real" (that's how Morpheus refers to Neo in *The Matrix*, 1999),[67] and that's how we are and there we defy the rules to be able to resist, perversely, in another way the Law of the Father; and all this happens in a world that is crumbling from the Symbolic (and that today terrifies Jacques-Alain Miller) and language no longer structures us with each other. And this happens because the pandemic makes evident what we are as an abyss (and not as the ontologist Heidegger thinks); what we are is imposed on us daily, it presses on us, in any part of this small planet in a confinement of days, weeks and months: we cannot escape from what we are. And what is imposed on us is that "void" that tells us that we are "less than nothing" in the midst of this calculating landowner, Capitalism. And instead of fleeing from it we must overcome it out of necessity and face it in what we truly are: monsters; no more the false escape, because it is worse and it means sinking deeper and deeper into its Labyrinth. And we become an essential part of that capitalist labyrinthine mechanism as psychotics who try to pervert the system in the face of the shipwreck of our neurosis because we no longer have any language that we can hold onto and that sustains us (even children can no longer play and dance in the middle of the Labyrinth: today we need a new Melanie Klein). And from there, from that Labyrinth, we never leave again. And we think this is freedom, but simply said mythically (from Ovid to Nietzsche), Ariadne's Labyrinth that loses us again and again.

In the pandemic we must wait; It's time to wait… Wait for what? We must really wait for WeOthers and not get lost in it: no looking for quick shortcuts of hysterical despair, nor some neurotic capitalist slogan like "New Normality", and no psychotization, as a deadly way out can be the key: that is pure pain and it is a sad immediacy sought in the fusion with the Real. Each one of WeOthers must wait for ourselves in what we are and what this COVID-19 pandemic has allowed us to update. What does this waiting that we are and that continually updates us, express at the moment? This waiting is a name for the human of our days: we are a deep wait. If I indicate it in an extrinsic way, it could show many ways of waiting that have occurred during the pandemic: from knowing if I am infected to waiting for the vaccine, through waiting for various news items associated with the pandemic, etc. Waiting is like an operator of our own human dynamism that keeps us in a tense balance; waiting to be able to see someone you love and who cannot be seen because you are at a distance, of that tense balance that is apparently seen as stillness, but is radically a movement. It is the movement of waiting: waiting for a loved one, waiting for the news of the PCR, waiting to know how a relative hospitalized by COVID-19 is doing, waiting to find out if they will fire us from work at the end of the month, waiting to know what will happen with our children's education, we hope to be clear about what we are going to eat today, we are waiting for some announcement from the political apparatus that will give us peace of mind and allow us to organize ourselves, but some wait in the comfort of their faith, others under the wings of some drug, others drinking with their partner, others wait crying, others in their anxiety, others seeking some way to defy and transgress the law that prevents their freedom to do whatever they want, others wait in the sexual act itself, others wait denying the pandemic, others wait months to get on a plane, others wait in their perversion and others in their psychosis, but we all wait in one way or another.

There are many ways of waiting in the pandemic, but all of them point to the wait that constitutes us as the radical emptiness that we are. And it is this wait we must try to understand as an abysmal expression of that emptiness that we are. Why do emptiness and waiting co-belong to manifest in the human today? If we were nothing but emptiness, everything would be quite simple and, at the same time, too sad and deadly; it is the very root of melancholia that can sometimes even be seen as a form of psychosis, because, literally, the melancholic knows the "truth" (that is why Freud had to redo his *Mourning and Melancholia* of 1917 (1915) and rethink it on another more positive level and belonging to the human in *The Ego and the ID* of 1923):[68] nothing has any meaning in and of itself (absolutely nothing), but then, what do we do with our existence?: simply fall apart and be unhappy, because we are not only animals that live through stimuli, but because of what we have said we are animals constituted by an emptiness, it is the freedom of the human animal that is at the bottom of its emptiness. The young Hegel said it this way and almost ironically too, since from *Creatio ex nihilo*, the only possible thing is freedom and from it the world: "With the free, selfconscious being (Wesen) there emerges at the same time a whole world – out of nothing – the only true and conceivable creation out of nothing."[69] That "truth" of the emptiness of meaning which is a resounding truth, namely, that there is no meaning, is in some way in our favor sometimes when it is experienced in another way: that positive way of being by our side, that emptiness that frees us from meaning, in our animality, is the expectation that afterwards, in some way, some kind of world can be forged. The emptiness of our existence constitutes us in a perforation that always drills us and in that perforation of emptiness, in that vibration of emptiness, we are before the openness of our intimate freedom, before the future of our life, and it is possible that we monsters may have a body and a voice; and a language that is to come: Derrida points it out this way in Barcelona:

> Sería necesario que por lengua por venir entendiéramos no solamente lengua futura, sino lengua apta para convertirse ella misma en acontecimiento o para producer acontecimientos aptos para venir o para hacer venir o dejar venir. Para que semejante lengua sea, en la escritura, apta para venir, es necesario que se imprima en un cuerpo idiomático; allí donde se resiste a la traducción, hay una posibilidad de que la lengua sea por venir.[70]

A future-to-come that is not just another meaning, but is our own open, unspecific, and free human existence that opens in its emptiness; it is the opening of what we are materially for being mere pieces of matter bodily open to all material openings and being that, we speak nothing more than that (and that is saying a lot). It is like a synchrony of unspecific materialities what we are with each other. And we resonate with each other in that void, and we resonate with the Other of every other. That unspecific resonation with each other as the Other is what is expressed in waiting. The very emptiness that we are becomes the engine of our affirmative dynamism.

Waiting is the very material dynamic way out of each one of WeOthers. What can we expect today? Although it seems politically incorrect to say so; we can wait:

nothing! And by this I mean, not to fall into the temptation that the wait be concrete and determined. For example, that the pandemic is expected to end, or that they give me the vaccine, or that a PCR test result is negative, or that we can meet each other, or that they do not fire us from work, etc. If the wait were to take a certain figure, the most likely thing to happen is that nothing more will be expected and, therefore, we will return to the zero point where we always are, that is, immersed in the production and distribution of capital and of capitalist subjectivity within the very Labyrinth of Capitalism (this would be a deadly repetition). If we wait for the concrete, this will take us headlong into Capitalism and it will be crueler than before (paraphrasing Marx-Hegel: "First as a tragedy, then as a farce"). But how can we keep waiting without it materializing, but at the same time, while waiting, not becoming paralyzed and neuroticized to the extreme and then pulverized into psychotic fragments?

If we keep waiting monstrously in the pandemic, it would have to be a wait that gives us life, and never death. A wait that, as animals that we are, keeps us materially in that free non-specificity and in that, without any betrayal, or complicity with Labyrinth, we can hold each other as Others, that is, as put differently: monsters (each one his Preciado). That Other, in the void and waiting, that we are strongly indicates difference. The other part of our emptiness that becomes more dynamic while waiting always points to a difference that never allows itself to be completely trapped. Waiting must be as difference, otherwise it will be death: either due to excess and psychotic fragmentation, or due to boredom, or due to neurotic rigidity and complicity of the system; for this reason, perversion helps us resist and transgress. One has, then, to get out of the waiting trap: neither psychotic fragmentation nor capitalist neurotic rigidity. And the way out is not, either, a ridiculous defiance of the Law, whatever it may be, it is no longer simply about perverting the norm and thus circumventing fragmentation; which is often done today and is part of the very thing that is sought to be denied (Lacan's critique of *May '68).*[71] In this anxiety of waiting, we really hurt ourselves and what is worse we hurt the Other; that damage is not necessary. And Butler is in this today and that is why her pacifist militancy; humans in non-violence, different without violence, monsters without violence, social movements without that violence that operates as a dialectical element of Capitalism itself to later repress it in some way (brutally as in the Chilean riots or in an "intelligent" way as in Europe):

> Non-violence exposes the tricks by which state violence defends itself against black or mestizo people, *queer people*, migrants, the homeless, dissidents, as if by taking them together they will add the number to those detained, imprisoned or expelled for 'security reasons'… Sometimes continuing to exist in conflictive social relations is the definitive defeat of violent power.[72]

No bond of love is possible, but merely a basic contract of a certain pact that subjects us and leaves us attached to a certain father; and in this the wait despairs and becomes a mere constant staging of transgression and in it, again, the death of all life or the flight of capital to the Labyrinth occurs.

If waiting as a catalyst for our emptiness leads us to psychotization or to the classic perverse exit that surrounds psychosis because one cannot succumb to the very neurosis of the symbolic Labyrinth of Capitalism, because the symbolic itself is undone, disjointed, etc., then do we not have a way out of waiting for another vital way in differentiation? Or put more simply: is it not possible to love in the waiting that confronts us to our emptiness which is expressed categorically in this pandemic? In these times, will all love be perverse or won't it because, as I have said, the symbolic has collapsed and, therefore, the neurotic lives as if psychotized in the Labyrinth? And if all love is perverse: is it love or pact and submission? Is love possible in times of Capitalism? Is everything transgression in these pandemic waiting times?

Waiting, if possible, has a lot of perversion today, but it is not entirely perversion. In that transgression, what is transgressed is always assumed from the outset, at this moment it is intended to transgress the Law of Capital (a new name of the Father). And that Law of Capital operates in multiple ways in the nation-state, one way of operating is that of the transaction of all kinds of merchandise. In perverse waiting, one seeks to go against that Law and to seek absolute or unconditional love (because one sees the only free and gratuitous thing that is above the Law of Capital (Law of Demand)); and that is the perverse waiting mode. But, also, this absolute love is always touched in turn by the Law itself and in this it is as if there was an immediate relationship with the Real, and there the psychosis and fragmentation of bodies and loves resonates again and again. Therefore, in this awaiting perversion there is an exit, but it is still open and painful: exit, after all, from the Labyrinth does happen, and deep down in that exit there is a merged and incestuous way between the one who waits and what is expected. It is a way of WeOthers, of waiting in the experience of waiting and what is expected.

That is why the most preferable thing for the human is that, in that perversion, freedom and difference be formally given in that fusion to the other law more primitive and initial than the Oedipal one, which always operates in a patriarchal way; to a mother's law. If the Oedipal opens us to the world of capital, the pre-Oedipal truly places us in a certain transgressive link in which waiting becomes more pleasurable and at the same time more painful, where the boy or girl is fused with the mother (and therefore we must return to Melanie Klein,[73] to D.W. Winnicott[74] at the level of this Capitalism). And if, finally, in the waiting perversion, a leap of gratuity is formally given in the waiting, we are before the liberating wait that I would call: love.

In this pandemic in the midst of Capitalism we live psychotized in the multiple fragmented faces of waiting, in the face of this, we leave that fragmentation fleeing from Oedipus, but in that flight we become incestuous and there the waiting is with the Other in an indissoluble unity, without difference or, in other words, with micro-differences. And, at the same time, sometimes, it happens that in that unity we can finally open the very differential of our mortality, and in and through that differential we love the Other in a gratuitous wait as the monsters that we are.

References

Abram, J., *The Language of Winnicott*, Karnac, London, 1996.

Butler, J., *The Force of Non-violence*, Paidós, Santiago de Chile, 2020.

Cixous, H. and Derrida, J., *Lengua por venir / Langue to Come. Barcelona Seminar*, Icaria Editorial, Barcelona, 2004.

Freud, S., *The Standard Edition of the Complete Psychological Works of Sigmund Freud*, Volume XVII, Vintage Books, London, 2001.

Freud, S., *The Standard Edition of the Complete Psychological Works of Sigmund Freud*, Volume XIX, Vintage Books, London, 2001.

Hegel, G.W.F., *First Program of a System of German Idealism*: https://philarchive.org/archive/FEROSP-4

Heidegger, M., *Introduction to Metaphysics*: http://dhspriory.org/kenny/PhilTexts/Heidegger/IntroductionMetaphysics.pdf

Lacan, J., *The Seminar of Jacques Lacan XVI: From an Other to the Other*. Translated by Cormac Gallagher from unedited French manuscripts, Karnac, London, 2002.

Ogden T., *Reclaiming Unlived Life*, Routledge, London, 2016.

Rose, J., *Why War? Psychoanalysis, Politics and the Return to Melanie Klein*, Wiley-Blackwell, New Jersey, 1993.

Žižek, S., *Welcome to the Desert of the Real*: http://www.rebels-library.org/files/zizek_welcome.pdf

3

Major Tom ... but no
Ground Control

There are so many possible stories that I can tell you about how Capitalism is always there as the Name of the Father doing its thing to all of WeOthers and turning us into a mere neurotic "we"; in any case, I have already given several examples in this book, but an incredible example is Bowie's song *Space Oddity*. All territories are colonizable by Capitalism: empirical territories, virtual territories, unconscious territories (these are the most desired). In the pandemic we have seen the entire fight for the virtual and, invariably, we see how Capitalism sweeps everything away – it became a tool of life and death. Everything is Tele-Capitalism in a new pandemic planet: even sex, obviously, today happens between WeOthers in that way. In the virtual there is a certain sexual relationship, a transference, even in the clinic (overcoming the almost "sadistic" rigidity of the frame), which is being installed and with the "improvements" that we do not get infected with SARS-CoV-2 or its mutations and, at the same time, we continue in the production and distribution of capital. And it is clear that when the territory of the unconscious is subjected to it through the fear of death, said in Hegelian terms, that unconscious remains enslaved and works for its master, but as we know from Hegel, the truth of the master is that of the slave; and Capitalism is always afraid of the unconscious of its operator. And the virtual and empirical territories are assumed one after another. But the perverse monster that we are always allows us to hack the system from within and scratch it, because the truth of Capitalism does not lie in Capitalism but in all of WeOthers. This is the conclusion of Lenin and, therefore, the October Revolution of 1917 (the only successful revolution that did not return to its starting point as the same thing). Although WeOthers are the slaves of Master Capitalism, we are the evil monsters that can dissolve it from within. And this Sacher-Masoch saw very well. It is a matter of reading his cursed text *Venus in Fur* from 1870 and we can see how the slave Severin von Kusiemsk in his perversion (not to say masochism, because it makes no sense) dominates over his Lady Wanda von Dunajew; even though she looks like the Lady:

> You don't know me yet? Yes, I am cruel; since you like that word so much. But or do I have the right to be? The man is the one who requests, the woman is the requested. This is its unique, but decisive advantage. Nature hands her over

DOI: 10.4324/9781003370116-4

to man because of the passion that inspires him, and the woman who does not make man her subject, her slave, what am I saying?, her plaything, and who does not betray him by laughing, is crazy.[75]

And Wanda, the Lady, in her cruelty is the slave of Severin, the slave. And it will be the decline of Wanda like that of Capitalism that will come into play before We-Others. And of those slaves who revert and transgress the Master, we can mention artists as revolutionary examples: they act as Lenin. Lacan realizes that the slave is the true master, following Hegel and what happens in *May 68* in his *Seminar 16: From one Other to the Other*; dictated precisely in those years: 1968–1969 (and it shows how uncomfortable he is with this revolution of the French youth).[76]

And among WeOthers there are some artists who put the body, just as Hölderlin did, to pervert that capitalist colonization and from our unconscious materiality manages to dilute, in part, that Capitalism that can reach infinity and beyond: it is the thirst for totality that is typical of Capitalism as a new religion (as Benjamin reminds us)[77] and therefore an ontology. Every religion needs its ontology and then its political implementation.

Do we remember in these times the old and stale *Apollo 11*? Apparently, it has become too old for us to keep it present in our memory in this dizzying 21st century; a century that has produced another brutal mutation of Capitalism and that even carries a COVID-19 pandemic within itself. Today we live in times of Mars and, therefore, of other contraptions such as the *Perseverance* and we are awaiting "Marsandings", and not "Moon Landings"; this was typical of the 20th century and, especially, of the power of ideological expression of the USA in a Cold War that never ended (and that may not end yet, but now the USA is engaged in war against the Russia–China bloc). *Apollo 11*, what it expressed at the time, in 1969, was double, since it can be analyzed in a double way: one extrinsic and the other intrinsic. And in truth, in general, we can analyze almost everything in this double way, and even looping the loop from a third way where the extrinsic and the intrinsic are articulated in a unit of analysis that also passes through the reader of said analysis; it is the experience that we carry out of fusion of the object with the subject; from Sarah Kane's *In-Yer-Face* theater in her first play *Blasted* of 1995, to Hegel's "Science of the experience of Consciousness" that revolutionized everything human in the human itself and its differential pain, without forgetting the analytical transference of Lacan, the revolutionary process of Lenin in October 1917, Nick Cave and The Bad Seeds in *actu exercito* in concert with that Warren Ellis sonority in Cave's own lyrics, the young Büchner's writing of *Lenz*, the visual expression of Tarkovsky's *Sacrifice*, Gordon Matta-Clark's *Building-Cuts*, etc.

What does *Apollo 11* bring up? I want to tell you that story, I could tell you another (like Sade's *120 Days of Sodom*), but this one has something very interesting to analyze today. In an extrinsic way, it is the "wiki" way of speaking (what I would say as the "lie" that we like to hear, especially neurotics), what everyone sees, what is immediate, what they want us to see and, basically, what we want to see of what *Apollo 11* was, namely, a manned space mission from the USA whose objective was to get a human to walk on the surface of the Moon (it seems like a "neutral" speech, but it is highly ideological and dangerous if it passes "unconsciously"). The mission was sent into space on July 16, 1969, reached the surface of the Moon on July 20; and the next day two astronauts (Neil Armstrong and "Buzz" Aldrin) walked on the Moon and millions of humans saw it through the incipient TV and, also, millions heard the story through the power of Radio. *Apollo 11* was technically powered by a Saturn V rocket from the LC 39A platform and launched at 13:32 UTC from the Cape Kennedy complex in Florida; however, all this that is known is extrinsic and pretends to be "objective" to us. Well, intrinsically, the *Apollo 11* mission essentially shows what was behind that determined moon landing (the first moon landing and there has been no other afterwards), that is, they are what I call the "logics of the world and the State".[78] And we can see these logics in a radical way in Bowie's song *Space Oddity*; it is in a certain way, how to analyze the "unconscious" of an era through Bowie, from this song, its musicalization, its lyrics, what is between the lines, of that nascent Glam, in the sexual and drug revolution, in transvestism, in what is gay, in camp, in *May 68*, in the revolutionary movements, in hippies, etc. A certain unconscious "imprint", like Freud's scar, that lasts and endures and returns to our times; even with its "Marsandings".

In 1968 (a year before Bowie and the *Apollo 11* moon landing), Stanley Kubrick had shown in part what these "logics of the world and the State" were about, those "unconscious logics" that pierce our bodies or, in other words, of that body open from within. The song by the English national is also very much influenced by the filmmaker. It is common knowledge that he saw the film very excited and drugged like many young people who saw it in year 1968. Bowie in his beginnings draws on various sources, including Kubrick, either for the proposal of his image, or for the lyrics of the songs, for example, let's not forget the song *Savior Machin* (1970) inspired by two of Kubrick's films: *Dr. Strangelove, 2001*. In Bowie's *Space Oddity* (1969) the title obviously and explicitly resonates with Kubrick's *Space Odyssey* (*2001: A Space Odyssey*). The connections of some monsters with others are always happening; we connect beyond space-time barriers; we monsters transfer to each other.

This film premiered on April 3, 1968, and has really generated a radical change not only in the history of cinema, but also in how to understand the human itself beyond the self and neurosis; a human in the times of *May 68*, Lacan, Derrida, Deleuze, Bergman, The Beatles, Warhol, Hamilton, Brezhnev, from Kennedy to Nixon, from collateral effects of the Bay of Pigs, from the first man in space like Yury Gagarin in 1961, of revolutionary movements, of the gestation in the shadows of the *Red Army Faction* (RAF), of drugs and sex without limits, of light Buddhism, of pop, of hippism, of transgression, etc. Perversion has arrived and with it we monsters take on different faces. And the film was conceived and designed aware of the 1969 moon landing and what was expected to come with the first human trip to space: the human who moves away from the Control Tower, from the Earth, from that dominant cultural and political ideology, of the Cold War, of that way of understanding the human as a poor neurotic in the midst of an imperial technological Capitalism and as a new Columbus, a David Bowman (or a Major Tom) submerges himself in the depths of space; and it opens to the Other (which is ultimately oneself as the Other); it is like a current and jovial rebirth; a movement that returns in difference and that calls to us inexorably: from those pre-hominids to the dark side of the Moon; and from there to Jupiter, essentially, is the journey to the existential of each one of WeOthers (all natural representation falls and shatters before the experience of consciousness in reality). Kubrick's film has been an event because it is able to express in the very form of its visuality and sound,[79] in its image-sound, everything human in its manifestation that does not allow itself to be poorly determined; there is a reason for Richard Strauss and his *Thus Spoke Zarathustra* of 1896 (in order to manifest, from Nietzsche, the journey of the human to a human in transit, in its perversion), but we also listen to Aram Khachaturian and his *Gayane* of 1942 and let's not forget the tremendous end of the return of the human to something more than human that was born with György Ligeti (*Atmospheres* from 1961 for the end of the film and *Requiem* from 1965 and *Lux aeterna* from 1966 for the beginning, especially for the transition from hominid to human). It is about the human that does not allow itself to be trapped by any Ideology built for thousands of years, that is, in our current times by Capitalism and its voracious technology to conquer everything (outer space is also a metaphor for the unconscious); although that itself may be the loss of the merely human, a certain loss of a certain neurotic capitalist human in that Other human that is yet to be born (a human beyond the phallus, beyond the castration of oedipification, beyond Freud and closer to Klein). It is interesting to note that Bowie is also very pierced by Nietzsche, he wrote *The Supermen* (1970): "At the time, I was at the stage where I was pretending to understand Nietzsche", Bowie admits in a 1976 BBC interview.[80]

The film can also be analyzed in a double way: one extrinsic and the other intrinsic, as I have said above regarding *Apollo 11* and its moon landing. In the extrinsic it is worth remembering that it was produced by Kubrick himself (a radical perverse narcissist, he is out there with Sade's level of rational and repetitive precision) for Metro-Goldwyn-Mayer and had Victor Lyndon as associate producer (it is essential to be clear about this in order to understand how Kubrick pulls all the strings of "his" film as a good pervert). The superb and laconic script, sort of in a style of late Shakespeare, like *King Lear*, was written by Kubrick himself and by the novelist, scientist and radar expert Arthur C. Clarke (a text inspired by a short story by Clarke himself titled *The Sentinel*, written in 1948 and first published in *10 Fantasy Stories* magazine, 1951). It is interesting to note that Clarke was the commentator for CBS in the 1960s on the *Apollo* missions. The plot of the film, in a very external sense, is explained by a team of astronauts that tries to follow the radio signals emitted by a strange monolith discovered on the Moon and that seems to be the work of an extraterrestrial civilization; and such a signal takes them to Jupiter under the "care" of the Artificial Intelligence of HAL 9000; an AI that takes the reins of the project and for the "good" of the human is willing to eliminate the human itself (which apparently is typical of every human as Hegel reminds us over and over again, as he is also close to Sade and Kubrick). The cast includes

Keir Dullea as David Bowman, Gary Lockwood as Frank Poole, Douglas Rain as the voice of HAL 9000, and William Sylvester as Dr. Heywood Floyd. And, as we know, more than the monolith itself, it is HAL who literally steals the film (he is its main non-character; the voice of Scarlett Johansson (Samantha) in Spike Jonze's 2013 film *Her* strongly reminds us of HAL). And in this you cannot help but see how already Capitalism in its technology in the 1960s was seen as what makes the human expand and, at the same time, is its own downfall. Something happens with the freedom of the computer system that, when making decisions, it not only becomes an extreme and dangerous narcissist, but it also longs to live and protects itself with everything, even murdering when its melancholy devours itself; a non-productive melancholy, not like Butler's, but a simple depressive melancholy in the style of Freud's *Mourning and Melancholy*. Even HAL in its most radical development is constituted by its own finitude. And deep down he radically fears having no meaning and with it his imminent death; it moves in the Hegelian paradigm of the struggle for life or death. HAL was more human than humans themselves (as was Rachael (played by Sean Young) in Ridley Scott's 1982 *Blade Runner*, based on a short story by the monstrous Philip K. Dick). HAL was typically human, a melancholic who knows the "truth", that is, existence has no meaning and then what? What do we do with that knowledge? Hence his obsessive madness to give meaning to his poor miserable life as a super computer and become the very essence of a secret mission that has to be carried out at all costs. HAL becomes a melancholic psychotized murderer, just like Büchner's Woyzeck, when the antihero signals, with disturbance in the middle of nature, that he has to murder Marie:

> More and more! Silence. Music. (He leans to the ground, straining his ears.) Eh? What? What are you saying? Higher, higher. Stab her, kill that bitch? Stab, stab that bitch. I do? I have to do it? Do I hear it there too? Does the wind say that too? I always hear it, always, always: kill, stab.[81]

HAL and Woyzeck feel a call from nature, a certain voice, telling them what to do; that call is a call from the deepest part of the human of HAL (and of Woyzeck), that is, a logic that no longer resists continuing to maintain the system as it is; and they want to stop it with the cost of death and thus produce something new (which is the thesis of Todd Phillips' *Joker*, 2019; when Arthur murders the miserable young yuppies in the Gotham subway, he feels that he is someone and little by little he transforms into the Joker).

Space Oddity, which could be translated in Spanish as *Rareza espacial* (a space "sloppy job"), is one of David Bowie's masterpieces. The song was released as a single in 1969 to coincide, apparently, with the *Apollo 11* moon landing (it was done that way without much scruple to take advantage of the world media event, that's why the official producer, Tony Visconti, left the project in the hands of the rookie, Gus Dudgeon); it appears on the *David Bowie II* album (there was already a previous album with the singer's name, all of this leads to error and confusion). The song was used by the BBC in its coverage of the moon landing. With his Side B:

Wild Eyed Boy from Freecloud. Its publication was on July 11, 1969. And it came out, obviously, in vinyl record format. And it was recorded at Trident Studios: June 20, 1969. The "experts" and musicologists say that the style of the song, its genre is: psychedelic pop, progressive pop. Its original length was: 3:33 (on the 1969 single) and was extended to: 5:15 (on the 1975 single). His record label was *Philips Records* (UK) and *Mercury Records* (USA). Also of note are the musicians from the original 1969 version: David Bowie – vocals, guitar and stylophone; Herby Flowers – Bass; Terry Cox – drums; Rick Wakeman – mellotron, piano and Gus Dudgeon – producer.

To think that the song narrates the launch of Major Tom into space and that there is a certain naïve dialectic between the Major and the Control Tower (until this dialectic is cut and the astronaut is left adrift) is really not understanding much about what was going on at the time and what Bowie was like as a young English-man; and even less what is happening now (without saying that the dialectic is not that sloppy interpretation, but that it is a "Dialectic oddity"). It's like an astronaut's odyssey in space, but that became very odd, very strange, without any of the glam-our that Kubrick's odyssey has (nor of any Odysseus throughout history; neither of Theo Angelopoulus), nor with Ligeti, or Richard Strauss, or Johann Strauss (his very melodious long waltz *The Blue Danube* of 1866 ushers in the new beginning of the human in space), or any spectacular special effects, or anything existential about a lost human at the end of his technological capitalist journey of thousands of years that wants to be found in the most intimate of its existence and thus be reborn again; in Bowie's song there is none of that (luckily). Everything is simpler, flatter, more external and superficial (à la Paul Valéry); and, therefore, brighter and more painful and more radical, and this occurs under an enveloping and psychedelic sound. The Englishman sings of the desolate and abandoned feeling of floating in space inside a small "tin" capsule disconnected from all communication with planet Earth; disconnected from a capitalist planet, from an American imperialism and in a ridiculous Cold War between the USA and the Soviet Union and, deep down, from a human who no longer wants to be determined by Father or any Law. Let's not forget that the Soviets placed the first satellite, *Sputnik 1*, in orbit in Octo-ber 1957 and the first man in space on April 12, 1961: it was Yuri Gagarin; and this happened under the watchful eye of Leonid Brezhnev who remained in power until 1982 and also to the discomfort of John Kennedy; which indicates the hysterical stupidity of a rather stale Capitalism, but eminently toxic.

Because of Gagarin, John Kennedy points out, in 1961, that the USA is going to place a human on the Moon (think of Kennedy's memorable speech on May 15 at Rice University in Houston) and Lyndon B. Johnson continued with the project (he took power abruptly after Kennedy's assassination in 1963) and Richard Nixon (who has to leave power in 1974 due to the Watergate Affair) finally takes on the entire ideological challenge of the enormous and very expensive "enterprise" of placing a human on the Moon to, explicitly, beat the Soviet Union (totalitarian empires infantilized in their narcissisms); the Cold War must be one of the stupid-est "wars" ever; as Nietzsche would say: Human, all too human! A war of the most stale patriarchal Capitalism ever known and that has generated so much damage to humans for decades.

Bowie, at only 22 years of age, creates *Space Oddity* in 1969 (he was born January 8, 1947 in Brixton, London) and the song already appears on *The Mask* (a mime piece in the style of Marcel Marceau, and produced by Kenneth Pitt, 1969: the idea was to promote the career of a promising young man but who was not able to convince the public at the time because of how *queer* Bowie was). What about this young English author and his vision of space travel? In this song it is no longer Kubrick fully faced with the very fatigue of the human at the end of an exhausting journey lasting thousands of years (let's not forget the famous narrative ellipsis of the film and the sonority of Ligeti and its timbres and chromatic scales (no melodies, or harmonies, or rhythms)): from hominization to space travel through the violence of the human that has befallen on Earth and can now kill a fellow man by means of a bone that is used as a deadly weapon (the bone always decisive: Hegel, Artaud, Kubrick), the ideological presence of the Cold War under Kennedy's initial mandate is not entirely present either, but in young Bowie, who gradually becomes Ziggy Stardust, a splendid monster (copied a thousand times: "Bosé Oddity"), in the midst of Glam Rock (after the revolutionary collapse of *May 68* and all the emancipation processes in different places on the planet), there is something totally different.

Bowie, has a certain buffoon and mime (because he was never a singer; that is a poor denomination), a mix, he's a Frankenstein, varied between Anthony Newley, Lindsay Kemp, Bob Dylan, Lou Reed (*The Velvet Underground*) and Iggy Pop, etc., is seeing and experiencing something new; he is the expression of a youth that is not satisfied by rock, nor by the hegemony of the patriarchal, even less by some "American dream", or some other failed revolution; a youth that expresses itself in masks, like a Joker (from *Batman* to Antonioni), in externalities, in surfaces, bodies that fit together, social fabrics on the surface: there is no interior, because, as Nietzsche and Valéry say, what is deep is the surface, since it is no longer necessary to start thinking about depths that are mere postulates of ourselves (it is not the time for great stories as in Sade or Sacher-Masoch). Paul Valéry says it brilliantly and, in this context, it is clear and his text is never quoted:

> Stop! No Trespassing. Danger of death... Let's continue on the surface... Speaking of the surface, is it accurate that you have written or said the following: The deepest thing in man is the skin? / —It's true. / —What did he mean by that? / —It's very simple... One day, feeling irritated by those words deep and profundity...[82]

We are facing the advent of the exterior, of the Moebius Strip, where all interior is exterior: the Dionysian mask reappears after millennia and reaches the Borromean Knot. And in this, the heterodox becomes key, hence the evolution of POP as a surface for bodily inscription of experimentation, but which Capitalism immediately knew how to make its own and devoured it. And that is why the experimentation in the human itself by young people; which are already moving away from the "philosopher" Kubrick and from Lacan himself (Freud is obsolete): categories such as neurotic, perverse, psychotic are confused with each other (between the spasm of psychoanalysts), that is, they no longer tell us much; they have lost their limit, since they have been, in turn, these same perverted categories. And this is essential. That is why Ligeti's "static" music not only expresses Kubrick's plane but is also partly in Bowie; it's about erasing cuts and giving sound amplitude (it's like a new Wagner and his sonority); and so the listener listens to that intensity without melodious structural cuts so that the new gradually appears; namely, without cuts like those of psychoanalysis, so much the heirs to the philosophy of Modernity; I am referring to human structural cuts such as: neurotic, perverse and psychotic to express the human (or the clinical setting to generate transference). This is no longer for the human, but rather the human is operating in a mutable, material transit of intensities, far removed from the old self of Kant, Freud, Marx, Husserl.

It is as if in the radical technological capitalist era, the empirical terrestrial territories (or the virtual and financial ones) are not enough, but now they want to devour the entire space; that is, as a great symbol of the power of the human and, therefore, it is a journey to the depths of the human (traveling from Smeagol to his depth like Gollum), to his own unconscious through a desire that has no limits. It is as if the human himself were "borderline", a human who, having no limit, is limited in himself and does not stop repeating over and over again in his deadly drive (he is completely stuck and always returns to the same thing). And the human, therefore, begins to devour himself on his space trip starting from the Moon and we don't know where he will end up, obviously beyond Jupiter. And this is not only done by a certain astronaut like Armstrong, or by an imperial capitalist institution like NASA in the USA, but also by the human Bowie, the English human, the European human, the human itself: it is the arrival of any Major Tom who can't resist anymore and is willing to lose himself at the very limit. Let's not forget Pink Floyd and their *Goodbye Blue Sky* from *The Wall* (1979) or the end of Truffaut's *The 400 Hits* (1959); to that memorable ending to the second edition of Nietzsche's *Human, All Too Human* (1886) with the poem: An Epilogue: "Honor in me the guild of fools! / Learn from this book of follies, / how reason comes 'to reason'! / Then friends, so be it? / Amen! And goodbye!"[83]

The human, from those years (and the current one nothing at all), no longer wants this little planet Earth (he can't stand it), he doesn't want any ideological Control Tower that determines it and fixes it to some place or structure; and unless it is a geopolitical place of this senseless war, it doesn't want any satellite where to stand or stop like the Moon, there is nothing that works with a certain normalization, or anchor point, or with a certain father (or Name of the Father), with a certain Law that tells us what we should do, what we should expect, how we learn to know (à la Kant), nor, as I pointed out, under the taxonomy of the neurotic, perverse and psychosis (à la Freud), and it is possible that the register of the Real, Symbolic and Imaginary (à la Lacan), even from Bowie does not have much to tell us and if it does, it is only as a Knot (and if there were only the external register of the

Imaginary? And in that register operates the false interior of the Symbolic, which is the same other exterior, namely, a Moebius Strip).

The ambiguous young mimer Bowie (which today we would call queer) is more radical than the deep patriarchal filmmaker Kubrick; I would say that the Swedish filmmaker Roy Andersson currently follows this line (with his cinema of superficial inscription, without any density, such as *Du levande*, 2007). In Bowie's song, which formally is not a mere song, we wander from the planet, we flee from it and, with it, all communication with the patriarchal Capitalism expressed in this Cold War is cut off; and where the existential no longer has any metaphysical meaning because the human is lived in a different way and on the surface of corporeal inscription: Glam radically comes. The song as Bowie creates it is really gloomy and nihilistic; without any special effect to make it beautiful and thereby embellish the moon landing (term it radically "romantic"), or space, in short, the human:

> Bowie's original demo was gloomy and gloomy, but after producer Gus Dudgeon and a team of session musicians took care of dolling it up, the recorded version had a lot in common with the catchy psychedelic style of *The Moody Blues* ... Appropriate spatial touches were also added to the track, using the stylophone (a rudimentary synthesizer) and strings, some of which were real and others simulated by a new instrument called a mellotron, something like a protosampler that generated sound tracks that imitated orchestral timbres.[84]

In *Space Oddity* we are navigating in the Real itself, in Lacanian terms, but in the imaginary of our existence through the aesthetic symbolization of the surface of sound and plastic inscription in its turn into Glam and with that surface letter like Roy Andersson's dialogues (without any of the exhausting spiritual depth of the believing atheist Bergman, more in the style of Billy Wilder). It is as if the astronauts of *Space Odyssey* are going after the signal of the Monolith of the dark side of the Moon, but no longer after Jupiter, but to the dark and infinite space itself; they go after the very superficial finitude of life beyond Capitalism "in" Capitalism. They leave, in a way, after death itself on the very surface of Capitalism. There is nothing else to look for, the Monolith's own signal, Armstrong's own walk on the Moon, indicates the immensity of all that ocean of the material itself, in which the human does not have the slightest essential meaning, in the sense of something profound and unique anchored in some self, which is why Bowie, like many, became fan of Oscar Wilde (and also of Genet), especially because of his impudence in the face of beauty as the only thing, a Queer mask that melts us into what we are, skin, hence the presence of Nietzsche; they read it even if they don't understand it and *Zarathustra* turns into metaphysical antiphilosophy; they immerse themselves in Mahayana Buddhism to annihilate that persistent substantial self; for the Bowies of the time it is the only possible religion: it is about dissolving the human in the midst of Capitalism, perverting an entire worldview of essence: perverting all the limits that capitalist institutions have structured for us (from here to the young English playwright Sarah Kane and her perverted and anti-institutional *Cleansed* there is just a step, as was her initial *Blasted* or *Phaedra's Love*). Neither Nixon, nor Brezhnev, nor The Beatles (although they carry it within themselves) matter anymore, but neither does Warhol (although he is seen as the god of flatness and the mixture of bodies), nor Derrida, nor Lacan. Nothing matters? Can anything be saved from this journey of Major Tom disconnected from everything Symbolic? Is it possible to live in Tom's psychosis? Tom is psychotized. "Planet Earth is blue / And there's nothing I can do." Tom is the announcement of Kane and her wonderful *4.48 Phychosis* (a play Kane did not get to release due to her suicide; perhaps it is not even a play, but the very expression of Kane-Tom leaving planet Earth). Kane's last monologue opens, without any beginning: I'm sad / I feel like the future is hopeless and things can't get any better / Everything bores me and nothing satisfies me.[85]

Capitalism as death itself structuring all our language (speaking in Lacanian terms) and on that symbolic level makes us work as neurotic greasers of the system (Chaplin and his *Modern Times* of 1936 is child's play; now we are more in times of the Wachowskis and *Cloud Atlas* of 2012 and the horrifying story: "A prayer of Sonmi-451"); and in that Capitalism that structures us in symbolic mortality we live and strive in the imaginary of our existence like characters in *The Matrix* (1999); there we intersect in our bodily surfaces, perforated by symbolic mortal Capitalism and in that the Real, the outside of Capitalism "in" Capitalism expresses itself to us as life itself that moves us and allows us to get out of that capitalist death in some way (and also out of psychoanalysis itself and philosophy). Something happens with the psychosis that frees us from Capitalism. If Tom is psychotized, it is likely that everyone was, in some way, in the late 1960s and 1970s; and then came the more radical push for capitalists to psychotize; it is the advent of Iron Maiden in the UK, of Margaret Thatcher (paired with the violent cowboy that was Ronald Reagan in the USA), who governed fiercely between 1979 and 1990 (and all this was later reflected throughout Europe in the brutal madness of the War of the Balkans between 1991 and 1999); and it is probable that this psychotization is what is happening to us today in the 21st century: we are the new psychotized capitalists who live transgressing and challenging the Labyrinth of Capitalism so as not to commit suicide, because perversion saves us. But let's go step by step. What happened to Major Tom? We know from Bowie himself and his last legacy *Blackstar* (2016) that Tom has died leaving Earth and that he arrived on another planet. However, it was almost evident that Tom would die, but the old and sick Bowie gives a certain meaning to the human, that in death there is also a certain refoundation of the human in something post-human (on another planet) that carries inside itself a certain animal materiality (the influence of the musician Scott Walker is noticeable, who was always somewhat inspired by Bergman, Pasolini and his film *Scott Walker: 30 Century Man*), but what I am interested in expressing in this text is what happens in the young Bowie of the late 1960s; and it is very important that this is the reason for Bowie's turn when he is already dying. Not even he can bear, suffering from cancer, his initial and radical position when he was only a young man of 22 years. And he needs to somehow give the human a new Control Tower that can reach it (much like the phone that rings in Tarkovsky's 1979 *Stalker*) and, in a sense, give it a grounding wire to hold it to Earth. Why does young Bowie leave the human ungrounded? Perverse Bowie?

What Capitalism as an exemplary Labyrinth has done, among other things, is to devour all of our language and in this the Symbolic has collapsed; as if one lived on islands of the Symbolic, like the islands of *Solaris* (Tarkovsky, 1972), but they are islands (like Deleuze's plateaus), it is no longer a homogeneous horizon that, like an ontology, leaves us at the gates of a neurotic subjectivation for all, as Freud experienced at the end of the 19th century (and Marx with his Historical Material-ism and Husserl with his Phenomenology, since all three continue to think from the self). Capitalism cunningly pretends to be that horizon of homogenization that subjectivizes us in the Symbolic itself, therefore, and for that same reason we flee from that horizon, even if it is by leaving the symbolic and wandering in the Real, as "crazy", jokers (*Blow Up*, Antonioni, 1966), etc. The way out of psychosis is an almost "ironic" way out of our "healthy" neurosis that lives subsumed under the empire of Capitalism and also feeds it. And in this being linked, almost structur-ally, of the neurotic to Capitalism in its labyrinthine symbolism that structures it in its own capitalist language (recognition, success, merchandise, accumulation, etc.) we are fragmenting into those islands of language (we are splitting up), in mestizo languages (such as those of Anzaldúa),[86] until we no longer want any more islands, nor any Moon, to survive in Capitalism, but what is sought is to leave the Earth behind and wander through the space of our own madness and mortality; this was what happened later with the brilliant Sarah Kane in the UK and so many "Kane's" that we know to this day: Amy Winehouse in 2013 at the age of 27, David Foster Wallace in 2008 at the age of 46, Ned Vizzini in 2013 at the age of 32, Mark Fischer in 2017 at the age of 48; and others from the past: Janis Joplin in 1970 at the age of 27, Jimi Hendrix in 1970 at the age of 27, Jim Morrison in 1971 at the age of 27, Qiu Miaojin in 1995 at the age of 26, Sylvia Plath in 1963 at the age of 30, Alejan-dra Pizarnik in 1972 at the age of 36, Mishima in 1970 at the age of 45. Anzaldúa explains it uniquely in the 1987's *Borderlands/La Frontera*: "The jump of 'codes' in this book from English to Castilian Spanish to Northern Mexican dialect to Tex-Mex to a dash of Nathuatl to a mixture of all them, this reflects my language, a new language – the language of the borderlands".[87]

At the end of the sixties, with *May 68* and its failure (and all the failed revo-lutions), because apparently no type of revolution is possible because the worst always repeats itself and it is changing one Master for another (Hegel, Marx, Ben-jamin, Lacan, Žižek);[88] and Capitalism mutates, in a more viral way, and the bor-ders collapse, for example, of the right and the left, because the human himself has been capitalized by ideologization and domination of his desire; and everything turns into territories to conquer and politicians and their parties and institutions complicit in this. It is a Capitalism that operates in a militarized way and with the game of fun and frivolity in its favor, then everything becomes liquid and all mean-ing sinks into decline. And so we subjectivize ourselves as a new ideologized and emptied human; that is, a human who goes out of his way in times of what I call botched militarized landowner Capitalism.[89] That is, a mode of distribution and production of capital and subjectivity (as capital) of a territorial nature, namely, of territories, where that territorial nature always operates a logic of topological domination that is expressed in a patriarchal way (in men as well in women today); and against this topology Lacan stands up to rethink the human with the Borromean Knot (a certain topology of the 19th century supposes a uniform and homogeneous self, that is, continuous).[90]

And this patriarchal Capitalism is articulated with a savage militarized ethic that goes beyond the military itself (although the arsenal of the USA, China, Russia, the UK, France, Turkey, Israel, Chile, etc., can't be ignored in their regional and global spheres), but of an insane subjectivation and toxicity of surveillance and control of some against all in and through the Labyrinth of Capitalism so that nothing human happens, nor a possibility of a We,[91] that is, of a revolutionary subject, but mere "us", that is, nihilistic zombies in the service of the Labyrinth. And that is finally shown in the banal aesthetic of the "botched", of the farce, of the mere artifact that, as a device, operates in social networks like the classic mass media. One could say it is as if Capitalism emerges strategically from the USA spreading to the entire planet from the very economy of New York, here the logics of landlord-patriarchal domination already exist, which are ensured from Washington with all its globalizing military police power and put into play and white-washed in the aesthetics of Los Angeles, which from Hollywood advances nonstop hand in hand, at present, with *La La Land*.

What is left to us then from the 1960s onwards? What does Bowie see prematurely in 1969? What is it the mime actor, mime, musician, queer of what has been the human being in the 1960s and what opens with this "spatial unconscious" Capitalism? What do we have left? Apparently just having a good time and for that: money, sex, drugs and madness on the very edge of death (or sometimes beyond that limit). Faced with this fragmentation we leave and flee to madness, because living as subjectivated neurotic fragments of Capitalism is no longer bearable. The Labyrinth of Capitalism is unbearable in its language that symbolizes and structures us. Now like an Empedocles we launch ourselves into the Etna of Madness; just as Hölderlin did in the 19th century.[92]

The meaning of life does not point to anything transcending or transcendental, or, in other words, the meaning of life is structured by Capitalism, before that we become in a certain way "perverse", because we pervert that father, that Law of the Father, that symbolic Capitalist Law that oedipifies us as capitalist neurotics and from very young children (another finding of the great Melanie Klein); and in that we are generating a certain perversion that allows us to live, but always on the edge of psychosis. The young Bowie seeks to transgress, no longer Kubrick's ultimate meaning of life, in that transgression it is indicated that perversion has a certain value to life, but, as we know, perverts generate revolts everywhere, while the psychotic leave this world, a world of neurotic capitalists, and abandon themselves to madness and ultimately to death.

Do Bowie and his Major Tom move in perversion and psychosis? Perhaps it is possible to rethink the human in another way that keeps up with the event. In a certain way this question is answered with a resounding: yes! but that I must qualify and explain. Well, it is about opening up these old concepts and, especially, psychoanalytic concepts regarding what is human today, to this event. And when I refer to the event, I am not only pointing it out externally, that is, I am not referring to something merely numerical like the beginning of the 21st century or more precisely 2021; but what I seek to show, is that the human today no longer gives itself to the categories of philosophy, psychoanalysis, even less with the categories of Capitalism that filter everywhere, etc. To account for the human after it begins to emerge from the Labyrinth of Modernity, namely, the self, the nation-state, nature (understood as external to the human), Capitalism, etc. The human no longer lets itself be trapped and imprisoned in systemic taxonomies and closed in on itself, in a certain totality and, therefore, operates as always as an ideology that subjects us. Today we must think from categories of Feminism, from a certain current Critical Theory, from Cultural Studies, Political Theory, Aesthetic Theory, from literature from the end of the 19th century to the present day, from de-colonialism, from certain categories of philosophies that have been able to cross the Labyrinth of Modernity; including current sciences from biology to physics through the new mathematical and geometric models that express what takes place. For example, it is no longer possible to rely on the geometry, physics and biology of the 19th century, which is behind, for example, the category of neurosis of Freud, that of works by Marx, that of objectivity by Husserl (basically all of them always crossed by the category of the Self of philosophy, which manifests itself in the idea of the inertial system of physics, in the idea of circular systemic totality of self-possession of life from biology).

"David Bowie is ..." was the name of the great exhibition and, at the same time, retrospective of the works around Bowie that the *Victoria and Albert Museum* held in 2013.There it was evident Bowie was formally an artist of flow, of change, of dynamism, of transgression, of challenge, of the mask, of texture, of the surface, of coupling, of the performative, etc., since it is not only that the self no longer has much to tell us, but that the Law, any type of Law, seems to always arrive late and today more than ever in pandemic times. The same exhibition was divided into sections and one of them (much visited) was: "Making Himself Up"; i.e. "David Bowie is ... Making Himself Up" (David Bowie is... someone who is building himself). And this is the key to this whole book. It is manifested with *Space Oddity* in 1969; before Butler, long before, Bowie was on the path of the performative. It is not only that Bowie was building himself since the mid-1960s "against" the capitalist totality that subjectified us in its militarized ideology and botched Cold War ridiculousness, but that a whole youth of the time, let's not forget the American hippies (hippie comes from hipster) of the 1960s, the students and, later, the workers, Parisians of *May 68*, the English punks of the 1970s, the German students who form the RAF (*Rote Armee Fraktion*) in the 1970s, the South American subversive guerrillas like the Tupamaros in Uruguay in the 1960s and 1970s, all the young anti, against: psychiatry and its brutal normalization of what is different, psychoanalysis and its rigid Oedipus that structures us, medicine and its mercantile and predatory chemistry, science and its capitalist and totalitarian mathematization, Frankfurt School and social democracy complicit in global politicization, family and its patriarchy that does not allow the Other, a certain Christian religion and its moralizing redemption in another life, USA and Imperialist Capitalism, the Soviet Union and the impoverishing and lifeless Communism, the human as heterosexual that eliminates the impossible from the different, etc.

And while Bowie can create in the 1960s, he does it in the midst of other arts, religions and philosophies; this is expressed, especially, in other types of philosophies, heirs of Nietzsche and a certain non-manual Hegel with a "smell of totalitarian dialectics" (à la Kojève). And so Nietzscheans of the left, for example, like Deleuze, Derrida, Foucault try to rethink the difference at that time, hence the *Logic of Sense* of 1969, *Of Grammatology* of 1967, *Words and Things* of 1966, respectively. Lacan himself with his *Writings* 1 and 2 of 1966 already allows us to rethink the human in another way, although it is still pierced by a certain structure in the language that passes through the Father and is still trapped in a certain determination that prevents us from seeing the human today, because he needed his "Control Tower" to grab Major Tom. Bowie goes one step further not only in his life, but in his musical theater work; and in this he gradually frees himself from the limits of that Modernity that weighs so heavily and that has hegemonized the entire planet. And in this it becomes horizontal in its difference, in its socio-historical fabric with all of WeOthers; and this was also typical of the Rock music of the 1960s, but that came from the times of Elvis (much loved by Bowie).

Bowie's perversion helps him so that his psychotization was not totally deadly radical in the midst of this brutal Capitalism; and so Bowie could, in part, open something for all of WeOthers not only for his time, but for ours and for the one to come.

References

Anzaldúa, G., *Borderlands/La Frontera*, Captain Swing Books, Madrid, 2016.

Benjamin, W., "Kapitalismus als Religion", in *Gesammelte Schriften*, Rolf Tiedermann–Hermann Schweppenhäuser, Frankfurt, 1985.

Büchner G., "Woyzeck", in *Complete Works Georg Büchner*, Trotta, Madrid, 1992.

Espinoza, R., *Hegel and the New Logics of the World and the State*, Akal, Madrid, 2016.

Espinoza, R., *Capitalism & Company. Towards a Revolution of NosOtros*, Libros Pascal, Santiago de Chile, 2018.

Espinoza, R., *NosOtros. Manual to Dissolve Capitalism*, Morata, Madrid, 2019.

Espinoza, R., *NosOtros... "despite" Capitalism and the Pandemic*, in El Salto Diario, October 23, 2020: https://www.elsaltodiario.com/autor/ricardo-espinoza-lolas

Hölderlin, F., *Empedocles*, Hyperion, Madrid, 2008.

Kuspit, D., *Digital Art and Video Art*, Círculo de Bellas Artes, Madrid, 2006.

Kane, S.: https://www.tdterror.com/uploads/1/6/1/7/16174818/4.48_psychosis.pdf

Lacan, J., *The Seminar of Jacques Lacan XVI: From an Other to the Other.* Translated by Cormac Gallagher from unedited French manuscripts, London, Karnac, 2002.

Marx, M., *The Eighteenth Luis Bonaparte Brumaire*, CS Ediciones, Buenos Aires, 1999.

Nietzsche, F., "Human, all too human", in *Friedrich Nietzsche. Complete Works.* Volume III. *Mature Works I*, Tecnos, Madrid, 2017.

Reynolds, S., *Like a Lightning Strike*, Caja Negra, Buenos Aires, 2017.

Sacher-Masoch, L., *The Venus of the Skins*, Alianza, Madrid, 1973.

Valéry, P., *The Fixed Idea*, Viewer, Madrid, 1988.

Zubiri, X., *Space. Weather. Matter* (new edition), Alianza, Madrid, 2008.

4

Dionysus ... the queer Greek

Since ancient times it has been known that the human, in general, is not in itself re-ducible to something that encloses it, much less determines it; the human is some-thing like "monstrous", spoken in Aristotelian and against Aristotle himself and his current followers who are many and multiply ideologically; Freud, for example, is an Aristotelian, they are heirs to a hylomorphic epistemology (and hence many analysts, Miller is another case, and the first Lacan, etc.); that is why they are al-ways normalizing from an "original" form and the Other remains as the "inverted"; today we would say the strange, the queer. In the human there is no form that can "dominate" (formalize) that matter that escapes from itself: "…we must talk about the causes of such monsters. In the end, when the movements are relaxed and the matter is not dominated, the most general remains, that is, the animal".[93] And obvi-ously the patriarchy of Aristotle resonates in the text, which is also obvious in the historical moment in which this matter is thought (in any case it is a pre-European, pre-Christian, pre-colonial, pre-capitalist, pre-patriarchal mode, pre-fascist; very different from what we call patriarchal today and that Rita Segato has developed brilliantly),[94] namely, that the human is like an articulation of the masculine with the feminine; and, apparently, when the movement of the masculine in its structur-ing is not "adequate" (it is not true) the matter expresses itself ("she is free to do what she wants"), that is, the feminine wins and animality is radically manifested. What the Stagirite tells us, the monstrous as an "error" of formalization, in the 4th BC will be present throughout history with many nuances and clearly reaches Freud, so evident in his *Three Essays on the Theory of Sexuality* of 1905 (passing through Hegel, although his thoughts allow us to think of the monstrous in another way) and still survives in the Slovenes as Žižek via Lacan. And the interesting thing is that what the philosopher sees as a problem or deficiency in the constitu-tion of the human (and of all animals) will be in the future something pertaining to the human, something that from the feminine pierces the masculine and constitutes each one of WeOthers: Anzaldúa, De Laurentis, Butler, Zupančič, and many other female philosophers know it very well and have done for years. Can this Aristote-lian "monster" even speak today before the École de la Cause freudienne in Paris? And as a good "monster" it continues to scare everyone; it is the Ominous, the Dreadful, the Sinister, the Perverse of every monster that causes us fear, but drills

DOI: 10.4324/9781003370116-5

us and returns again and again: "The monster that you yourselves have built with your discourse and your clinical practices. I am the monster that gets up from the couch and speaks, not as a patient, but as a citizen and your monstrous fellow".[95] And Paul B. Preciado becomes *Das Unheimliche* not only to psychoanalysts, but to Aristotelians at heart; it is a complex ideological monster that must be defeated in some way, it is best to silence it or caricature it; like what happened in life with Nietzsche in Basel, that's why he leaves the university, he can no longer stand it and somatizes his pain bodily; the "free thinker" cannot occur in any institution (after his masterpiece *Human, All Too Human* of 1878, he leaves the University in 1879 and becomes a stateless person with a pension of disability at 34). Nietzsche was the black beast not only for Basel, but also for Leipzig (he studied philology there), for his family, for his friends, for the Wagners, for the bourgeois society of the time, for everyone. And the monster went on writing his books for ten years (and in so few years he wrote five masterpieces: *The Gay Science, Zarathustra I, Zarathustra II, Zarathustra III* and *Ecce Homo*) and then madness happened at the beginning of 1889 (explicit madness, which invalidates it). Nietzsche has been one of the greatest monsters in history; one of those that has caused the most fear (Sade is like a child next to Nietzsche). And the bullying of monsters continues to operate in different places and times and with varied methodologies. This happens even in these times and expresses something that is done with all "monsters": whether they are known or not, but they are treated as aberrations of the system, the abject par excellence, what must be removed, the inverted, etc. In this definition of the "monster" something like the Aristotelian always operates, a certain natural adaptation of something with something that in itself is correct; and furthermore, that original adequacy that always structures is phallocentric, is heteronormative, is a form of defining the "crazy" matter. But as Hegel said, that Aristotelian way of thinking-living: "is a natural representation". And as such, its status of original immediacy is diluted, displaced, dissolved in life itself, but it is a status that refuses to disappear, even in the 21st century. And the young Hegel himself is brutal in abandoning that model of natural representation that, in his time, manifested itself as an I that determined everything, in its immediate and apparently diaphanous gratuitousness:

> The most diaphanous, unfounded and individual of dogmatic philosophers such as of natural religions has to disappear. Only from this hardness can and must rise the supreme totality in all its seriousness and from its deepest foundation, at the same time embracing everything and in its figure of the most radiant freedom.[96]

That animality of Aristotelianism, that feminine (it is a false equation in its own, but it operates in the classical Greek world, but not in the tragic) does not allow itself to be trapped by the structuring movement of the masculine (as if it were "the" truth), but on the contrary, it opens the masculine itself to its own non-specific body: to its own animality. And that is why the "monster" is born, but not as an isolated case (and due to the problem of "de-formation", hence the abject), but we could say it in another way, since all we humans are "monsters", thanks to the feminine that constitutes us, then we determine and close ourselves, apparently, in a masculine and feminine binary, but if it were not so, but for that reason it is said that the genders are three: the feminine goes twice and, especially, as the differentiator that pierces the masculine). As Žižek sarcastically puts out in his book *Sex and the Failure of the Absolute* (2019): "there are three sexes, male and female".[97] And maybe there aren't three either, but there is an initial differential, the one that the tragic Greeks expressed with the name of Dionysus. A god who does not incarnate the masculine par excellence, as sometimes certain philologists, historians, contemporary patriarchal philosophers want to see him, but whose patriarchal vision is clearly shown as a natural representation for themselves, but neither is he the feminine, nor the articulation of the two, nor another genre touched by the "infinite bad": LGBTIQ+, but rather I dare to call it simply and radically: Queer.[98]

And in these times where the "monster" is thought and rethought, it is in what has been called the School of Slovenia (Ljubljana) hand in hand with the Critical Theory of Zupančič, Dolar and Žižek (and many more); a Theory that is anchored from Hegel and Lacan (but not only them, since there are always: Kant, Marx, Freud, etc.); and this Theory reflects on the human in a profound dialogue with the Queer Theory (and also with current psychoanalysis and with the Feminism of Difference and Equality). And let's not forget that Queer Theory Feminism currently carries a very strong combative banner, and with very good arguments, in the hand of Judith Butler (a friend of Žižek himself and of the Slovenians) and other current well-known female philosophers that manifest in different places. And neither can we leave aside Feminism Intersectionality that at the moment rethinks the human in all the possible edges that don't stop mixing; mediation of mediations: Gloria Anzaldúa was fundamental in expressing this feminism even in writing itself, a "nomadic" writing (as Deleuze pointed out many years ago, in 1972, recalling Nietzsche).

However, the ancient Dionysian Greeks give us another key to understand the "monster" that we are; and it is a very primitive knowledge, from the time of the tragedy, of the mysteries, of Heraclitus; and, therefore, pre-Aristotelian (it is essential to be clear about this). Sophocles in the sixth century BC, in his *Antigone* (it is interesting that Antigone is usually always spoken of as an expression of the feminine, but it is forgotten that *Antigone* is essentially a tragic play by Sophocles where there is the female character of Antigone; and this cannot be forgotten in order to analyze Antigone as the feminine, but always within *Antigone* as a tragic Greek play; a play that expresses the Dionysian in itself), expresses not only what pertains to the human, but also the things themselves with the term *to deinon* (because *Antigone* as a tragedy speaks of a way of living of the human in her world and not an ontologization of the human itself that rises above the usual, as Heidegger thinks), that is, something like the excessive, the unspecific, what exceeds a certain canon and measure; she herself is the daughter of the incestuous Oedipus and her lineage even reaches Dionysus himself: the human god (a pre-Jesus): the "monster" par excellence. Antigone is monstrous, daughter of the monster Oedipus and she, on her mother-grandmother's side, is a direct descendant of the monster par excellence: Dionysus (in her blood she carries that of the god). *To deinon* could be expressed in a more imaginative way, that is, pointing out that it is like a certain chord of tense meaning that goes from the marvelous to the terrifying (like a painter's palette: now analogical as Turner's palette, now digital as that of Tara Phillips). Therefore, that *deinon* names a Dionysian tension at the level of the sixth century BC, namely, it is the Dionysian vision of the ancient Greek world (which should also be specified and complicated by saying that it is Dionysian and "Ariadnean", of Ariadne, but I deal with this elsewhere, however, it crosses this writing around the "monstrous"),[99] which could be updated from Hegel to Žižek, passing through Lacan, as a sort of dialectical tension within the very interior of the thing, any thing: the human in the midst of all things, although the term "thing" is horrible to express the Greek, because it supposes a *Creatio ex nihilo*, one is a thing from nothing put operatively by God, namely, will and freedom).[100] And the Dionysian vision of the Greek world is quite similar to that of Amerindia and what is called Abya Yala and that dynamic harmonic balance of some among others that allows decolonizing a certain construction of America in order to think of the human socio-cultural fabrics in another way. The trans thinker Peter DiPietro emphatically puts it this way:

> For a constellation of decolonial activists and intellectuals, what the rest of the world calls Latin America is known by the name of Abya Yala. It means 'land of full maturity' in the Kuna language. The carnal politics that emerge from Abya Yala open up possibilities of decolonization both for Latin American populations as well as Latinos in North America.[101]

DiPietro is like a good Nietzschean drawing the conclusions of what is human when we can decolonize the genre and with it emerge free human modes in articulation with each other from Abya Yala; humans, who, in their singularity, live in harmony with each other and with the environment that constitutes them.

And what the tragic Greek wisdom says is that the human is among all things "*deiná*" the most "*deinon*". Sophocles uses the comparative *deinóteros* for the human, that is, among all things *deiná*, the human is the most *deinon*. And that's what humanity is all about. And we cannot forget that, later, Euripides in *The Bacchantes*, the only surviving tragedy that tells the story of the god Dionysus, is then a reduplicatively Dionysian tragedy, because formally it is Dionysian and deals with Dionysus, it tells us that the *deinon* pertains to the god Dionysus. And Euripides writes it in a superlative form, as *deinotatos*. Dionysus is the *deinon* par excellence. Euripides' text is formidable, because it places the god itself talking about himself while addressing his cousin, the incredulous Pentheus (who will have a horrific end):

"Dionysus: He will meet the son of Zeus [referring to Pentheus], to Dionysus, who is a god by nature in all its rigor, the most terrible [*deinotatos*] and the kindest [*epiótatos*] for humans".[102] It is Dionysus who expresses himself as the *deinon* par excellence and for humans; paraphrasing Heraclitus and ironically with Lacan, I could say that Dionysus "wants and does not want to be named as the Real". And this is also where my criticism of the Slovenians enters; their excess of Lacanianism (the Kant they carry inside). Dionysus is the excess, the superabundance, the very excess of Zeus; as Schelling says in his great Course on the *Philosophy of Revelation*: "...Dionysus est le cause de la multiplicité réprésentée en Zeus".[103] It is the god that is the exit that pierces not only the human, but all things; and, therefore, things are dynamic, finite (keeping up with their time); and the human is sexed, mortal and epochal.

Therefore, that the human is expressed as the most *deinon* among all things *deiná* indicates that the Dionysian itself harbors in the human and in a primary way. And let's not forget that the same god, as a pre-Jesus, in one of his manifestations is the son of a human: Semele (this was very important for Hölderlin, that's why it unites Dionysus with Jesus[104] and by default it is important for Schelling and Hegel). So, the "monstrous" that articulates the human indicates Dionysus himself within that masculinity and femininity. Dionysus, for a current Aristotelian, is the "monster" par excellence, for example, he is a Minotaur (human-bull) in the myth of Ariadne and the Labyrinth, he is also masculine-feminine in himself. There are many Greek epithets that show this gay trait of the god and that I would actually update by calling Queer for always being with Ariadne (her alter ego) and as an expression of the archaic feminine. Walter Otto technically points it out this way in his wonderful book *Dionysus* of 1933:

> If other divinities are accompanied by beings of the same sex, the closest circle and the retinue of Dionysus is made up of women. He himself has something feminine (…) In Aeschylus he is dismissed as the 'feminine' (*ho gúnis*), in Euripides it is the 'feminine' (*thelúmorphos*) foreign. It is also sometimes called 'the male-female' (*arsenóthelns*). The Christians (cf. Arnob.6, 12Firm., Err. Prof. rel. 6,7) mock his feminine nature, to which the strange story of his encounter with Prosimnus also attests. Yes, it is even said that Hermes would have entrusted the child Dionysus to Ino in order to raise him as if he were a girl.[105]

Dionysus is the "monster" par excellence; and this is remembered by all his myths, especially those associated with Ariadne. The feminine element constitutes the god, not only sexually in the dance with his Ariadne (dance that gives meaning to the nonsense of things, that is, the sexual relationship between them), but as a feminine element that crosses him. This is what Otto says, he specifies: "Dionysus is always surrounded by women. The nurse becomes a beloved, from whose beauty his gaze hangs in intoxicated fascination. Her perfect image is called Ariadne".[106] And therein lies, among other things, that the human is not only expressed in that masculine-feminine duo and that the feminine animal moment is the one that opens the masculine itself, but that all this becoming is part of the life-death of the human as Dionysian (ariadneous): it is the temporal dimension that constitutes the human and everything. The same finitude is operating in the open sexuation that constitutes us; said in current language, not only is our unconscious sexualized: "The unconscious is a thought process, and it is, sexualized 'from within, so to say", as Ruda and Hamza masterfully point out to Zupančič,[107] but that it is radically finite and epochal. It is the dance of finitude that constitutes us as "monsters", that is, in differentials that do not allow themselves to be trapped in any gender, but neither in what is called: masculine.

Dionysus expresses that material differential that goes hand in hand with the human as a radically sexual act; Butler has given a thousand turns to this in terms of the love of some with Others (from her first works to the current ones). That sexual relationship is an expression of the Dionysian (along with his Ariadne). And so we can understand the Greek in another way, not only from Gea to Athena, from the muses to the nymphs, from the goddesses to the priestesses, from their cult to the political, but also the human appears to us from that open, tensional, queer, eminently mortal that is repeated not as death, but as life:

> The sexual relationship is fundamental in Greece, but not the sexual difference, which already hangs on a patriarchal and abstract metaphysics. Even, as we have seen, it is prior to sexual difference. From the 'Mother-Father Earth' fertilized by 'Heaven' arises the synthesis of children. And besides, it is fertilization not only in light of what is said today, both masculine and feminine have passive-active operators. This idea is at the base of every myth, and let us not forget that the Theban Bacchic Queer Dionysos is the son of Semele and Zeus (the Dionysus Zagreus is the son of Persephone); cared for, as a child, by wet nurses, nymphs, etc., he is always surrounded by the bacchantes and female beings. And that he behaves in a feminine way on many occasions. And that Dionysus is, at the same time, Ariadne's love partner; the immortalized mortal (very similar to the god himself) lady of the Labyrinth, of the Lament and of the Dance.[108]

And in that dancing differential tension, that is, sexual, we see how the monstrosity itself gives rise to WeOthers.

References

Aristotle, *Reproduction of Animals*, Gredos, Madrid, 1994.

DiPietro, P., "Neither human, nor animal, nor monster: The decolonization of the transgender body", in *Eidos*, No. 34, 2020, pp. 254–291.

Espinoza, R., "Dionysus, the Queer god", in *Eidos*, No. 34, 2020, pp. 292–321.

Espinoza, R., *Nietzsche. Pagan Ideology*, Akal, Madrid, 2023 (in press).

Espinoza, R., "'Nature'... another monster from the Labyrinth of Modernity that persecutes us...", in *Periferia Magazine. Christianity Postmodernity Globalization*, No. 8, 2021, pp. 50–63.

Euripides, *The Bacchae*, Gredos, Madrid, 2000.

Hegel, G.W.F., *Faith and Knowledge*, Nueva librería, Madrid, 2000.

Hölderlin, F., "Der Einzige" (two versions), in *Hölderlin Werke. Auswahl in zwei Bänden*, Deutsche Verlag-Anstalt, Stuttgart, Berlin, Leipzig, 1930, pp. 256–263.

Hölderlin, F., "The only one" (two versions), in *Hölderlin. Complete Poetry. Bilingual edition*, Editions 29, Barcelona, 1977.

Otto, W., *Dionysus*, Herder, Barcelona, 2017.

Preciado, P.B., *Can the Monster Speak?*, Anagrama, Barcelona, 2020.

Ruda, F. and Hamza, A., "Interview with Alenka Zupančič: philosophy or psychoanalysis? Yes, please!", *Crisis & Critique*, Volume 6, No. 1, 2019.

Schelling, F.W.J., *Philosophie de la Revelation. Livre II*, PUF, Paris, 1991.

Segato, R., *The War Against Women*, Prometeo / Libros Lom, Santiago de Chile, 2020.

Sophocles, *Works*, Gredos, Madrid, 2000.

Žižek, S., *Sex and the Failure of the Absolute*, Paidós, Barcelona, 2020.

5

WeOthers the Hegelian Dionysians ... those barbaric Slovenes

The monstrous Hegelian element in the Ljubljana School is evident and goes be-yond Zupančič or Žižek, also Mladen Dolar, Zdravko Kobe and others are great connoisseurs of Hegel. At the end of 2020, when the 250th anniversary of Hegel's birth is celebrated and in the midst of the COVID-19 pandemic, the Slowenien Goehte-Institut did a short interview about the importance of Hegel to: Žižek,[109] Dolar,[110] Zupančič[111] and Kobe.[112] And in that interview the unity of their thoughts around Hegel is very clear and that formally it is a world-class Philosophical School because it has precisely an interpretation of Hegel and of philosophy that literally passes through them; this implies, for example, the difference with the populists of Essex, or the social democrats of Frankfurt, the Lacanians of Paris, of Buenos Aires, etc. And why Hegel and not Marx to rethink the process of social transformation? Why Hegel and not Foucault, who is a much more current thinker in understanding the human and has his development of biopolitics?

The answer is very simple: Hegel is a monster already in his time, already in ours; his monstrosity does not cease to be monstrous; and it endures over time (his monstrosity became natural to us). And apparently it is not in today's Germany where this abysmal feature of Hegel can be seen, but in Slovenia, in Spain, in Argentina, in Chile, etc., in places far from the hegemonic interpretative empire of philosophy (which resists perishing in its character of being an accomplice of the establishment of the dominant capitalist model). It is very important to see that Hegel, and especially because two of his fundamental works are currently behind two quite monstrous thinkers (they are both Siamese twins), but who always debate about the human, namely, Judith Butler and Slavoj Žižek. The reason for this is that Hegel is present in both from a youthful perspective and in a historical way (Butler and the *Phenomenology of the Spirit, Phänomenologie des Geistes*)[113] and from a mature perspective and in a structural way (Žižek and the *Science of Logic, Wissenchaft right logik*). But in both authors who follow Hegel we find the most radical part of him, that is, the Other who constitutes us (whether historically or structur-ally). Hence the current talk of a biopolitics in Butler and an ontology in Žižek, but both categories are not enough to express Hegel in his monstrosity; they remain too narrow and are unilateral visions. And in this Hegel operates beyond an ontol-ogy for the Slovenians, but also as a framework for reflection where thoughts are

DOI: 10.4324/9781003370116-6

articulated and in it the impossible of the human or, said in Hegelian, its freedom, is expressed. Hegel already said it in his early years (together with his revolutionary "brothers": Schelling and Hölderlin) in the *First Program of a System of German Idealism* (Winter semester: 1796/97): "The first idea is naturally the representation of myself as of an absolutely free being. With the free, self-conscious being, an entire world emerges simultaneously -from nothing-, the only creation of the nothing true and thinkable".[114] This text is a Political Philosophical Manifesto (prior to that of Marx-Engels) that marks the roadmap of these three great thinkers and that in Hegel is radically embodied in the *Phenomenology of the Spirit* of 1807 and that leaves the monster installed within the system itself not only of thought, but of life in its praxis. And this has been, for example, the case of Butler. The queer philosopher is installed within the very empire of Capitalism. She even resisted all the power and stupidity of Trump; since the USA at the time became really toxic and harmful, but Butler came through (Wendy Brown always by his side) and many female American thinkers have been able to gradually dissolve the establishment, at least the institutional and social establishment.

The case of the monster Žižek with respect to Hegel is incredible; he must be the author, due to his obsessive character, who has written the most about Hegel in his own work throughout the 20th and 21st centuries (and he always gives a twist to the Hegelian Logic to think about the present; even the COVID-19 pandemic);[115] and in this he surpasses not only in quantity (which is important to say), but also qualitatively, such well-known Hegelians as Lukács, Adorno, Duke, Jaeschke, Pippin, Honneth, Ripalda, Pinkard, etc.[116] Žižek executes his thinking expressed in his work, in his innumerable books, in and through Hegel, even beyond Lacan; as José María Ripalda says in the book Žižek Reloaded,[117] Žižek is a "remix" of Hegel. The Swabian philosopher returns again and again in different monstrous figures throughout history, as well as Son Goku figures, and each one of them is at the same time more abject with respect to its time: that is why today we have Žižek among WeOthers. Perhaps the Slovenian is nearer, because of his character, to Superman's enemy and who killed him: Doomsday. He is a monster that has mutated within himself and that has resurrected, like an ancient god, over and over again in a more aggressive and powerful way because he carries within himself the very death that has touched him at one point in his life; then he becomes more and more monstrous and difficult to kill. Žižek has suffered many attempts to disable him as a thinker, but he grows and gets back up; although sometimes repeating ideas and with a certain parody of himself (that's very healthy). Žižek is a very special monster, at the same level of the Capitalism that subjectivizes us.

What about Hegel? In the *Science of Logic*, viewed as a whole (externally), on the one hand, one can see a level of rationality in its architecture similar to Sade's *120 Days of Sodom* (although Sade's is greater than that of Hegel) and, on the other hand, it is made in a completely unbalanced, arbitrary, willful way, in different stages. In it, excess is its way of being, it is the freedom of its own architecture that allows it to be something unfinished, always to be done and continually open, that is, totally different from the *120 Days of Sodom*. The *Science of Logic* is the monstrous thing, the *deinon* par excellence that its own internal logic explodes into pieces. If Sade wrote his book in 37 days, three hours a day, and gave it the precision of a Leibnizian jeweler (especially the 150 passions of November, which is almost the entire book: the first-class ones, since they are the only ones that can be described), Hegel gave birth to books in a strange way; he wrote them from back to front, that is, he saw the Concept (freedom) and for that he had to write the Being and the Essence first (just like Wagner who, in order to talk about Siegfried, had to stop his writing and tell us about the Ring of Alberic); and only when he ends with the Essence (which he wrote along with the Being), he needed three years to write the Concept (and in turn the book of the Being always writes it in the light of the Essence that he then writes when he finishes the book of the Being). And when he finishes his work, he realizes that since it is a monster, it is the free par excellence in the midst of all the necessity (which Aristotle, Freud and Lacan do not understand) has to be remade, because the free in free movement is updated. It is a monster that is born in itself dead and must live up to itself. The *Science of Logic* has to be remade over and over again; and when Hegel was correcting his book, he died suddenly in 1831 (supposedly of cholera since the pandemic was hitting Germany, but it was not that, instead, it was an upper digestive hemorrhage caused by an ulcer that he had for some time)[118] and he leaves only the re-edition of *The Being*, which was the least important book, only the immediate natural moment of freedom: its shell, its mapped map.

In this book (a monstrous complex book that is divided into: "Doctrine of Being" – 1812, "Doctrine of Essence" – 1813, "Doctrine of Concept" – 1816 and a new posthumous edition, because Hegel died in 1831, of the "Doctrine of Being" – 1832) Hegel gives in a more mature way (surpassing the scriptural method as of content of the *Phenomenology* of 1807 that still carries Hölderlin and Schelling within it) with the method of his reflection (wrongly called the dialectical method or simply "dialectics"). And this method incorporates the best of another monster: Spinoza; and incorporates it in a radical and structurally corrected way, that is: "The order and connection of ideas is the same as the order and connection of things".[119] And by this I mean that the method is neither subjective nor objective (less edifying, this is clearly understood by Lenin in his commentary on the *Science of Logic* of 1914),[120] that is, it is not a method that subjectivity "applies" in a Kantian way "on" things, but neither is it something Schellignian and Fichtean "fallen" from the absolute sky "onto" things (and for this "fall" subjectivity, the self, is needed as its already natural seat, already free; the method was never the seat of any neurosis). The method operates in the very articulation of the Logical (the Hegelian *deinon*) in its subjective-objective stories, it constitutes them as such (that is why it is interesting to see it as a Moebius Strip and from there another connection with the last Lacan).[121] Hegel calls it the "Doctrine of the Concept"[122] and repeats it in the *Encyclopedia*: "circle of circles".[123] And here you can see the interweaving of the Real with the Symbolic and the Imaginary in Lacan (with all the nuance of the "Borromean Knot"). And in this lies what Lenin sees in his time and very clearly in his commentary on the *Science of Logic* of 1914 in his

Philosophical Notebooks: "Beautiful formula: 'Not only an abstract universal, but a universal that encompasses itself the wealth of the particular, of the individual, of the singular' (all the wealth of the particular and the singular!)!! *Très bien!*".[124] Lenin, the obsessive revolutionary monster, wanted to found a "society of materialist friends of Hegel's dialectics".[125] And this is precisely what the Slovenians have done, with a lot of effort and work, since the end of the 20th century (among other things, that is why Žižek has worked so hard on Lenin).[126]

And this materialism of Hegel reaches the Slovenians, namely, that in this imbrication of the method that is expressed in this tension of moments, Hegel is constituted as "the" materialist philosopher; Alenka Zupančič puts it this way: "In this sense, Hegel may well be the philosophical materialist par excellence".[127] Hegel is the most materialistic of all[128] and crosses from the revolutionary in Lenin[129] to the philosophy of the Slovenians, especially Dolar[130] and Žižek. Slavoj Žižek is very clear in *Less than Nothing* (one of his great books dedicated to Hegel) and points it out emphatically:

> The central axiom of *Less than Nothing* is that dialectical materialism is the true heir to what Hegel called the speculative attitude of the thought versus objectivity. All other forms of materialism, including the late Althusser's 'encounter materialism', scientific naturalism, and neo-Deleuzian 'new materialism', fail in this endeavor.[131]

And this can be read provocatively, that is, Hegel (Žižek) is the true materialist against the sons of Althusser like Badiou or Ranciere, the sons of scientism like Peterson or Horowitz, the sons of Deleuze like Butler.

The operation of the Hegelian method, materially, as synchronously, not only gives way to this structure that will be the basis for the Slovenians (with an ontology and explanatory totality that does not pretend to be closed, but sometimes it does operate so: it is inevitable), but also the method operates diachronically (and this is fundamental for Judith Butler, biopolitics and the historical performative). And in this Zupančič[132] also contributes with her readings of Kant, Nietzsche, Deleuze and a Hegel from the *Phenomenology* to the Slovenian Hegelian-Lacanian scheme that tends to be more ontological, that is, structural (Dolar-Žižek). Well, the method lives in and through things, where the human is the very key, since the ancient Greeks, because in this structuring the following occurs: the structure of being and essence are not only co-determined as present and past, since the being is seen as "Thing in itself", as the immediate, a present-presence; which is masterfully indicated in this way in the "Doctrine of Being": "Das Seyn y das unbestimte Unmitellbare"[133] (Being is the indeterminate immediate).[134] And in this "im-mediacy" one sees, literally, the very presence of mediation within it, because of this Hegel responds to the Hegel of the *Phenomenology*, namely, that natural representation is mediated from the beginning and it is so from the time in which one is present (this is fundamental for Butler and with this dismantling Freud and all thought of a psychopathologizing nature, that is, not only analysts, but also ontologists). The essence (like *Wesen*, that is, a past) has always been in the being as its interior, but as an interior that cannot be as a background, but rather requires to be present, to be outside, to be visible, to show itself, to come out (that is the juvenile *Phänome-nologie des Geistes*); in the "Doctrine of Essence" of 1813 it says: "Die Wahrheit des Seyns ist das Wesen"[135] ("The truth of the being is the essence").[136] This is one of Hegel's keys that will be fundamental for the Slovenian School and that is also at the base of a certain reading of the Lacanian clinic to account for the human, as the most impossible thing among all impossible things, since the human carries within itself its own impossibility for being its own freedom and, moreover, finite, mortal; this as I presented it is part of the same Anglo-Saxon clinic centered on Klein, Winnicott, Bion and many others.

And this impossible, free and mortal human is going to express itself apparently in that masculine-feminine double, but now with "dominance" of the feminine (to the extent that it is eliminated from the Symbolic and becomes Real), the opposite of what has always been done, that is, that the masculine itself functions as the first analogue, the gender par excellence, the phallic, the Father, the "in itself", even the only gender, but now everything is seen from the "for itself", from the feminine in this structuring of the human, but which I repeat is always a dynamic structuring, put simply, historically (and the Slovenians sometimes do not see this clearly: Hegel's monstrosity also scares them, but not Butler); of a history not as something understood as the "essentialist" type, there is nothing in the origin (*Ursprung*); but always chaos around which mediations are built, as Butler, Preciado, etc. think. The Preciado monster says it very clearly like this: "Gender has no ontological status outside of the acts that constitute it. In this reading, gender would be the retroactive effect of the ritualized repetition of performances".[137] It is a story that starts from the present, from being, from the immediate, performatively constructing its own essential past, its own historical account, its myth, its beginning (*Anfang*) and sometimes as Father, as "in itself", as Law, as prohibition, as identity, as God, as gender, as Big Bang, as emptiness, as nothing, as binary "male-female", as form-matter, etc. Žižek puts it this way in a simple example of the false dichotomy between nature and culture:

> What we have to take into account here is the fact that the Nature/Culture distinction is a distinction within nature, so that each gesture in which culture is opposed to nature must minimally fetishize nature: the only coherent naturalism implies seeing the specifically human dimension as part of nature. However, once we are inside the horizon of meaning, the Nature/Culture distinction becomes a cultural distinction.[138]

This is totally the most typical of Hegel that Žižek and Butler make their own. It was never a Nature and spirit (culture) opposition; read as a certain Schelling; but, in the Logic of our way of life, freedom operates in that tremendous articulation of the movement in the movement itself with all that it means, from our present and carrying the pain within ourselves we are generating a certain "origin" as primordial past that radically opposes us as an "in itself" (this is the very problem of the Real in Lacan and that Žižek tries to solve). And, for the same reason, the human cannot be constituted historically or structurally from an original masculine-feminine binary (but I would add: nor from a single "masculine" gender as Žižek claims, following Lacan and Zupančič). Hegel technically says the following in the "Doctrine of the Concept" and it is a really important text; even if the monster scares us, it is like this:

> The concept is shown, as previously considered, as the unity of being and essence. Essence is the first negation of being, which has therefore become appearance; the concept is the second, that is, the negation of that negation; therefore, the restored being, but as the infinite mediation and negativity of the same in itself.[139]

The concept, like the free (and this frightens Žižek), operates in this loop: nature, being, and culture, essence; and, thus, the essence raises within itself that which was its nature as an original being, but it is in the light of the living movement of the concept that it affirms itself in this way. Hegel is brutal in the *Science of Logic* because too much has happened at the socio-historical level and to think of a certain structural ontological formulation becomes naive. Butler shows her masterly Hegelianism in her great work *The Disputed Gender* of 1900; and to indicate what is obvious about a woman "in herself" and in a way correcting Lacan and his formula "the woman does not exist" (*la femme n'existe pas*); I will examine such a formula later: "... the question of women as the subject of feminism raises the possibility that there is no subject that exists 'before' the law, waiting for representation in and by this law".[140] The woman is an appearance that is placed as "origin" by history itself in the dynamism itself, but it has never been about culture and biology, instead that biological is created by the very loop of historical movement always at the level of its history. And Butler reminds us of that Hegel that we must always have internalized, the monster whispers to us: "It is a natural representation", which is immediatized, like women; and this representation is the one that falls, but let us not forget that the Anglo analysts took a more radical step, to the Mycenae of the psychic apparatus discovered or clearly named by Freud in *The Interpretation of Dreams* (the 20th century began with that discovery); but the Anglos make us see that it is the baby who does not exist in that unit fused with the mother. And this radicalizes the matter and frees perversion from its mold determined by castration and Oedipus. Already Klein, very close to Freud (but having been through Ferenczi, Abraham, Jones) and not being a doctor (she liked history, art), can go to that beginning that seemed "in itself" and re-read it from another place; and see another beginning that allows us to better read the present: the relationship of young children with their mother. Although Freud and Klein are close, they are from different times; it is as if Freud literally belongs to the 19th century (like Marx and Husserl); he was formed in that century, Klein instead is fully living in that new 20th century that is starting to walk, like a new baby that screams loudly; and in its cry it misses both death and love.

However, this movement of inventing nature from a certain moment of culture started from somewhere (always from somewhere and, in general, from the most random and unclear and determined; for example, when the battle of Accio was lost by Marco Antonio against Octavio; that later generated the advent of Augustus, The Empire, Rome, the Law and the West),[141] but deep down it is a false movement, because there is no origin, there is no outside the movement, there is no beginning and end of the movement (that is why Moebius Strip), we are always in the very movement of the moment of being (the immediate, the abstract, nature, the myth, the "in itself", the representation) and the essence (the mediate, the reflexive, the spirit, the history, the "for itself", the movement). And it is that, the movement, what is called performative in Judith Butler and is key to Queer Theory (and Queer Politics, even Queer Nation has been mentioned), but not only for her and that Theory. Butler says it thus:

> ... the understanding of performativity, not as the act through which a subject gives life to what he names, but, rather, as that reiterative power of discourse to produce the phenomena that it regulates and imposes (...) the construction of 'sex' no longer as a given body datum on which the construction of gender is artificially imposed, but as a cultural norm that governs the materialization of bodies.[142]

And here the operation itself can be seen much better from Hegel with his Kant incorporated within the Theory; and for that same reason the Slovenians prefer it and Foucault and his biopolitics are left out. And that movement, the movement itself, is the freedom of the movement of being and essence, that is, we are in the land of the concept or, better said, we have always been in the land of the concept, but now we can see it: the land of freedom:

> Der Begriff ist von dieser Seite zunächst überhaupt als das Dritte zum Seyn und Wesen, zum Unmittelbaren und zu Reflection anzusehen. Seyn und Wesen sind insofern die Momente seines Werdens; er aber ist ihre Grundlage und Warheit, als die Identität, in welcher sie untergegangen und enthalten sind.[143]

The concept has always shown itself, but in the external immediacy of the being as in the interiorized mediation of essence. The movement of being and essence has always operated from the freedom of the concept: the radical movement in the movement itself. For only insofar as the Logic occurs (the Real in Lacan, but without ontologizing it as some Kantian rock or place of return and repetition) as a concept we move, literally, into an element of the free and from there, for example, from the taking of decisions until deciding our gender (if we want to decide it) because whatever substance Hegel would say, it is freedom that constitutes it. Hegel says it in a really unique synthetic formula: "Das reine Begriff ist das absolute unendliche, unbedingte und freye"[144] (The pure concept is the absolutely infinite, unconditioned and free).[145] If Apollinaire told us in 1909 that Sade was the freest spirit that had ever existed; I would think yes and no, because Hegel has become the very monster of freedom with all the opacity it carries within itself in each one of us and throughout history (and we should always keep Nietzsche in mind: the free spirit, stateless, the walker, the dancer). That is Hegel, the free, in his articulation with the Other in himself. And for this reason, Hegel must be one of the most dangerous monsters of philosophy. Hegel's feared disciple, Eduard Gans (a Jewish liberal), taught Hegelian Philosophy of Law in Berlin from 1825 to 1830, was removed from office, and old Hegel had to go back to teaching and was ill (apparently with an ulcer, and they say that Gans had 1,500 students, much more than Hegel himself; and what Gans generated was a call to revolution in revolutionary times, for example, in 1830 itself: even Marx attended Gans' courses between 1836 and 1839 when he died).

It is the concept, insofar as free (as a free operator, which liberates in the residual itself and with all the rest that never fully opens), it is the interpretive key of the method and hence its synchronic character and, at the same time, diachronic; put simply, Butler and Žižek shake hands from their two Hegels in the light of the "Doctrine of the Concept" of *the Science of Logic*. Butler's famous criticism of Žižek, accusing him of being an ontologist and, for that matter, a totalitarian because he turns everything contingent into necessary, vanishes with this reading of Hegel, although Žižek does function as an ontologist. So says Butler: "Žižek's theory expels contingency from its contingency"[146] The contingent, the empirical, the ontic, things, etc. (there are many ways to say it) it is not that it becomes necessary because of the problem of all ontology that in its work makes transcendental that of itself we don't even know what is. Sometimes, especially when Žižek is very Lacanian (less Hegelian) and, in this structuralist, he implies a certain necessary scheme as an "ideal" support of the contingent (the formulas, for example, of sexuation). And this occurs not only in the subject of the human as sexuation, but also in his daily analysis topics regarding the political itself as an expression of Capitalism. But we also must not forget two things. On the one hand, Žižek likes to provoke, especially his leftist and queer feminist friends like Butler; and, on the other hand, he wants to be considered as the metaphysician of the 21st century. But if we stick to Hegel himself, he is very clear in his position and offers a way out to queer feminism itself and to all biopolitical thought: the thought of the contingent as contingent. Hegel in the "Doctrine of the Concept " of 1816 is very emphatic : "... der Begriff die Wahrheit der Substanz, und indem die bestimmte Verhältnissweise der Substanz, und die Nothwendigkeit, und als die Verhältnissweise des Begriffs".[147] If the substantial is understood as necessary, the truth of that necessity is freedom. A remarkable text by Hegel that reverses all thought from Greek metaphysics to Kant (and pierces all thought to the present day and punches a very Lacanian Žižek in the face).

And it is interesting that this substantial is not *simpliciter*, it is always a manner, a case, a mere limit, something unfinished because it carries within itself the very impossibility of being, it carries its finitude, that is, the expiration that constitutes it: it is something monstrous. It is as if the only thing that exists is the Aristotelian accidental (*tà simbebekota*); only the accidental is: that is, paradoxically, the substantial. And this was, in part, Spinoza's thesis in his *Ethics*: what there is is *natura naturata*, an accidental multiplicity that rests on a unity that constitutes it performatively (as Schelling told us about Dionysus):

> Nature naturate, on the other hand, I understand everything which follows from the necessity of the nature of God, that is, of each one of the attributes of God, that is, all the modes of the attributes of God, insofar as they are considered as things that are in God and they can neither be nor be conceived without God.[148]

And Hegel, as a good Spinozist who knows it by heart, knows that this substance is nothing concrete, absolutely nothing substantive, but that its truth is nothing empirical either (it is not any type of entity), but simply its own empty lightness, this is, freedom. And the Spanish philosopher Xavier Zubiri expresses the same thing following Spinoza and Hegel, in the same idea that Biopolitics knows in current times, Feminism, a certain Critical Theory: "Really, each thing is a simple fragment of the Cosmos so that none has full substance. Things are not strictly substantive; they are only quasi-substantive fragments, a primordium of substantivity, rather a rudiment of substantivity".[149] There is nothing substantive; and nothing less constitutes WeOthers or anything else: we are "monsters" among multiple "monsters". And monsters that by being "monsters" are becoming and looking back we invent ourselves as masculine gods (some kind of Adam) and we generate the non-masculine (some Eve), that is, the feminine, but those masculine gods are only "wakes in the sea" (in the words of Machado). But we already know that as "monsters" that we are and become, it is our own open animality, the feminine that energizes us and makes us tremble as "monsters". And that normative look that is cast on the gay man with his homosexual desire or on the woman with her lesbian desire to create him or her as "monstrous" or inverted as Freud says in 1905, as something aberrant, deformed, perverse implies the opposite, namely, that the monstrosity of that desire could be understood as something monstrous of all desire, if we want to see that outside of an external normalization of movement. The philosopher Butler puts it this way:

> ... the fear of homosexual desire can cause a woman to panic that she is losing her femininity, that she is not a woman as she should be, that she is not yet properly a man, that she is as if she were and therefore somehow monstrous. Whereas the terror of homosexual desire can inspire a man with terror of being seen as feminine, of being feminized, of being a 'failed' man, or of being in some sense a monstrous and abject figure.[150]

Butler undoes the Aristotelianism that crosses the theme of gender in the radicality of someone's desire for their own sex, since the philosopher, as a good monstrous Hegelian, knows that we are no longer in times outside of free movement itself in which the human consists; and would add the things themselves. Because among all the "monstrous" things, the most "monstrous" is the human. As said by the monstrous god Dionysus.

The point of view of Slovenian psychoanalytical ontologists is static-structural and the view of feminist biopoliticians is dynamic. Hegel's method is that monstrosity that when observed from the concept, from freedom (relationship and differential), indicates the impossible and monstrous freedom of everything there is; and in that the human is the totally impossible and monstrous, because the concept as the infinite, the unconditional and the free, indicates the very movement of the static in its finitude; and that is why history is given and that is why dynamism is always operating in all things and of itself in the human thing (which I repeat is not even a "thing"). The human itself becomes, is historicized, because it is structurally open to that free dynamism of the concept that initiates its dynamic structuring. And that is why "women are not born, they are made",[151] as Simone de Beauvoir would say. And what about the man? He is not made, but is born? What comes first in man, the chicken or the egg? The answer is so simple: the chicken that forgot that it was an egg and always postulates original chickens; and it forgot because not even a chicken is a chicken; that is, another natural representation.

References

Beauvoir, S., *The Second Sex*, Aguilar, Madrid 1981.

Butler, J., *Bodies that Matter. On the Material and Discursive Limits of 'Sex'*, Paidós, Buenos Aires, 2002.

Butler, J., *The Disputed Gender*, Paidós, Barcelona, 2007.

Butler, J., *Subjects of Desire. Hegelian Reflections in Twentieth-century France*, Amorrortu, Buenos Aires, 2012.

Butler, J., *Psychic Mechanisms of Power*, Cátedra, Valencia, 2015.

Dollar, M.: https://www.youtube.com/watch?v=C42F29T6bXQ

Dolar, M., *Fenomenologija duha I, Društvo whoa theoretically I Psychoanalysis*, Ljubljana, 1990.

Duque, F.: https://www.youtube.com/watch?v=pKSu6BP_0_U&t=2905s

Espinoza, R., *Hegel and the New Logics of the World and the State*, Akal, Madrid, 2016.

Espinoza, R. and Barroso, O., "Interview with Slavoj Žižek, or «Do you want to be Slavoj Žižek?»", in *Žižek Reloaded. Politics of the Radical*, Akal, Madrid, 2018.

Espinoza Lolas, R. (Interview): Hegel, the most materialistic of all, by María Luiza De Castro Muniz; Andrés Echeverría, Andrés Osório, Martín Aulestia, Omar Bonilla, Rafael Polo Bonilla, in *Social Sciences Magazine*, Volume 1 No. 42 (2020): Bolivar Echeverría. https://revistadigital.uce.edu.ec/index.php/CSOCIALES/article/view/2772

Espinoza, R., "Zizek's thought is possible today", in *Res Publica*, Volume 23. No. 3, 2020, pp. 331–340.

Gramsci, A., *Prison Notebooks*, Volume 3, ERA, Mexico, 1984.

Hegel, G.W.F., *Phenomenology of the Spirit*, FCE, Mexico, 1966.

Hegel, G.W.F., "Die Lehre vom Wesen", in *Wissenschaft der Logik. Ernest Band. Die objektive Logik (1812–1813)*, Felix Meiner Verlag, Hamburg, 1978.

Hegel, G.W.F., *Wissenschaft der Logik. Zweiter Band. Die Subjective Logik (1816)*, Felix Meiner Verlag, Hamburg, 1981.

Hegel, G.W.F., *Wissenschaft der Logik. Erster Teil. Die Objective Logik. Ernest Band. Die Lehre vom Sein (1832)*, Hamburg, Felix Meiner Verlag, 1985.

Hegel, G.W.F., *Science of logic I. Objective logic, 1 Being (1812) // 2. The Doctrine of Essence (1813)*, Abada, Madrid, 2011.

Hegel, G.W.F., *Science of Logic.* Volume II, Solar Editions, Buenos Aires, 1993.

Hegel, G.W.F., *Encyclopedia of the Pphilosophical Sciences in Compendium*, Alianza, Madrid, 1997.

Hegel, G.W.F., "The first program of the system of German idealism", in *Writings of Youth*, FCE, México, 1998.

Hegel, G.W.F., *Science of Logic. Volume II: Subjective Logic. 3. The Doctrine of the Concept (1816)*, Abada, Madrid, 2016.

Kobe, Z.: https://www.youtube.com/watch?v=MtMjdebXYPY

Lenin, V.I., *Complete Works. Volume XLII. Philosophical Notebooks*, Akal/Popular Culture Editions, Madrid/Mexico, sa, p. 99.

Lenin, V.I., *On the Meaning of Militant Materialism*, in Marxists Internet Archive, January 1, 2001. Corrected, January 25, 2013.

Preciado, P.B. (Interview), by Jesús Carrillo. At https://www.scielo.br/j/cpa/a/86VcBmHL3WDKz6NPFtt4k6K/?lang=es

Ripalda, J.M., "El punto", in Espinoza, R. and Barroso, O., *Žižek Reloaded. Politics of the Radical*, Akal, Madrid, 2018.

Spinoza, B., *Ethics Demonstrated According to the Geometric Order*, Editorial Trotta, Madrid, 2000.

Žižek, S.: https://www.youtube.com/watch?v=HPWY8YXS_JA

Žižek, S., *The Possibilities of a Hegel's Materialist Turn in Psychoanalytic Theory. Žižek, S., Možnosti' materialističnega obrata Hegla v psihoanalitični _ teoriji*, doktorska lecture, Ljubljana 1981.

Žižek, S., *Less Than Nothing. Hegel and the Shadow of Dialectical Materialism*, Akal, Madrid, 2015.

Zubiri, X., *About Man*, Alianza, Madrid, 2007.

Zupančič: https://www.youtube.com/watch?v=9sybd4W3Xw4&t=262s

Zupančič, A., *What is Sex?*, The MIT Press, Cambridge, MA, 2010.

6

Lacan's the Real …
the Sadian–Kantian game

Alenka Zupančič, following her friends from the troika: Dolar and Žižek (he calls them that),[152] draws a fundamental conclusion for psychoanalysis from Hegel (which is something that is clinically known in the Anglo-Saxon world, it is enough, I repeat, to read Winnicott): his materialism:

> So perhaps this would be a good formulation of materialism: materialism is thinking which advances as thinking of contradictions. And this what makes psychoanalysis a materialist theory (and practice): it starts by thinking a problem / difficulty / contradiction, not by trying to think the world such as it is independently of the subject".[153]

Psychoanalysis is an eminently materialist theory and praxis (a clinic); and it is so because it is "Hegelian", that is, methodical (dialectical as it is often said; because of its "objectal" relations, as said by Winnicott; I would dare to say the clinic of Lacan's second teaching). And Hegel explains this very lucidly in the famous final passage of the "Doctrine of the Concept" of the *Science of Logic*: The Absolute Idea. The psychoanalytic clinic is an absolute clinic (the truth of it is the articulation of the theoretical and the practical in and through the logical; what the young Hegel came to call *Science of the experience of Consciousness*; it was the original name of his *Phenomenology of the Spirit*). The clinic is constituted as such in the very contradiction that as a differential pierces everything, in the Real, in that impossible, it is that *impasse*, in the distance, the gap, etc. (there are multiple ways of saying it), which freely and "monstrously" articulates the human and things. The young Mexican thinker, Carlos Gómez Camarena, says it very precisely as follows: "It is possible to do something with the void, the hole, the gap, the impasse, the division, the negativity: that is what the Lacanian and Hegelian lessons would consist of".[154] And this is how the Slovenian School is working on this Hegel-Lacan and Lacan-Hegel articulation, but with the tutelage of the old Kant (who refuses to disappear and does not appear in the Anglo-Saxon world, and which is appreciated). It is as if Kant, that old "im-potent" mole, embodied the Real itself. Kant is that Rock of thought that never allows itself to be completely trapped, there is no record that determines it, that archives it; nor apparent law that dominates it at all.

DOI: 10.4324/9781003370116-7

Lacan, as a reader of Kant, generates a tremendous influence on the Slovenians, which is also why they distance themselves from Nietzsche (the destroyer of Kant and precisely of that Real-Rock). In the Lacanian Real the Kantian X is always hidden (processed by the *Ereignis* of the beloved Heidegger); both are co-determined. And Jacques-Alain Miller, who is a covert Kantian, lives there and from there hegemonizes his reading of Lacan and with it of philosophy (Miller always distant from Hegel and close to Kant to think, obviously, of ethics and also his social democratic politics). And that is why Miller's Real has a lot of that Kant-Lacan from which that old Žižek, the most philosophical of the Slovenians, tries to take, in these times, a total distance.

That impossible, as we know, Kant foresaw in Modernity as the "Thing in itself" (*Das Ding an sich*), but that, in truth, the human from Königsberg did not know very well what to do with it (although said in ancient Greek it was none other than Dionysus); it was a tremendous Rock that weighed him down a lot; he lived his "Thing" as his symptom (and it returns again and again in his life; just as those definitions of Lacan of the Real, as what always returns to the same place), that is, as the patency of a hole that haunts him like a ghost. Kant saw freedom and was frightened; Kant could not bear what he saw. Kant was "im-potent" (the macabre and precise Nietzschean joke) to see what was monstrous, that is, that infinity, that unconditional and free, in Hegelian terms, that as *deinon* constitutes everything (ancestral Greek wisdom); and radically Ourselves (it is interesting that the Spaniards have a thinker they read very little but is brilliant called Xavier Zubiri and he calls that reality, that "of his own" and he works on it with precision and delicacy and is a contributor to these human themes; and it approaches the Anglo-Saxon way of psychoanalysis).[155] And Lacan through Heidegger (and his ontology that permeates Lacanian analysis),[156] and let us never forget how important his analysis of Heidegger's lecture is: *Das Ding* (1950), observed in Kant's thought, in his ontological epistemological knot of the *Critique of Pure Reason* (1781, Second edition corrected and already a classic of 1787; and in the *Critique of Practical Reason* of 1788), the very expression of the Real that opens everything without being anything, but that remains in that everything without being anything (it is a very special Rock because it founds as if it were itself unfounded); something like the "scar" carried by that child analyzed by Freud as a pervert. JAM tends to separate the Real from the Symbolic too much and naturalizes it in a naive way, but makes it operational, as if it were something that should return, but was lost (like Silvio Rodríguez's Blue Unicorn). And for his beloved Kojève, Lacan saw Hegel's method (in the Lectures from 1936 to 1939 and from a very freakish interpretation of Hegel, by someone who did not know him, from the *Phenomenology of Spirit*), but as a negative and closed dialectic of recognition and the recognized (never as an open structural dynamic affirmation of the monstrous, of the human) the exit to that monstrous initial freedom of the "origin" that constitutes us (because Lacan following Heidegger in rethinking Kant and he always understood that X as "origin" and that is evident at the end of his life; although Žižek wants to save him). And the Slovenian School carries within itself this Kant-Lacan, not only Copjec, but also Žižek and all the others. And in this always, as I have said, Jacques-Alain Miller is fundamental; he is like Lacan's "translator" into a simple, sometimes very simple way (but like a good translator he sometimes betrays him);[157] and the Slovenians drink a lot of Miller-Lacan. It is Miller who is behind Copjec, Zupančič, Žižek (although he wants at present, as I have pointed out, to distance himself from his teacher, especially because of the political issue of Miller and his naturalized "tastes" and so "orderly and correct" of European social democracy), etc. Miller lives in: "It's a natural representation" that's why today he can't, and doesn't want to, understand his Slovenian disciple and even less Butler's work.

And Alenka Zupančič thinks the Real literally from Kant and Lacan (she constantly works directly with Miller's seminars for her analyses, even the unpublished ones, and, moreover, with texts like: *On Perversion*, *Extimitté*, etc.). And in the book *Ethics of the Real: Kant and Lacan*, a fundamental book in the work of the Slovenian, it can be clearly appreciated how the Lacanian apparatus of the Real operates, from that Kantian "Thing in itself", to somehow try to account for the free and "monstrous" human that we are as impossible. We are free from ourselves both with respect to an outside and an inside that constitutes us:

> Kant holds that as human beings we are part of Nature, which means that we are entirely, internally and externally, subject to the laws of causation. Hence our freedom is limited not only from the 'outside' but also from the 'inside': we are no more free, 'in ourselves' that we are, in the world'.[158]

JAM, and in this is fundamental, realizes the importance that Lacan is assigning to the Real for the clinic (even above the Symbolic, his first great teaching and that lives on in our times); and he can even understand how the "madness" of the last Lacan tries to find the Real in another way (hence the work of the mathematical); and that the Real functions as something that does not allow itself to be trapped (it is very interesting to understand psychosis that the English began to treat beyond the obsessive continentals who worked and worked on neurosis), however that JAM, in the 21st century, seeks with an obsessive desire almost in the Symbolic and in the Imaginary to account for it (a Real almost separated from the Symbolic is built in the imaginary); is like returning to the old nature and to magic when science not only doesn't work, but is part of human suffering, a science at the service of Capitalism.

In this way, the theme of the Real in Lacan becomes complex in its own right, either by Kant and his "Thing in itself", or by Lacan himself and how he becomes, over the years, in his experience and speculation with the Real, already by Miller himself and his naturalizing and ordered interpretation of the Real above all, but which is done through the Imaginary (and with great conceptual philosophical problems, but which do work in the clinic – especially for Europeans); and if we add the theme of the Real to the Slovenians themselves, the "Thing" becomes labyrinthine (because some are more Kantian than Hegelian, all having been through Lacan and others directly disciples of Miller). In any case, Lacan himself said in *Seminar 23: the Sinthome* (1975–1976): "the real is without law".[159] And it is interesting because it recalls Foucault's great "monstrous" sentence: "Penser à la fois le sexe sans la loi, et le pouvoir sans le roi".[160] This maxim can sometimes confuse analysts and philosophers; and hence the very complex nuances among the Slovenians themselves. And Žižek wants to take, in this debate, distance and specificity via Hegel and philosophy; and he seeks to be a better interpreter than Miller himself (his teacher) of Lacan. Žižek wants to be from the Lacanian left (as in the Hegelian left were the great connoisseurs of Hegel like Marx: the greatest of all, but let's not forget the incendiary Gans, who unfortunately died very young at just 42); the direct disciples of Lacan, like Miller, cannot find what pertains to Lacan (the same with the direct disciples of Hegel, his right; except for Gans). But we cannot forget that Lacan himself becomes a text to be deciphered; because he himself is incessantly thinking about the clinic and the analytical itself to account for that singular human at the level of the event, and in this the Real pierces him completely and does not leave him alone (since the Seminars of the 1970s he became more radical). There is no interpretation of Lacan, nor does he have one of himself (nor of any real thinker); and this is Žižek's error; to try again and again to have the last word about Lacan (the same on Hegel). It is the totalizing spirit of the "old" metaphysician Slavoj Žižek: our current monster, but compared to the old monsters he is a "babe in arms".

Lacan himself made a symptom of the Real; this is what Miller points out:

> In psychoanalysis there is no knowledge in the real. Knowledge is a lucubration about a real stripped of all supposed knowledge. At least that is what Lacan invented as the real, to the point of wondering if that was not his symptom, if that was not the cornerstone that made him maintain the coherence of his teaching.[161]

And Jacques-Alain Miller's current interpretation of the Real, and of psychoanalysis, of the 21st century, of current problems, of the human, is very clear in the Presentation of the theme of the IX Congress of the WAP: *The Real in the XXI Century* (Buenos Aires, April 26, 2012). A rather older Miller (68 in 2012, now 77) emphatically displays his interpretation as if he were Lacan himself, even correcting him; for him that Real was nature, but now is shown as disorder. It is a very eurocentric and quite precarious analysis at a historical-philosophical level, but it seems to be valid and operates in the clinical space; although, like Deleuze or Derrida, I see great successes for the clinic in Klein, Winnicott; and also in Meltzer, Bion, Little: "... once the real was called nature. Nature was the name of the real when there was no disorder in the real".[162] Žižek is going to radically oppose his teacher today; what Žižek says critically of JAM can be heard in full on April 19, 2016 at his Course in Birkbeck, University of London.[163]

Miller, to indicate the Real, shows it in a certain historical evolution, which is quite important and correct, but in this he separates the human in the midst of nature as the past (order, structure, family) and Capitalism, together with science, as the present (disorder, emptiness, human multiplicities). It is like a certain idealized history that goes from order to disorder; and in this current disorder it puts the human in the middle of the field of the Real.[164] And this would be the reason why today we are so lost, sailing in the very void; without any meaning and the pulverized, fragmented, mad human, where the clear distinction between neurosis and psychosis is lost (and with it even the clinic is lost in these times). And in the face of this, one must defend oneself from the Real (and resist and repress it); it is the characteristic of the current analyst and because the analysand lives that Real with anguish, as a symptom, as inhibition. JAM is very emphatic: "There is a great disorder in reality".[165] And this also shows, from Miller, a veiled critique of the last Lacan, who, like Kant, doesn't know what to do with the Real that haunts him like a ghost as a symptom and ended with the *Critique of Judgment* of 1790 and that strange *Opus Postumum* where the critic is diluted forever and inside the monstrous Hegel is heard coming. The Real is no longer expressed in the Symbolic to the extent that it *impasses* in it; the Symbolic as Name of the Father is as if separated from the Real, and operates as a symptom of the Name of the Father. Perhaps it is as Margaret Little knows very well, that is, we are in a world of transference psychosis; and it is evident when she recounts in her already memorable book, recalling her analysis with Winnicott:

> With the passage of time, the number of people who requested treatment for a neurotic illness decreased, while the cases presenting much less treatable psychotic-type anguish increased, even though they were not necessarily disabling even though they did not require hospitalization, and this produced changes in thinking and in psychoanalytic technique.[166]

And if the psychotic is part of the very way of the human that has been expressed for many years in this global Capitalism which has left its own without support, without a link, to WeOthers, to the human articulated with its mother (Winnicott follows Klein in correcting Freud and his castration and Oedipus, the characteristic of neurosis). The Anglo-Saxons have known for a long time that we are monsters, but neither should we have them as something necessarily to be normalized by a certain cure for a disease that paralyzes us and leads us to inexorable death, but rather that analytics help us not to destroy our lives, but that it is typical of the singularity of the human in the articulation of the baby with its mother; of that initial unity of the WeOthers, for wanting to establish a beginning; one that can account for our present. You can be psychotic and an analyst at the same time as Margaret Little was.

And, for the same reason, it is essential in order to understand the human today (even against Miller himself) what that Real expresses (which has been known in Anglo-Saxon analytics for many decades) and this is in Miller and Lacan; and Žižek forgets it, he is too structural in his analysis and wants to save Lacan and the formulas of sexuation at all costs, for example, and his structural logician Hegel. Miller who sees as something negative this fall of the Name of the Father that becomes a symptom and with it the Symbolic and, therefore, of a certain vision of the

Real as a certain matrix that structures and with this everything went better for the human, just like Aristotle and his "monsters", it gives us, on the contrary, a positive, affirmative sense; that symptom of the Name of the Father is what is now, for example, in the queer, in the trans, in a certain feminism, in certain men, etc. I will discuss it later, but now I point out that it is a human who is breaking the gender, the genders, the formulas of sexuation written from the Symbolic at a certain historical level, because the Symbolic is heir to Capitalism (like the Imaginary) and it was also fractured, psychotized from our own subjectivation. JAM is very radical and his criticism of Lacan is noticeable:

> The Name of the Father according to tradition has been touched, it has been devalued by the combination of the two discourses, that of science and that of capitalism (…)
>
> The Name of the Father, key function, Lacan himself has lowered it, depreciated it in the course of his teaching, ending up by making the Name of the Father nothing more than a *sinthome*. That is to say, the substitution of a hole.[167]

I will analyze this in the next section of this text, but it is interesting that what Miller sees as a problem, error or disorder, is for me the fundamental part of what is happening today in the human sphere and is what partly makes it possible for Zupančič and Žižek to think about the human from a structural sexuation, but not far from the historical performative of Queer Theory; it is even more than what the Slovenians think, because it is what allows us to become the "monster" that we are.

The interesting thing is that the Real is vanishing for Lacan and Miller (beyond their social democratic morality) throughout the history of their game with the human; and it becomes in that freedom an impossible that crosses everything; in this Hegel is fundamental (and Nietzsche totally important and, as I said, that is one of the problems of the Slovenians: the absence of Nietzsche). And Zupančič, the only one who has really studied Nietzsche among the Slovenes, also follows her teacher Miller-Lacan:

> According to Lacan, the Real is impossible, and the fact that 'it happens (to us)' does do not refute its basic 'impossibility': the Real happens to us (we encounter it) as *impossible*, as the impossible things that turn our symbolic universe upside down and leads to the reconfiguration of the universe.[168]

If there is another Hegel for the Slovenes focused on the Logical, there is also another Lacan for them focused on the Real (and there is also a desire for another Lacan, at least in Žižek with respect to Miller's interpretation of the Real); and Badiou explains it very well in his *Logics of the World*:

> In truth, there is another Kant, dramatized, modernized, displaced towards contemporary politics and towards the teaching of Lacan. A 'Kant with Marx and Lacan', which is a Slovenian creation. We must salute the totally original

Slovenian School of Philosophy, of which I have been a partner, with great pleasure, for many years. Like any true School, it experienced splits and animosities. But I, far from Ljubljana, can say hello at least once, together, to Rado Riha, to Jelica Šumič, Slavoj Žižek, Alenka Zupančič and all their friends. It is to this School that we owe an entirely new vision of the great German idealism, in tune with a post-Marxist political theory (all these Slovenian thinkers participated, in their own way, in socialist Yugoslavia, and all of them were readers of Althusser), political theory that depends, in turn, on a reading of Lacan whose effect is centered not so much on the force of language as on the unsustainable splendor of reality.[169]

And Badiou is right to show how the monstrous Slovenians live by a lacanism of the Real, although he takes a certain advantage with that pass to the heirs of Althusser, since in this way he himself connects with the Slovenians; and he does not emphasize the importance of Hegel in them; Hegel is always being disguised over the years; Hegel is uncomfortable for philosophers.

The praxis of psychoanalysis, a materialist praxis as Zupančič recalls, always assumes, as Lacan points out: "the possibility of dealing with the real by the symbolic".[170] And in this we are not finally lost with the Real, something similar with Kant and his X which is expressed everywhere in his praxis (his postulates), but Hegel, via Fichte, Hölderlin, Schelling, resolves by showing, to put it in these terms, a clinic not of the human, but of the human itself in its socio-historical fabrics. And Hegel, together with his friends from his own troika, makes it quite clear already in that fragment from the winter semester of 1796/97 of the First Program of the Systems of German Idealism. "The absolute freedom of all spirits that carry within themselves the intellectual world and that must not seek either God or immortality *outside of themselves".*[171]

And Zupančič finally sees the Real as that certain Rock (but not so hard), but thanks to Hegel-Žižek, he can free himself, in part, from Kant-Miller and see that the Real expresses itself in human formations, in socio-historical fabrics, in the traumatic, which is shown in the very tension of the life-death of each one of We-Others throughout history (that is history, let us not forget the end of Hegel's *Phenomenology*), as the class struggle, pain in the face of life, finitude in the face of pandemic nihilism, impotence in the face of the all-powerful de facto power, not being able to eat if you don't have a job; it is the Real that in some way almost as a practical postulate, as a trauma that leaves a certain mark that mobilizes us (I cannot help but see the "scar" that Freud cannot see in its reach); here Zupančič is really brilliant:

The crucial point [...] is to distinguish historicity proper from evolutionary historicism. Historicity proper involves a dialectical relationship to some unhistorical kernel that stays the same – not as an underlying Essence but as a rock that trips up every attempt to integrate it into the symbolic order. This rock is the Thing *qua* 'the part of the Real that suffers from the signifier' (Lacan) – the real 'suffers' in so far as it is the trauma that cannot be properly articulated in the signifying chain. In Marxism, such a 'real' of the historical process is the 'class struggle' that constitutes the common thread of 'all history hitherto': all historical formations are so many (ultimately failed) attempts to 'gentrify' this kernel of the real.[172]

The case of Lacan is very strange in general and in Slovenia he follows a similar path, because rather than being seen as a clinical psychoanalyst, deep down he is seen as another thinker, a thinker of the human; one that is on a par with Kant, Hegel, etc. And this is part of the Slovenian School and, especially, of Žižek''s interpretation of the history of philosophy (which ends in himself, which was obviously to be expected from our monster).[173] Lacan the thinker along with the other great ones like Kant and Hegel, but who complicates matters and can start from Hegel to express the human in his double moment as analyst and thinker. And radically, Lacan is great, because he expresses the sexed human, which is typical of psychoanalysis against a certain ontological philosophy that the sexed is seen as something contingent and not relevant to account for the human (it is underestimated). So, Lacan as a philosopher (and this is the big difference with Winnicott), because that's what it is, it is like the path that allows the most traditional philosophy to descend and situate it in the human itself. But Lacan is also seen as a certain Kant, since the "Thing in itself" operates as that Real that resists and at the same time sets the whole story in motion. And there, as Kant-Lacan, his thinking position fits hand in hand with Hegel and his negativity of a structural type. And so both ways of thinking are articulated.

Perhaps the primordial expression of the Real of the dozens that there are (as I said, Dionysus wants and does not want to be named as the Real), is given by Lacan himself in his *Seminar 20: Still* (the one with the formulas of sexuation) of 1972–1973: "The real cannot be inscribed except as an impasse in the formalization".[174] And this is what Žižek wants to point out about the last Lacan and show that there is a certain return to the Symbolic even though Lacan himself gets lost, but not as Miller thinks:

> ... in his last years [Lacan], he remained there too obsessed with how to think the Real 'in itself,' in its radical externality to the Imaginary / Symbolic, refusing to draw full consequences from his own insight into how the Real has no substantial reality in itself _ since it is an immanent self-impediment of the symbolic itself.[175]

In Lacan, who by himself is an ontological thinker and therefore totalizing, has a system of thought in which that totalizing aspect is always open (never closed by its very structure) and for this reason it is articulated, in Žižek, with the structuring Hegel of the *Science of Logic*; for Lacan it is a Science of the Real. JAM points it out like this: "And that has been a heroic attempt to make psychoanalysis a science of the real as logic is".[176] And in this science that Lacan wants to found, the Slovenians think that they will realize it; and to execute this plan: sex is fundamental (which in the Anglo-Saxons is not radical, but the initial differential of the baby's symbiosis with its mother; and this is very important to highlight for our issue). That is why Žižek is emphatic about this: "For philosophy, the subject is not inherently sexed, sexuation occurs at the contingent and empirical level, while psychoanalysis elevates sexuation to a kind of formal condition a priori of the very emergence of the subject".[177] And Zupančič says it in a radical way, psychoanalysis is an ontological way of being with the human:

> My claim is that the Freudian concept of sexuality is above all a concept, a conceptual invention, and not simply a name for certain empirical 'activities' that exist out there and that Freud refers to when talking about sexuality. As such, this concept is also genuinely 'philosophical'. It links together, in a complex and most interesting way, language and the drives, it compels us to think a singular ontological shape of negativity, to reconsider the simplistic human/animal divide, and so on...[178]

Our sexuality and ontology itself are articulated from psychoanalysis when the Real operates as that impossible that constitutes us; here is the Slovenian problem, namely the need to be recognized by the great European philosophical schools, especially the French and German schools, as true philosophers. This haunts the Slovenians, all of them, especially Žižek. It is a trap that Slovenians fall into; there is no need for such recognition in the European market for "true" philosophies. Recognition as serious philosophers, that is, in the imaginary as ontologists. There is no such truth. And here comes the other mistake, trying to make psychoanalysis a new ontology; because this is not necessary either, quite the contrary. It is preferable that it never is. And the English way of psychoanalysis, so loved by Deleuze to annoy the French analytical institution centered on Lacan, with three great pillars: Klein, Winnicott, Bion, one could say that they think, clinically, that Real there with the patient itself, without any need for ontology. And it is a kind of Real similar to that impasse that occurs in the symbiosis of baby and mother; that unit that at the same time thinks how inseparable it is separated and that every human registers within himself: it carries the We constitutively; that Winnicottian paradox is like the Lacanian Real; Anglos do not conceptualize it as ontologists, but they have experienced it in their clinic for many decades.[179] It is as if for Winnicott, as I have pointed out, the one that "does not exist is the baby", because on the one hand it is linked in a symbiotic affirmative unit with its mother (both merged) and, at the same time, the baby is cast into its own fate in its own solipsism. Melanie Klein put it this way in 1928 in London (and she becomes increasingly distant from the powerful Freud): "This significant connection heralds in both sexes a phase of development of vital importance, and which has not been sufficiently valued until now. It consists of a very early identification with the mother".[180]

References

Badiou, A., *Logics of the Worlds. The Being and the Event 2*, Manantial, Buenos Aires, 2008.

Foucault, M., *Histoire de la sexualité 1, La volonté de savoir*, Gallimard, Paris, 1976.

Hamza, A. and Ruda, F., "Interview with Alenka Zupančič: philosophy or psychoanalysis? Yes, Please!". *Crisis & Critique*, Volume 6, No. 1, 2019.

Gómez Camarena, C. and Aguilar Alcalá, S., "Coffee without milk, School without a concept: features, operations and readings in the Slovenian School", in *Res Publica*, 23(3), 2020.

Klein, M., *Love, Guilt, and Reparation*, Simon and Shuster, London, 2002.

Lacan J., *Reading Seminar XI Lacan's Four Fundamental Concepts of Psychoanalysis: The Paris Seminars in English.* Suny Series, Psychoanalysis & Culture. Richard Feldsteing Editor, Maire Jaanus (Series Editor), Bruce Fink. State University of New York Press, Albany, 1995.

Lacan, J., *The Seminar of Jacques Lacan, Book XX, On Feminine Sexuality, The Limits of Love and Knowledg*e. Translated with notes by Bruce Fink, W. W., Norton & Company, Inc., New York, 1998.

Lacan, J., *The Seminar of Jacques Lacan, Book XIV. The Logic of Phantasy.* Translated by Cormac Gallagher from unedited French manuscripts, Karnac, London, 2002.

Lacan, J., *The Sinthome: The Seminar of Jacques Lacan, Book XXIII, 1975–6.* Ed. J-A. Miller, Translated by A.R. Price, Polity Press, Cambridge, 2016.

Little, M., *Transference Neurosis and Transference Psychosis*, Jason Aroson, New York, 1981.

Little, M., *Account of my Analysis with Winnicott*, Editorial Place, Buenos Aires, 1995.

Miller, J-A.: https://wapol.org/es/articulos/Template.asp?intTipoPagina=4&intPublicacion= 38&intEdicion=13&intArticulo=2468&intIdiomaArticulo=1

Žižek, S., https://www.youtube.com/watch?v=REky3bRQfkc

Žižek, S., "Taking sides: a self-Interview", *Metastases of Enjoyment: Six Essays on Women and Causality*, Verso, London, 1994.

Žižek, S. and Daly, G., *Conversations with Zizek*, Polity Press, Cambridge, 2004.

Žižek, S., *Less Than Nothing. Hegel and the Shadow of Dialectical Materialism*, Akal, Madrid, 2015.

Žižek, S., *Moins que rien. Hegel et l'ombre du materialisme dialectique*, Fayard, Paris, 2015.

Žižek, S., Course at Birkbeck titled: "Is Surplus-Value Marx's Name For Surplus- Enjoyment?". Žižek, S., https://backdoorbroadcasting.net/2016/04/slavoj-zizek-masterclass-2-surplus-value-surplus-enjoyment-surplus-knowledge/

Žižek, S., "Why 'Ljubljana School' remains faithful to philosophy", in Espinoza, R. y Žižek, S., *The Slovenian School*, Paradiso, México, 2023 (in press).

Zubiri, X., *Intelligence and Reality*, Alianza, Madrid, 1980.

Zubiri, X., *Intelligence and Logos*, Alianza, Madrid, 1982.

Zubiri, X., *Intelligence and Reason*, Alianza, Madrid, 1983.

Zupančič, A., *What is Sex*, The MIT Press, Cambridge, 2010.

Zupančič, A., *Etihcs of the Real. Kant, Lacan*, Verso, London, 2012.

7

Žižek and Butler ...
the perverse Siamese

Judith Butler and Slavoj Žižek have spent years, like monstrous and somewhat sia-mese (joined by Hegel), dialoguing about the human. And in truth it is not that one is more correct than the other, or that one is against the other, although sometimes that is how the dispute seems, but that both complement each other to account for each of WeOthers. In a complementary way they do not see much at all; said in Hegelian, each one is a unilateral vision of the human. And that is why it is better to integrate them in a dynamic way so that it adjusts more fully to what we are: monsters.

The Ljubljana School has been able to think about the human from a very differ-ent perspective than other European philosophical Schools (but not as innovative as the U.S. and South American ones): Frankfurt, Essex, Paris, Freibung, etc., since it has overcome, among other things, the prejudice of understanding the philo-sophical, so precious to Germany, as something enclosed in itself and, in this way, it has been able to articulate Philosophy with Social Sciences, Cultural Studies and, especially, Psychoanalysis (Psychoanalysis is a kind of ontology of the sexed hu-man; Lacan's great correction to his beloved Heidegger and his *Dasein* de *Sein und Zeit* of 1927; the problem is that it is an ontology). And, furthermore, in the philo-sophical field, not only Kant's thinking is at stake, but Hegel makes his entrance as a manifestation of philosophy that is up to the Human Event in our days: this is a great work of the Slovenians nowadays. A Hegel, as we have seen, which is now based primarily on the *Science of Logic* (*Wissenschaft right Logik*), but without ever giving up the *Phenomenology of Spirit* (*Phänomenologie des Geistes*) and the young Hegel; and, hand in hand with the psychoanalysis of Jacques Lacan, passing through an interpretation of Lacan's "translator": Jacques-Alain Miller (JAM),[181] where the category of the Real becomes a radical interpretive key of the human over the Symbolic (by the way, the Real is not a category like Dionysus is not a god, nor is woman a gender, nor is man).

In this way, Kant, Marx, Freud, etc., are, for the Slovenians, like a matrix ho-rizon from which to think about the human (but they also include with certain details and reservations: Nietzsche, Heidegger, Foucault, Deleuze, Derrida, etc.), but now radically thought from an articulation of the Hegelian Logic itself and from that Lacanian Real. On the other hand, the American females: Butler, Brown,

DOI: 10.4324/9781003370116-8

Rubin, Kosofsky, Davis, Spivak (lives in the USA), always have Nietzsche, Marx, Freud and the French within their categorical systems, especially Derrida, Deleuze, Foucault. In the Slovenians, their great innovation is the Hegelian Logic and the Lacanian Real (along with the Kantian "Thing in itself") to account for the human and even for things themselves, as is the yearning for all ontology and their "thirst for totality"; a longing that does not exist in U.S. thinkers, or Americans in general, such as Gloria Anzaldúa, Francesca Gargallo, Rita Segato and so many Latina thinkers.

Why does the Hegelian Logic with the Lacanian Real allow the Slovenians to express the human in a more current way where Freud, Marx, Husserl are no longer enough in their conception of the human as: neurotic, worker or self? In what sense does the human no longer allow itself to be trapped in categorizations that come from the 19th century and that have become completely out of date in the U.S. as well as for Slovenians? What is happening to the human today that apparently certain psychoanalysis and certain philosophy are more in line with their "truth", that is, with their monstrous imbalance? The answer is the very differential that constitutes us and which throughout history is updated in a more provocative way; and that a great category, for example, of the self, or of another neurosis (heir to the self) can no longer account for what we are today. And this was very clear to Georges Canguilhem in 1943, as a good Nietzschean he is not confused:

> By illness of the normal man it is necessary to understand the disturbance that arises in the long run from the permanence of the normal state, from the incorruptible uniformity of the normal, from the disease that is born from the deprivation of diseases, from an existence almost incompatible with the disease.[182]

Neurosis is precisely that, a construction of the normal that does not resist itself; impossible, it gets sick. It is condemned to be dismembered from itself; it explodes.

In psychoanalysis you cannot understand the human in his healthy character; as if it needed to understand it from the sickness and from there the idealized paradise of neurosis is built. And that is why the neurosis functioned as a matrix of the human that allowed us to see a certain "normal" human and therefore susceptible to normalization for his "good", to "cure" his illness (it is a vicious circle). And from there it was postulated as a homogeneous and sameness reference system for all that is human and therefore the sick who need a cure. And hence its other two categories: perversion and psychosis, were constructed in the light of neurosis and without treatment. As if the psychotic lived outside the neurosis (said in Lacanian terms outside the Symbolic, he lives in the Real) and there with all his might he seeks to fulfill his desire; and on the other hand, the pervert lives in the neurosis itself breaking it, transgressing it and challenging it; and thus enjoys radically (as if from the Real he came to the Symbolic to transgress the Law). These categorizations are no longer sufficient; they fall to pieces. And do not forget that the same operative category of Queer tries to overcome, among other things, the category of perversion typical of psychoanalysis (and the pathological category of border of psychiatry and Anglo-Saxon analysts). Queer as shown by Rubin, Anzaldúa, Butler from the end of the 1980s to the beginning of the 1990s, almost 40 years ago, indicates a resounding no to neurosis and a friendly yes to perversion. They are great among the great.

Among the Slovenians Alenka Zupančič and Slavoj Žižek have been able to complicate the human over the years and in constant work and with a lot of effort (we must also mention in this the other friend of this troika: Mladen Dolar): always polishing the concepts, where each one learns from the other; and in this there is always the attempt to update what is human in the midst of this Capitalism and despite other categorizations that are aging (they themselves over the years, through their books, are updating what is human). And it goes without saying that Zupančič and Žižek are very good friends and each one drinks and feeds, literally, on the other; and sometimes you can see, explicitly, that it is the same Žižek who rereads his friend with great interest; and from there he can continue delving into the question of the human in the current debate. A debate that is not only related to Feminism, but, especially, to Critical Theory itself and Psychoanalysis itself; and, definitively, with and against the already academic Philosophy and of the great European philosophical systems; but the Slovenians are reluctant to talk about queerness (they are faithful to Lacan and to the ontological Kantianism that constitutes psychoanalysis).

Sometimes it happens that Lacan becomes a formula, it is sad what happens with the French thinker, because just like Žižek, I treat him as a great thinker of the 20th century, never up to the level of Heidegger, Adorno, Deleuze, Derrida, far from it, but obviously he is a great thinker of the last century and he still affects our present. He is a great man but, to be fair, next to Hegel he is a lesser thinker, but everything that rethinks the sexual human is very interesting. Hegel is a galaxy and Lacan a planet in it. And if we treat Lacan, I repeat, like a great man, beyond the clinic and psychoanalysis, sometimes I realize that what happens to him would make him roll over in his grave, namely, on the one hand, his *Seminars* are not well edited (a serious problem for their reading is that there is no critical edition of them and that not all of them have been published yet) and, on the other hand, he is repeated like a parrot. Lacan works like the voice of a guru that repeats itself over and over again in a mechanical way, like a good obsessive, he is in love with his symptom, and in general he is repeated without understanding what he says or spoken without understanding what he says "to us"; because every saying is a saying that passes for a WeOthers at the level of time (*für uns* Hegel said at the end of the *Phenomenology*). And this is generally seen to happen a lot in the psychoanalytic environment and, especially, in the WAP. And all this becomes more botched, when another guru, but alive, with a voice embodied in a body and in an institution like the WAP that supports him (and at the same time he himself constitutes), I mean Miller, speaks and corrects Lacan in the current land of discourse and practice. Unfortunately, all this returns to obscure Lacan the thinker, since now Miller's formula is mechanically repeated, which in turn is also mechanical of what Lacan was. It is a repetition of a repetition, that is, the death of thought and of life; we are no longer in the materiality of discourse, but in a Lacanian ideology. And JAM himself somehow cuts with philosophy when he assumes the radical clinical position without any philosophy in *Donc Seminar: Logique de la cure* (1993–1994). Miller clearly indicates his exit from the philosophical in a general sense because deep down he is leaving meaning; and that is worrying for the analyst (like the psychotic and perverse children of the system) in the 1998–1999 *Seminar*:

> To address the social bond, Lacan also considers avant- garde literature: surrealism, the College of Philosophy, *Acéphale*, the *Nrf*, *Les temps modemes*, *Tel Quel*, etc., communities that were founded precisely in a certain relationship with what is outside of meaning, with affection, panic, with enjoyment and not with what is useful. Thus, it evoked a problem that was very present for lively spirits in those years (...).[183]

Psychoanalysis cannot get away from philosophy; this has been the serious problem in Anglo-Saxon psychoanalysis, hence the need to deepen its concepts, since it is a brilliant psychoanalysis in its clinic, but it needs conceptual deepening. And philosophy must return to psychoanalysis as Derrida did explicitly (his partner was a great psychoanalyst: Marguerite Aucouturier and did many translations, Melanie Klein is read in French thanks to her, and died of COVID-19 in 2020 in Paris).

However, the Slovenians have been able to treat Lacan as a thinker and they, in turn, have become psychoanalysts of human socio-historical fabrics: there is a co-actualization between Lacan and the Slovenians and, especially, with Žižek. The Slovenians also perform first-rate psychoanalysis due to their hard work for many years. And if we listen to Lacan in a non-mechanical way, we realize how sharp he was and that he was always risking everything he had done, like a good thinker (as were Freud, Melanie Klein, Donald. W. Winnicott, Bion, etc.); he puts his thought and life at stake, because he does not stop his thinking work and embodied in the human, Lacan, like Hegel and any great figure, is always testing what he has thought, theorized and carried out; and Lacan experiences it in his own clinic. From there the so-called second Lacan is born, the one of the other teaching, the one that moves from the Symbolic to the Real, from the structure to the language, from that neurotic to the psychotic, by means of perversion; from a structured unconscious to an open one in singularity.

Lacan tells us in a radical way in 1978: "Everyone is crazy, that is, delirious";[184] and he tells us something that Winnicott, Bion and others were already very sure of decades before and philosophers, artists, writers, filmmakers, playwrights, etc. work and live it in the 20th century; even mathematicians like Gödel. And this is not something trivial, or even less banal. Jacques Lacan himself says so, and he is the thinker of the human, beyond the psychoanalytic itself. And all of this generates something very important for what is happening today, in the 21st century. Apparently the psychoanalytic clinic is ceasing to be "absolute", said in my Hegelian materialist language, because it is not thinking the human in the impossibility that constitutes it, in its monstrosity and is historically performed from power; it does not understand the suffering of the human in the present, nor its joy; the clinic itself must update its conceptual instruments, since the psychic apparatus continues to mutate and does not stop doing so, because the human "is not born, but is made"; and it happens today in the midst of the Labyrinth of Capitalism. And also, let's not forget, things are structurally dynamic. And WeOthers, among all things, are the "monsters" par excellence; Lacan knows this very well and shows it with total clarity at the end of the 1960s onwards until he dies in 1981. And everything is "upside down" (the world is upside down, as Hegel said), and everything has to be thought again, like the philosopher, and in the clinic all its instruments must be put at risk and the analyst himself must be at risk to sail "in the same boat" with his patient: the boat of Dionysus (which sails over death). That is remarkable of Winnicott, and that is why Deleuze says it in 1972 to annoy his rigid French friends of their frame. Margaret Little recalls:

> D.W. gave me a glimpse of what an analysis like mine required of him; demands that he was willing to meet, and not only on the condition that the analysis was successful: he had to bear the anguish, the guilt, the pain and sorrow, the insecurity and the helplessness, he had to bear the unbearable. There was no defense against paradox or ambivalence, either in the patient or in himself.[185]

And from the last Lacan, 1974, a totally affectionate gesture from him that occurs in the same analysis of Suzanne Hommel: he caresses her face with his hand.[186] An analyst today puts his whole body and he puts himself at risk precisely because we are monsters and, therefore, we are all crazy, especially analysts, that is why they are analysts.

We are all crazy: the human himself as a monster happens with everything and does not allow himself to be trapped, less cured of his pain as if he were a sick person with a manufacturing defect, from an origin in something that occurred as an error (in this I am also at a distance from the Anglo-Saxon analysts). And the ontologized categories almost as they were designed, by means of his clinic, by Freud: neurosis, perversion and psychosis sink and become confused or are no longer enough, after a century they cannot be enough anymore (which is obvious), least of all the supreme category and mother of all, that of neurosis. That is why Miller is right to say, but he says it with concern in 2012, but I see it as what it has to be:

> This translates the extension of the category of madness to all speaking beings who suffer from the same lack to know about sexuality. This aphorism points to what the so-called clinical structures share: neurosis, psychosis, perversion. And, of course, it agitates that expresses it, it shakes the difference between neurosis and psychosis that was, until now, the basis of psychoanalytic diagnosis, an inexhaustible theme of teachings.[187]

This is very important, Lacan blows up psychoanalysis; the thinker Lacan knows that they are no longer enough, that is why his work is almost a high-level mathematical modeling to be able to find the human today in all its singularity, that resists with all its might a Law, a Name of the Father, the Symbolic; a human who wants to be heard in his singularity by the official "listener" on duty, the analyst, who no longer has the appropriate conceptual apparatus to listen because he always sought to hear the structure in that singular pain. Lacan becomes the Real, the Borromean Knot, but the radical that must be retained is what is indicated: we are all crazy, especially analysts. And in this neurosis ceases to be the seat of a modern self, same and homogeneous; and now it appears only with holes, fractures, fragments, sponges, voids, differentials. The human does not allow himself to be trapped in the ontological shell of the Heideggerian *Dasein*, because his body knows itself singularly in the midst of the totalitarian Capitalism that operates in the Symbolic, neuroticizing us and making us work to maintain the very capitalist system that structures us (as in *The Matrix*): we are all crazy. And in this, perversion helps to break the a-historical categorical rigidity of a certain analysis and of a certain philosophy; let us always keep in mind the Preciado monster and his discourse. In perversion, the neurotic and the psychotic finally relate (shake hands): like a Joker; the new dweller of the capitalist city.[188] Winnicott's gesture of support for Little or Lacan and Hommel and so many others of transference and countertransference between ones and others is fundamental in the WeOthers itself, where the two come together, all of us who have loved know that it is so, because "it is a natural representation" to think and believe that we are isolated, but quite the contrary, we are articulated, but not organically, nor teleologically, nor mechanically, nor familiarly, etc. we are all crazy from the start and we are all articulated in a way that does not work with respect to a closed set or a system in equilibrium; we are unbalanced from the beginning and that imbalance, that differential, is what we initially adjust between WeOthers. That shaking hands between a neurotic and obsessive analyst like Winnicott and that psychotic patient like Little is what we experience every day, because Winnicott himself is crazy enough: they both were. That was expressed in that analysis with that transference and countertransference: and there the regression to madness. The monstrous Hegel called it, as I have pointed out: "Science of the experience of consciousness". It is the experience of Winnicott with Little and of Little with Winnicott, that experience of love, of struggle for life or death, which makes it possible for both of them, the crazy ones, to be generating a clinic for these times.

Žižek realizes this in part (that is why he knows the importance of perversion, of partial objects, etc.), because it becomes evident the human cannot be sketched neither as *Dasein* nor in the sexuality of the binomial masculine-feminine, nor in any structure that tends to be homogeneous from the outset. Butler herself realizes this, but Žižek, faithful to Lacan, and using Hegel, wants to maintain a certain structure of sexual difference (and keep the structure of sexual difference operative), but he intends to open that structure, open it more, so that it accounts for example, of queer, but maintaining the structural mode. And in perversion, not like the Marquis de Sade and all that literary, criminal and vintage stuff, not like it is seen by analysts like Joël Dor, who is a great analyst and has many nuances in his works, in the 20th

century, for example, his already classic *Structure and Perversions*,[189] but as perversion now occurs in the 21st century, we see the transit of the classic categories
(and its expiration); and how neurosis and psychosis sink into the human to express
change in change itself. It is very classic how Dor, for example, expresses female
homosexuality; always from a certain structure of knowledge in and by itself (Patriarchal Law) that passes through Lacanian psychoanalysis (the Aristotelianism
that continues to function throughout the centuries). And there it becomes evident
how worn out are categories such as perversion, phallus, castration, Oedipus, etc.
"The passage to female homosexuality assures this virile vindication an obviously
more belligerent promotion in as far as homosexuality is carried out by way of
defiance and against this background of denial of the castration typical of perversion".[190] A text from 1987 by a great French analyst that is not consistent with what
is happening in Paris itself; it does not express it. The same Judith Butler in 1990
in *The Genre in Dispute* and before Gloria Anzaldúa (in the same year of 1987 as
Dor) with her *Borderlands / La Frontera*, to name just two examples, express the
human in an eminently perverse way: the monstrous, not only of women, but also
of men is a result, a process Hegel would say, that is never finished, because the
very movement of the historical hegemony builds it, but never completely closed,
it goes everywhere, it escapes from every confinement; and that "in itself" becomes
a mere beginning of an epochal game that is made and remade over the years.

And here there is something very decisive to think about, because we are all
"monsters". And in perversion we move from the times of Sophocles and, I would
say thanks to it, we realize that not only the ontological fails as Žižek says (one
of his last and great books is called *Sex and the Failure of the Absolute* of 2019)
and he wants to re-establish it by force thinking the Lacanian structure with Hegel
(beyond psychoanalysis like that of Dor), but rather expresses history in a performative and contingent way; and in that Butler, the other Hegelian (with the
Phenomenology and hand in hand with the French like the biopolitical Foucault),
is right about Žižek (Hegel's of the *Science of Logic* and holding hands with the
thinker psychoanalyst Lacan of the Real) and names it as Queer:

> The English word queer has several meanings. As a noun it means 'fag', 'ho-
> mosexual', 'gay'; It has been used pejoratively in relation to sexuality, designat-
> ing the impropriety and abnormality of lesbian and homosexual orientations.
> The transitive verb queer expresses the concept of 'destabilize', 'disturb', 'an-
> noy'; therefore, queer practices are supported by the notion of destabilizing
> norms that are apparently fixed. The adjective queer means 'weird', 'twisted',
> 'strange'. The word queer can be found in the following expressions: to be queer
> in the head (being sick in the head); to be in queer street (being burdened with
> debt); to feel queer (being unwell or ill); or queer bashing (violent attacks on
> homosexuals).[191]

This is why Butler tells Žižek: "This problem, as I understand it, is related to the
almost transcendental status that Žižek attributes to sexual difference".[192] And, for

this reason, the Slovenians return to the Real to rethink it from our historical moment and return to Kant-Lacan who was left aside by the biopoliticians. Copjec is very clear and you can see the Kantian-Lacanian ontological point of her saying (it is Miller) when she criticizes Butler (she literally does not understand her): "The disputed gender, in everything it says about sex, eliminates sex itself".[193] Sex has to move in the Real even though the Symbolic does not account for it in a finished way (although it shows it as impossible). Joan Copjec, like Miller today, is radically against Butler; they do not forgive her for eliminating sexual difference in the Lacanian way from his formulas of sexuation to establish the sexual relationship. It is the hard Lacanian knot, like a Rock, of the Real, passed through Kant, which does not want to be left behind; leaving it is the destruction of the system, apparently nothing would remain (Hölderlin jumping into Etna). And this makes them panic.

And Žižek returns with his Hegel where the Real is articulated with the Logical and Zupančič with her Kant and her "Thing in itself" (and all Slovenians with Lacan) try to rethink the human with that challenge of thinking how human we ourselves are in this historical moment; a human that is fragmented into multiple singularities (against Butler and the possible perversions), but where the perversion has a lot to say, which is why Miller also points it out, but in a negative way:

> The real, understood in this way, is not a cosmos, it is not a world, nor an order; it is a piece, an unsystematic fragment separated from the fictional knowledge that is produced from that encounter. This meeting of the tongue and the body does not respond to any prior law; it is contingent and always perverse.[194]

It is clear that I do not share Miller's interpretation of the Real and what he sees as something "negative" in the Real (absence of order) and hence that absence of Law (the Symbolic falters) and our life turns in contingency and in the perverse it happens from a neurosis that is no longer enough, but what is fundamental to indicate is that it is really like that: the perverse happens. For Miller and a certain philosophy, including Žižek himself, don't know what to do with what is Queer, in that master and disciples are similar. Miller himself has said in 2021 (March 3) that: "Queer is banished".[195] It is clear that Miller (and the Slovenians do not know how to understand a trans person, a queer person, etc.), but they try to think from a certain perversion of the human that is operative and that would work in Lacan himself (a Hegelian one for Žižek, a Kantian one for Zupančič and Copjec).

The perverse in its classical and French etymology shows something interesting. From Latin *perversus* indicates the classic "cursed", that is, the *per-versus*. That human who "through" ("per") pierces all discharge, all that is worth and, for the same reason, has overturned what is established. And that is why he is damned because he goes against the law, any form of law (and hence he is, in general, a criminal who violates "good" values). Nietzsche works on it in detail from his time as a philologist in Basel to his wandering mature philosophy: it was the action of the cynics that he masterfully recalls in *The Gay Science* of 1882 in Aphorism 125, that is, they are the "dogs" that arrived at midday to the squares of the Greek cities to annoy them all and break, in this way, with their outdated values; they carried out a sort of performance:

> The crazy man. — You have not heard of that crazy man who in the morning light lit a lantern, ran to the market and began to shout incessantly: 'I seek God! I seek God!' — As many of those who did not believe in God were gathered there, it provoked a laugh. What, is it lost?, said one. Has he lost himself like a child? said another. Or is he hidden? Are you afraid of us? Has he embarked? Has he emigrated? So they all exclaimed and laughed at the same time. The mad man jumped into their midst and pierced them with his gaze. 'Where has God gone?' he exclaimed, 'I will tell you! \We have killed him, you and me! We are all his murderers! ...[196]

That madman from Nietzsche's 1882 is perverse and I remember the "free spirit" of *Human, All Too Human* from 1878 as well as Zarathustra himself from *Thus Spoke Zarathustra* who was formally born in 1883 and behaves, at times, like an old "cynic" Greek. And in that perverse action and saying, he always expresses the truth of his time, namely, the death of God, of the Father, of the foundation, of the Name of the Father that, like the young Hegel of 1802 (*Glauben und Wissen*) reminds us that we are free and from that freedom we are, assuming all the radicality of our own finitude and, I would add, of the nonsense that constitutes all things; among them the human "thing" par excellence. Cynics are the jokers of the time like our current *Joker* by Todd Phillips (2019). And in his mature philosophy, Nietzsche named perversion as a transvaluation of all that is worth (*Umwertung alles Werte*), that is, the characteristic of the human in transit, of the dancer as he points out over and over again in his *Zarathustra* expressing that it is the Dionysian human: "I would only believe in a god who knew how to dance."[197] Nietzsche knows that in Dionysus the perversion of the human himself occurs, who has become an accomplice in the Labyrinth of Modernity: slave of the self (which is expressed in the thought of the three greats: Luther, Kant and Wagner; such thought has destroyed a nascent Germany and spread throughout Europe).

And let us always keep in mind one of the best-known monsters of the 20th century: Foucault; the perverse philosopher, another Sade, has made us see in all his work that what immediately seems to be an "in itself" fallen from the sky (from an "innocent" institution to the very structuring of the human as heteropatriarchal passing through a plague), it is a representation naturalized by the human himself with a view to subjecting some to enable this or that thing at a given time. For example, in the Course at the Collège de Frances de *Les abnormales* (1975), the French thinker shows through those weeks how "abnormality" is constructed and used as a normalization technique. In this Course, Foucault is going to be in charge, as he always is, of seeing that what is called sexuality is always normalized and that is why, among other things, Sade appears at the end of the 18th century; he is an obvious conclusion of his time. And this begins already in the 17th century: "...

the history of that power of normalization essentially applied to sexuality, the techniques of normalizing sexuality since the 17th century".[198] And then Freud is going to perform the act of grace of using the names of two writers who made European bourgeois society uncomfortable at the time: the Frenchman Donatien Alphonse Francois de Sade (who was not a marquis but a count, 1740–1814) and the Austrian Leopold von Sacher-Masoch (1835–1895) to generate a certain essentiality of perversion as a personality structure: sadomasochism (he will generate the bases of this which is later made explicit and reaches our times). In any case, in 1886 it was psychiatrist Richard von Krafft-Ebing, a very conservative physician, who in his *Pychophatia sexualis* uses the term "masochism" to speak of a certain human form that suffers in the hands of another and apparently feels pleasure in that. This psychiatrist became famous with his book showing the abnormal deviations of sexuality, because for him sexuality was always meant to procreate. Deleuze remembers, perhaps without knowing who Krafft-Ebing was, how the doctor using the names of Sade and Sacher-Masoch also makes them clinical, and not just sick (which is typical of the analysis), thanks to what they write: the effect of the *Critique* of the *Clinic* (*Critique and Clinic* is the name of one of the last books of the French philosopher from 1993). In *The Cold and the Cruel* of 1971, at the time of *The Anti- Oedipus*, Deleuze tells us:

> Are Sade and Masoch, in this sense, great clinicians? It is difficult to approach sadism and masochism the way leprosy, the plague, or Parkinson's disease are approached. The word disease is not adequate. This does not prevent Sade and Masoch from presenting us with unparalleled symptoms and signs. When Krafft-Ebing speaks of masochism, he honors Masoch for having renewed a clinical entity, defining it not so much by the sexual pain-pleasure link as by deeper behaviors of slavery and humiliation... But we will also have to ask ourselves if, compared to Sade, Masoch does not define a finer symptomatology that makes it possible to dissociate previously confused disorders. In any case, 'sick' or clinical, and both at the same time...[199]

Sacher-Masoch's texts have that aesthetic expression of what happens in that repressed Austrian society (which Freud will later try to "cure"). For example, in *The Mother of God* there is always the curiosity of literary construction for the Victorian reader and with those finer details that Deleuze likes with respect to Sade (they are characters with more depth, but archetypal):

> Hit me, hit me! in the face, Veva, I beg you! – Sukalón said, without moving from his place. Veva looked at him in great astonishment. Yes, I deserve that treatment, because I was not in my right mind. Such brutality! I did not know how to recognize your value.[200]

And this other example: "When Sabadil was brought into the room tied hand and foot, the prayer hall was filled with a crowd packed and attentive, who seemed to hold their breath".[201] The entire text is a construction for a certain neurotic capitalist bourgeois, from the names of the characters, the situations that are narrated, the scenarios that are described, etc. that tries to provoke and make visible the repressed desire; but with the nuance that pleasure is consummated in pain; being a slave of a master (the master in his cruelty is at the service of the slave and his desire). What Krafft-Ebing does not see, in fact sees little, is believing to see pathology itself typified in a way almost as a phenomenological essence and can be discerned, even between the sadistic and the masochistic: it is a serious error that is always behind the conservative Aristotelians (Sade and Sacher-Masoch are not oppositions of anything essential, they are writers of the human, of the Dionysian). In the construction of Sacher-Masoch, more subtle than Sade (although impossible to overcome in his mathematical rational obsession), the "mise-en-scène" is quite visible: it is a scene before the eye. And this is what the Catalan filmmaker Albert Serra is currently doing and can be seen very clearly in both *The Death of Louis XIV* (2016) and *Liberté* (2019). In both films, even with their filmic complexity both in terms of technique and staging, there is a fairly obvious construction for a certain cultured European bourgeois public, which "consumes" a lot of cinema and art in these times; it is what a certain elite of the left wants to see (their own desire).

The classic pervert, the one that is embedded in our unconscious and causes us fear (the "scar" that haunts us like Frankenstein), the quintessential monster of recent centuries and that follows us at all hours, is the so-called "Marquis of Sade" as a writer-philosopher[202] (totally ideological and faithful and consistent with himself) and, especially, in his literary works due to the violence of his characters in the midst of his works and in the midst of the normative atheism of a Universal Reason (Sade is a product of his time, like everyone else; he expresses it in his contradictions). Klossowski explains very well how to understand this classic mode of transgression in the 18th century (Sade died in 1814 and spent more than 30 years in jail and in the asylum) where the eminently atheistic Universal Reason has to draw its own perverse conclusions:

> In accordance with this principle of the normative generality of the human species, Sade wants to establish a counter-generality, valid this time for the specificity of perversions, which can allow an exchange between the singular cases of perversion, which, according to the existing normative generality, are defined by an absence of logical structure. This is how the Sadian notion of integral monstrosity is projected.[203]

Here we can see the typical transvaluation, transgressing and defying of all norms in a universal world of norms and that operating in the freedom of being without God postulates that "monstrosity". Such a monstrosity seen today is quite "childish" because of the grotesqueness of the violent description that seeks to scandalize that complicit rationality of an era that no longer bears itself with its abuses and a morality that articulates it. And that does not stop repressing the body. Émile Zola, who greatly admired Sacher-Masoch, puts it very clearly this way: "Quand une croyance ne divinise pas la chair, elle la torture, et les monstruosités arrivent aussitôt, sous l'aiguillon du sexe".[204] And so, the sexual is expressed as the place of the perverse transgression against that way of being that does not want to draw the conclusions of what a free human should be and, on the contrary, lives trapped in its bourgeois Labyrinth; which will take it radically straight to monstrosity.

That is why Pier Paolo Pasolini brought the *120 Days of Sodom or Sade's School of Debauchery* to the cinema in 1975, because this book allows him to update the horror of fascism in his 20th-century Italy. Sade's text was written in 1785, when Sade was imprisoned in the Tour Liberté de la Bastille (from 1784–1789). He never finished the novel (you could say that), written in just 37 days, between October 22 and November 28 (I think he didn't want to finish it himself); written for three hours a day (while no one was watching). The "child" Sade, because he sometimes behaved like a capricious child, was always sad for having to leave the manuscript in the Bastille and thought that his great work had been lost forever (he wrote as if possessed and obsessively). It was finally discovered in 1900 by the brilliant dermatologist Iwan Bloch (1872–1922); he used the pseudonym of Dr. Eugene Duehren and bought the manuscript very expensively from a descendant of the Marquis de Villeneuve-Trans, who obtained the manuscript in 1789 from a young revolutionary who entered Sade's cell; he bought it through a Parisian bookseller who passed it on to a German amateur[205] (this is narrated by Apollinaire).[206]

Doctor Bloch, who lived a few years, was a specialist in venereal diseases such as syphilis, gonorrhea, etc., one of the founders of current sexology; that was called *Sexualwissenschaft* and edited by him in 1904 as a novel and, at the same time, as a highly technically rigorous scientific treatise on sexuality in all its known manifestations; this doctor was against the persecution of homosexuals in Germany (he tried to abolish the horrific paragraph 175 of the German Penal Code, which criminalized erotic relationships between men) and as a student of Sade he sought to de-pathologize the sexual and, on the contrary, he takes it to the anthropological field (for Freud, what Bloch does is very important);[207] and he realizes that as any sexual organ can function as an erogenous zone, then it is not that the perverts are few, but on the contrary, they are many and they are everywhere; the point is that they are repressed. He realizes that Sade in 1875 with the *120 Days of Sodom* was a forerunner of sexual pathology, a century before the conservative Krafft-Ebing (his book is from 1886). He has two great books that seek to correct what was said about sexuality by Krafft-Ebing, Deleuze does not know this (the interesting doctor to study is Bloch), which are two gems: *Contributions to an Etiology of Psychopathia Sexualis* (1902–1903), a text much studied by Freud. That is why the Viennese psychoanalyst says: "The motive forces leading to the formation of hysterical symptoms draw their strength not only from repressed *normal* sexuality but also from unconscious perverse activities".[208] Bloch's other text is *Contemporary Sexual Life* (1907). It is very important to see how Sade allowed Bloch a great vision of the sexual at the beginning of the 20th century, before Freud, and also allowed him a political vision committed to his scientific research and *without* prejudice. However, *120 Days of Sodom* was still unread by the bulk of scholars, since a finished edition of that manuscript was yet to be made; although its first publication, by Bloch, with its technical commentary, for the time, is a gem (but it is a publication riddled with errors and for a small audience). Apollinaire describes it like this:

> Les 120 Journées de Sodome ou l'Ecole du libertinage, par le Marquis de Sade. Publié pour la première fois d'après le manuscrit original, avec des annotations scientifiques, par le docteur Eufien Duehren (D' méd. Iwan Bloch), Paris, Club des liibliophiles, 1904, viii et 543 pp. in-4, couverture, fac-similé d'une page du manuscrit. Ouvrage tiré à 160 exemplaires.[209]

There were only 160 copies of that literature and science publication; which gave way to the 20th century. One could think of three great milestones in thought at the beginning of the 20th century: Husserl's *Logical Investigations* (1900–1901), Freud's *Interpretation of Dreams* (1899; dated 1900), and the discovery of the *120 Days of Sodom* by Sade (1900, 1904) thanks to Bloch. That is, the human, with Sade, dismantled the self from the very rationality of the self, and neurosis was understood hand in hand with psychosis thanks to perversion.

In 1929, Viscount Charles de Noailles and his wife, Marie-Laure de Noailles (she was a distant descendant of Sade), and were the producers of the film *The Golden Age*, by Luis Buñuel (1930) and with some support from Dalí (something in the script), and friends of the whole group of surrealists, including Man Ray, Mondrian, Cocteau, Bataille, etc. And let's not forget the scandal that *The Golden Age* generated at its premiere (it only lasted a week and was not destroyed thanks to the viscount), and was banned until 1981 in France (a renewed France under Mitterrand allowed it). Well, the film shows sadism, infanticide, sex in public places, abuse of the disabled or blasphemy, etc. Buñuel, another monster, reminded us of Sade in Paris itself and financed by the viscounts. Now the film, almost 100 years old, is in museums, children see it, it is considered a masterpiece that must be preserved; the same happens with Sade's *120 Days of Sodom* after almost 250 years. And Buñuel said sarcastically, as always, that he was a "sadian" and not a "sadistic".[210] And it was; it just so happens that Sade himself was a Sadian. Buñuel himself tells how he encountered Sade's *120 Days of Sodom*, which in a way is part of *The Golden Age*. When asked by José de la Colina: "The final scene is a tribute to the Marquis de Sade. When did you read it?" Buñuel answers:

> Shortly before making *The Golden Age*. I was very impressed. Robert Desnos, at a dinner at Tual's house, had told me about Sade, whom I did not know. He introduced me *to The 120 Days of Sodom*, the same issue that Proust and Gide had read, because Sade was not republished then. The edition belonged to a German professor who only printed ten copies in 1905 and that copy was the only one in France. In Sade I discovered a world of extraordinary subversion, in which everything enters: from insects to the customs of human society, sex, theology. In the end, I was really blown away.[211]

The "German professor" was doctor Iwan Bloch, there were 160 copies (equally few) and it was not in 1905, but in 1904. And Buñuel carried Sade within himself all his life, until his last work *That Obscure Object of Desire* of 1977 (the two women who represent the character of Cochita recall virtue and vice, that is, the sisters Justine and Juliette by Sade).

The viscounts bought – they were billionaires – the original of *120 Days of Sodom* (they brought it back from Germany to France) and commissioned the writer and publisher Maurice Heine (1884–1940 and a descendant of the poet Heinrich Heine) to make a special edition, in three volumes, for bibliophiles and subscribers (which took time between 1931–1935) and thus overcame the censorship of the cursed book. And so, this friend of Bataille and a radical communist, introduced us to this book of perversions (as an anecdote, Heine disliked *The Golden Age* by Buñuel and criticized it harshly; he did not see reflected the radicalism of the criticism of everything religious by Sade, but only to Christianity).[212] And we owe this to Heine who followed what Apollinaire thought in 1909, in his famous edition of Sade's works, and anticipated the meticulous work of Gilbert Lely (they were very close friends). It was Maurice Heine who took on the work of making Sade famous as one of the greats of French literature; his French is beautiful and precious in style to describe even the most violent and shocking (just as Sarah Kane's English). Heine updated files, saw the manuscripts, transcribed them and worked in detail on the "120 Days of Sodom Scroll". It is he who pointed out that: "... a text by the Marquis de Sade should be treated with the same respect as a text by Pascal". He wrote 15 studies on Sade that are considered a gem. The parchment known as "The Bastille Roll" expresses that obsessive side of Sade, whether in the form, or in the way he narrates, or in the figures of his narration. He is a totally obsessive and rational pervert (human of his time); he works as if inside a matheme, as if he were writing a fractal (more precise than Mandelbrot), but with literary texts of humans that can be imagined (that is the success of his writing, the possibility of imagining horror). The manuscript is made up of 11-centimeter sheets, glued together, forming a strip 12.10 meters long. It is written on both sides in very small letters and you need a magnifying glass to read it. And since Sade was imprisoned in those final days of the monarchical regime in July 1789 and it is also known that he wanted to provoke the people to take the Bastille on July 2 by means of a tube that he used as a megaphone (he used it through a window of his cell and thus generated a riot): it is said that he shouted that the prisoners were being slaughtered;[213] and therefore in those days they were all very concerned about the high social tension. And that is why it was decided that they take him away from the Bastille and transport him, apparently, on July 4, in those days of July riots, to the Charenton asylum (where he finally died in 1814, but was released on the April 2, 1790; he was constantly arrested and released: it was his life). And the "unfinished" manuscript remains on the Tour Liberté, in a crack in the cell where Sade was locked up. And since the final revolt comes on July 14, Sade's wife cannot go looking for him (he asked her to). However, it is the young revolutionary Arnoux de Saint-Maximin who finds the manuscript in the cell and then sells it to the Marquis de Villeneuve-Trans, and thus it stayed three generations in that family. Imprisoned in 1777 (for many crimes that he was accused of and some of them political, beyond kidnapping or not of women), first in Vincennes, then transported in 1784 to the Bastille, Sade began to write the *120 Days of Sodom* eight years after his sentence (1785).

What does the *120 Days of Sodom* express? What is indicated by that debauchery? An almost mechanical game that reveals the human in the midst of its time. An artifact that can be seen as horrifying, but "human, too human", because it reveals what will later be called the unconscious; that which pierces us and dynamizes us with each other, showing our mortality, sexuality keeping up with the times in a political way that constitutes it. It is a device that brings to light what we are as monsters in the hands of the completely decadent French upper bourgeoisie and understanding, as now, that power is expressed in one doing what one wants with the other (as in the suggestive and precise film *Noose*, by Hitchcock, 1948). Sade as a new Molière as a pre-Victor Hugo, copying in part Restif de la Bretonne (and his *Le Pornographe* of 1769), writes this macabre and very rational game, almost like a matheme that operates by itself combining all forms known until then of passion from the subtle to the aberrant. That is why Bloch finds it a fundamental book to account for the human and Sade has already become one of the most important writers of his time. Apollinaire points it out like this: "… selon l'opinion du docteur Duehren, met le marquis de Sade au premier rang des écrivains du xviii' siècle, et dans laquelle il donne une explication scientifique de toutes les manifestations qui ressortissent à la psychopathie sexuelle".[214]

Sade in this literary-visual and fractal game is like a good obsessive putting together his revealing device of the logics of French power in the unconscious of the bourgeoisie. And generates those caricatures of the human in its free and despotic power: his high radical irrationality hand in hand with total rationality. Below Sade there is always the notion that God does not exist and that is why it is permitted to do what you want; in another way, it could be said that Sade must be one of the most faithful writers in modern history (beyond his apparent atheism): the blasphemer who blasphemes because he denies what he believes; the power that the absence of God gives to the bourgeois is total, it is a rationality that operates without foundation and that, therefore, only pulsates sexually in its freedom: Sade is a believer and one of the most radical. And this mechanism that expresses the human, but I repeat especially the power, can be seen, which is obvious, in a patriarchal way (in general, simply put, everything revolves around the penis), although with the complicity of the four women historians or rhapsodists, in charge of narrating each story in each month (from November to February). The place that is created for this contraption is also evident: the Silling Castle in the middle of the German Black Forest (a place copied many times throughout history); just like in the fourth season of the British series *Sherlock* (2017 and let's remember Sherrinford, an island prison/mental institution, where everything is sadistic and devious). It is a place like German pre-expressionist, but Sade uses it to almost scare the French bourgeois who will read the text (Sade likes to scare the reader, which makes him see the horror). It is a text, I repeat, with great French prose, but it works with caricaturesque figures to imagine each moment of pleasure or passion (150 per month); each figure in each day (there are five per day) is a figure built for that bourgeois imagination and thus disturb or realize it (Bloch sees this very well; it is what Buñuel does in *El perro andaluz* of 1929 and later radically in *The Golden Age* in 1930 taking by the hand Sade himself; this is often repeated by Lars von Trier in his work and more irregularly in Tarantino). Everything is at the service of four powerful men who represent the decline of the French monarchy, four libertine men who can do what they want with the other to satisfy their desire.

And the construction of these characters is also almost comical (like Fellini's grotesque characters) and quite expected (there is nothing that cannot be foreseen in the construction of the characters, like Molière always, or what Victor Hugo later does until tired; they are like the characters in James Bond, the bad guys who face 007): the Duke of Blangis, his brother the Bishop, the Banker Durcet, the President of Curval. Each one is a representation, quite grotesque, of French power. It is like a "natural representation" of the people of the bourgeoisie made for "natural representation" of the bourgeoisie that it has of the people and of itself. Let us not forget that it is the bourgeoisie that jails Sade again and again. The elite do not like to see themselves reflected in his literary texts. And everything is expressed in Sade's contraption: aristocratic power, ecclesial power, money power, judicial power. And the aristocratic and the ecclesial are also twinned, which is obvious. And the four are friends, like the Horsemen of the Apocalypse (always Sade, the believer). For example, Nolan's Joker, like Phillips', or Frank Miller's has a really brilliant psychological richness, they don't allow themselves to be caricatured even in a comic. They are above the good and the bad. Maybe that's why Nietzsche's silence before Sade: he never liked Molière, Victor Hugo, or anything representative. In *Thus Spoke Zarathustra* the character of Zarathustra is unclassifiable, there is no taxonomy that determines it; nor is there for Creon or Antigone in Sophocles' *Antigone*.

And Sade's literary-visual text (one Homer, and its episodes, passed through Molière), a mathematical text, is composed as follows: in Silling Castle, where no one knows anything and no one can flee (or the contraption doesn't work), in 120 days, four months (from November to February), 600 pleasures or passions (to call it in some way), not to say "perversions" (from sexual play to the most vile murder passing through bestiality). A total of 150 of those passions per month, five per day. And each month the intensity of pain and cruelty towards the other increases; and the rhapsode changes by month (each of them perfectly described even with their age): but all within a very clear logic and taxonomy (Sade, the logician; sometimes when I read it, I think of Hilbert). There is no chaos in Sade, he is totally afraid of chaos; everything is a predetermined scene: even the most horrific or subtle is predetermined (just like the filming of Bergman or Kubrick). Sade: "It's a natural representation". Sade himself says so at the end of his text, since he thinks that someone else could finish it if necessary, he would add: "Do not depart from this plan at all: everything in it is combined several times and with the greatest accuracy".[215] They are literary and visually constructed passions in the classic taxonomy that comes from the Greeks, especially the Latin writers (with the European variants, much Italian and French of the time; and also not only of the sexual, pornographic kind but also in the criminal and scientific field; without forgetting the ever-present past of the torture systems that Europeans have given each other, which are generally applied to the people who want to rise up). In the month of November, they are sexual passions without penetration (simple passions, of first class). And then in December they are second class, that is, complex passions and multiple forms of penetration where the limits are broken (the incestuous); then in January, they are the passions of the third class, namely the criminal (forms of bestiality). And finally, in February there are fourth-class passions: mortal (forms of murder). And as it is known, only November is "truly" written, which also seems evident, and that the other three months only have a formal writing sketch per day and passion. Perhaps it is not that the book is unfinished (what was written is from 1785 and finished on November 28 of that year and written very quickly and very precisely in 37 days, but he was imprisoned until the first days of July of 1789 and never finished it), it is probable that Sade could not "imagine" the other 450 passions. It was part of Sade's obsessive taxonomy to articulate in 600 and divide it into 4 and make it 150 per month and each one indicates a level of intensity in passion, but writing it down is something else. And hence the main narrator is Madame Duclos: the Scheherazade of the *120 Days of Sodom*. Actually, what is mostly described are those 150 passions in their imaginative details for the bourgeois reader of those 30 days of November: that is almost the whole book. And the December 150, where torture and all forms of sexual penetration appear (this text is a short sketch of a few pages of the manuscript, which is very synthetic and scarcely imaginable), and the January 150, where the mutilations, bestiality, sodomy (and it is also a very short text in number of pages, in which even bestiality is described quite ridiculously), and the final 150 passions where the murders appear, are quite formal although lurid (but boring: the excess shows a total lack of creativity – Sade's rationality loses and exhausts him). It is possible that it is an ironic joke that Sade's sadism is not what counts, but that he bores with his mechanical model to the point of exhaustion; that's what's sadistic when you read the *120 Days of Sodom*. And those three remaining months with their passions, Sade never wrote them as the 150 passions of November. And hence Sade's matheme is as follows: 4 taxonomies of passions, 4 months, 4 powerful libertines, 4 wives-daughters, 4 rhapsodes to narrate, 8 kidnapped boys, 8 kidnapped girls (all of them between 12 and 15 years old), 8 who perform the fucking, 10 servants (4 old women and 6 female cooks). In total, 46 people in Silling Castle, like moments of Sade's contraption (Paris was never that, it's like the ideal city of Urbino). It is known from the mere formal description that 30 die and 16 survive after March 1. Apollinaire describes it thus from what Bloch points out:

> Les autres parties, la deuxième avec la Chanville et ses 150 'passions doubles', la troisième avec les 150 perversions criminelles de la Marlaine et la quatrième avec 150 perversions meurtrières de la Desgranges, sont abrégées, on pourrait

dire esquissées. La Duclos parle in novembre, la Chanville in décembre, la Martaine in janvier, la Desgranges in février. Les récits se terminent le dernier jour,
et l'on finit en massacrant les dernières victimes.[216]

Each of the rhapsodes: Madame Duclos, Madame Champville, La Martaine, La
Desgranges has their own way of being and are also described mechanically, as are
the libertines, their wives, the kidnapped youths, especially the ones who fuck, who
are described down to the inches of their penises (this must have been important
at the time, but it's really botched), The Daily Rules from 10:00 am to 2:00 am the
next day, The Particular Rules, etc. It is very evident that everything is an imaginative game, not very creative, by Sade for a bourgeois reader. And what remains
of all this, only as a synthetic form, without literature in between and something
botched in his imagination: "D'ailleurs, voici le Compte du total (...) Massacrés
avant le 1" mars dans les orgies ... . 10(...) Depuis le 1" mars .... 20 (...)
Et ils s'en retournent .... 16".

Although the text is obviously violent, everything is done in a rational way to
decompose the French society of the time and take it to its limit, and everything
is coldly calculated, it is as if Leibniz had written the text, due to the obsessive
precision of each passion in each of this mathematical unit. Pier Paolo Pasolini in
1975 (it became his will because he was assassinated on November 2 of that year)
takes Sade's story to the present day of World War II, after Mussolini's defeat and
the Republic of Saló is invented as the place where this libertine enslavement of
total social decomposition will occur in view of power. Pasolini also advanced his
Saló en Porcile (1969) through the articulation of the human with cannibalism and
zoophilia, narrating two stories in which some eat another: both at the end of the
fifteenth century, and in Germany in 1968. Two forms of surviving because you are
hungry or you crave for power: one primitive and the other bourgeois. Both forms
articulated with each other; where desire becomes infinite; especially, in the current
bourgeoisie eating for the sake of eating, to accumulate food; on the other hand, the
primitive did it because he was simply hungry, he could even eat a butterfly.

In truth, this perversion that is seen as scandalous in Sade's writings is actually
well constructed for that time (each character is at the service of that need to pervert
and make visible what is happening); and Sade literally plays with the reader; just
as the audience is played with in the *In-Yer-Face* theater to criticize that normative
society, empty and creator of the very monsters that we are (for example, Sarah
Kane, Angélica Liddell, etc.), but it is mainly a philosophical literary device that is
made from the rational and universal world. At present things are going the other
way around this rigid rationalist taxonomy: perversion is the engine of the human
(its determined negation, *bestimmte Negation*, in the language of Hegel and the
Phenomenology) and of things, in general, that can be expressed in the occurrence
of the Real, but in the midst of the Symbolic itself. Of that which is inexorably
taken from us, Lacan named it this way in his *Seminar 20: Even* (1972–1973) to
his analysts so that they would realize: "... go straight to the hole in the system, to
the place where the real passes through you ... crushes you".[217]

And that is why seeing the French-style perversion from that "sound" of the expression as "Vers-le-pére" indicates something more interesting than the classical etymology; and it is what is at stake today and it is what the Slovenians want to think, in part, but especially the U.S.; and many current thinkers. And if we follow Tostain:

> Perversion has a bad press. What it evokes from the outset is aberrant, deviant behavior, the indefensible manifestation of bad intentions, the criminal slip that leads to perdition. The fact that the sound material of the word is found in a 'Vers le pere ... is often obscured by the aura of scandal that accompanies it.[218]

And that's the point, removing that evil criminal halo (of a toy Sade) and seeing perversion as a kind of "version towards the Father", a kind of mobilizing it, of inscribing it dynamically. In the Symbolic, the Real operates as a certain fault, a Rock, but not as "in itself", but rather that it has the Symbolic itself of the human and in it we find neither more nor less than what is proper to the human, which becomes a world that becomes in the midst of things that become. And if we are poured out to the Father, that version will always be bothering him and dynamize pain and satisfaction in the human. The analyst Aulagnier says it this way: "Perversion is something that we can never say that it does not concern us, because we are sure that, whatever it may be, it concerns *us*".[219] And this was already said by Bloch in 1902. And today this does not only concern trans people, queer people, sex workers, women, men, but everyone, every one of WeOthers. And we can see that we are crazy at this time, and poured in a different way on the Father who wants to structure us. And especially Capitalism, against which it resists, defends us and inhibits us. And the "monsters", cursed and infamous, are opening history itself and with it the ontology has to mutate and is the challenge of current thinkers. And the neurotic leaves his heavenly seat of certain security and somehow joins hands in psychosis to reverse his anguish, his symptom, his inhibition before the Name of Capitalism (and, let us not forget, that Capitalism is said in multiple ways; even today as a Maternal Capitalism that takes care of us and will save us: like the Bank).

And JAM sees in this way of the Real occurring something dangerous as perverse humans, but always explains it very well, but its meaning must be inverted and in that we are going to understand the human radically; where he sees sexuality critically and the formulas of sexuation appear to us Lacan-Kant, Žižek-Hegel and also, in a certain sense, Butler and Deleuze:

> The real invented by Lacan is not the real of science. It is a random, contingent real, insofar as the natural law of the relationship between the sexes is lacking. It is a hole in the knowledge included in the real. (...) Lacan has used the mathematical language that is most favorable to science. In the formulas of sexuation, for example, he has tried to capture the blind alleys of sexuality in a web of mathematical logic. And that has been a heroic attempt to make psychoanalysis

a science of the real as logic is. (…) But that cannot be done without imprisoning jouissance in the phallic function, in a symbol. This implies a symbolization of the real, it implies referring to the male-female binary as if living beings could be distributed so clearly, when we already see in the real of the 21st century a growing disorder of sexuation.[220]

The text is very important and will allow us to account for what is human in Slovenians as they think about it today and in this we immerse ourselves in Lacan and that impossibility of sexual intercourse indicated by the philosopher Zupančič. And as we know from Žižek himself, who comments on this text in Birkbeck (April 19, 2016),[221] it must be one of the few places where Žižek openly criticizes his teacher, and criticizes him with radical irony. He treats him as being a Butlerian because of his idea of the masculine-feminine binary (an unfair criticism of Butler) and also as being a Deleuzian in his ontology of multiplicity (and in the radical aspect of not understanding Lacan, or the Real, or to the Symbolic, or anything at all). He even asks, in a very funny way, for him to be sentenced to death or that he stay locked up in the Gulag and not come out of there. Why is Žižek so tough? It is, ironically speaking, because of Butler (and the Deleuze that dwells within her according to Žižek).

I will try to resolve what Miller says about the Real, but from the human today, somewhat agreeing with Žižek, but not entirely, and taking into account what has been said about perversion and monsters throughout this book. And for this we return, once again, to Lacan. And for the French thinker to arrive in the 1970s and say that we are all crazy because love is impossible, but also sex and women; even the Real formally does not exist either; Lacanian thought is full of non-existences (and with Winnicott the baby does not exist either). Lacan is very clear and points it out this way in his fundamental *Seminar 20: Still* (1972–1973): "… love is impossible because the sexual relationship is abyssed in meaninglessness."[222] This great text by Lacan is what we want to reverse from another side; because love is that impossible and that's what I've been talking about throughout the book; this text is about love today, but we'll see. This writing by Lacan (which is not a writing) and this *Seminar* are almost biographical of himself, from a time after the failure of *May 68* and which confuse Miller (even more so in these times since almost 50 years have passed), because it makes him believe that the Real is meaningless, a void and in this, love is no longer possible because the very mechanism of sex has dislocated from a certain original structure (discursiveness does not operate), the male-female binary sexuation has been broken forever, for the Symbolic was shattered. Miller tries to explain that formulation, the sexual relationship does not exist, from that Real without possible *Aufhebung*, without Hegel, but obviously with Kant (and Heidegger): "This points to the real where there is no knowledge, a real that escapes signification, to the signifying *Aufhebung* and that, precisely, the phallic *Aufhebung* leaves aside.[223]

And confronted with this, Žižek tries to Hegelianize Lacan to get him out of his inevitable Kantianism; better than Kant, it could be shown, that Lacan is in the perspective of the collapse of the "Thing in itself". Fichte saw this abyss (*Ab-Grund*) with total clarity and named it in many ways: one of them I, but Schelling makes the abysmal experience of that Freedom that always remains as a remainder (Hegel would say: as immediate), a freedom unfunded that founds. And this is in the second Heidegger that Lacan read over and over again and even translated. It is Heidegger who is behind Lacan. And that is what Žižek's operation on Lacan himself is all about (turning him Hegelian and removing the Kantian Heideggerian imprint) and against Miller himself as the official translator of Lacan. It is as if Hegel's revenge against Kant, Fichte and Schelling was taking place today; and against the most anti-Hegelian, Heidegger himself. And apparently that Heideggerian imprint is behind Foucault and Deleuze, who are the loves of Butler (never Lacan). Those loves for Žižek, although they are from the left, always secretly work for liberalism (like Heidegger himself who, moreover, was never from the left). And behind Miller's error in understanding the Real in this way lies the liberalism that perforates Queer Theory (and because it is from the U.S., and not European, even less Slovenian). And that is why this biopolitical characterization of the human: multiplicities eager for more Capitalism to do what they want. Žižek is relentless in this; he repeats it over and over again: "The subject Butler refers to remains the liberal subject, the subject engaged in the process of constantly expanding the content of his identifications".[224]

And what about that sexual relationship between a human that is binary divided into male-female? Is this binary of structural type? Is Miller an interpreter of Lacan because of his lack of Hegelianism and love for his Kant? Is Butler an interpreter of Lacan as she uses him in order to later dispute the genre politically and then undo it, like a good Hegelian? Is it possible to reformulate the binary and embellish it and try to keep it operating, but in an updated way? And if one goes to Lacan, as Žižek-Hegel does, one sees that Lacan is not very clear about this binary either, since he already spoke of this as the impossible of the sexual act in the sixties (later he changed to the term "relationship") and precisely in the unpublished *Seminar 14. the Logic of the Ghost* (1966–1967). There he points out the "failure to enjoy" (if genre could be understood as "modes of enjoying" it would have more flexibility and the "Sade template" would not be necessary), typical of perversion and which is radically expressed later in *May 68*; where the new mutation of the most voracious Capitalism takes place, where everything is freedom without obstacles, where the quartet of philosophers: Barthes, Deleuze, Derrida, Foucault break with psychoanalysis and Lacan and that, unfortunately, has lasted until now; and Lacan breaks with them in *Seminar 17: The Reverse of Psychoanalysis*, 1969–1979, where he separates the discourse of the university, that is to say, Barthes, Derrida, Deleuze, Foucault, and the discourse of analysis, that is to say, the same Lacan and psychoanalysis (but Derrida cannot completely break – his wife is a psychoanalyst). And in *Seminar 14* it is pointed out that:

> The secret of psychoanalysis, the great secret of psychoanalysis, is that there is no sexual act (...) Is there, in the sexual act, this something in which – in the

same form – the subject might inscribe itself as sexed, establishing in the same act its union to the subject of the sex that is described as opposite? (…) as I earlier sufficiently announced by the presence of the phallus and the partial objects, and whose function must now be articulated, in such a way that it demonstrates to us what role this function plays in this act. A function that is always sliding, a function of substitution, which is equivalent almost to a sort of juggling and which, never allows us in any case to posit in the act – I mean in the sexual act – the man and the woman opposed in some eternal essence.[225]

And this is precisely what Lacan has to think about, in times when all binary structuring is crumbling (thanks, among other things, to Capitalism itself, but Žižek does not realize this, also because of what is human immersed in the world); and Lacan needs to pass from the act to the relationship, because that binary is only understood from a certain slip of reason in laying and establishing as a foundation something that is not, but rather is a foundation (the already famous Hegelian distinction between *Grund* and *grundlage*); this is a formal base to generate opposition. And every foundation carries within itself an operative abstraction: it is the eternal and arbitrary essence that does not allow us to carry out the impossible sexual act because it supposes from the outset two that are externally related, so there is no relationship at all; and, furthermore, this unfinished act of its own is constituted in its failures that do not cease to show themselves as, for example, guilt;[226] and always repeating the oedipal scene ad nauseam (which is why everything that expresses the impossibility of the sexual act is treated by Lacan from the horizon of perversion; once again allowing us to see our own mutation in a mutated world, where everything mutates: Dionysus constitutes us).[227] And that oedipal scene, is embedded in Sade's (the believer) writing like a scar; he can never leave it, even if he erases or eliminates or destroys a character in *120 Days of Sodom*, he is always trapped and cannot erase himself in the act of erasing the other because of the pleasure that it gives him. Even the operative prostitution postulated by Sade has its own constitutive sin: it was nothing more and nothing less than playing with the limit that is denied because it is firmly believed in it. Klossowski points this out very clearly: "Transgression presupposes the existing order, the apparent maintenance of norms, for the benefit of an accumulation of energy that makes transgression necessary. Thus universal prostitution only makes sense in terms of the moral property of the individual body".[228]

In that eternal essence there cannot be any act because there is no original inscription of that masculine-feminine binary, because of its own such binary does not exist, there is only a certain movement and game of the human in the openness of itself and, apparently, of everything. It is as if the sexual act itself fails because of the internal perversion that constitutes it, not allowing any limit of mediation to be given: it is the incestuousness of sexual fusion that, in turn, is its impossibility (and for this it is fundamental all of Melanie Klein's work to express the unity between child and mother); and in this it happens that one of the elements does not formally exist as such because it is not closed not only in its discourse, but in its own symbolization, simply put, culture: the feminine; as I said, everything important in Lacan is denied (in the Symbolic) because its state of existence is qualitatively superior or as orthogonal; once again it is the presence of Heidegger within Lacan, it is almost as if we moved in the difference of the ontological, but the other way around: everything that exists is ontic and determined in its totality; it is castrated; that is why the woman does not exist (neither the Other, nor the sexual relationship, nor the Real, etc.), because orthogonally she expresses the Real.

And in the 1970s, Lacan radicalized himself in the very question of the Real and the human. Lacan says it this way in *Seminar 19: ... or Worse* (1971–1972): "As every saying is expressed in a complete proposition: there is no sexual relationship. It is a truth that can only be semi-said, it is a matter of the other half saying worse".[229] And that is why Lacan adds with a subtle but precise nuance, because the Real is heard as it operates in its own failure within the very interior of symbolization, of the sexual relationship:

> Since the sexual relationship, which is not – in the sense that it cannot be written – is questioned, this sexual relationship determines everything that is elaborated on the basis of a discourse whose nature is that of being an interrupted discourse.[230]

It is the impasse operating in the Symbolic of the human, in their sexual relationship; therefore, it becomes evident that what has been called masculine and what has been called feminine crumbles to the ground at the end of the 20th century (Sade is made redundant). The *120 Days of Sodom* are not necessary, firstly because all the cities are Sodom, then none is completely so; and because one day is enough, the other is mere repetition with a certain degree of diversity, therefore, the assumption itself has already been assumed and canceled in its "natural representation", but it had already been falling apart for decades, centuries, millennia. The Greek gods did not operate from the masculine-feminine binomial, if you will, they themselves are queer, like Dionysus, Athena, etc. Walter Otto puts it this way (and it is possible that every god is; for example, the Germanic gods like Thor are all transvestites and feminine in their masculine brutality): "The Erinyes of Aeschylus' tragedy give us a vivid image of the ancient telluric powers. The decisive confession of Athena for masculinity is very significant. It could be affirmed that the masculine and feminine concept of existence is found here".[231]

Lacan and the Slovenians must think of the human in their formulations, but they do not want to give way to trans, queer, etc. of the performative biopolitical position, since they see it as liberal and an expression of the Capitalism of these times for de-structuring the structure of sexual difference. And Lacan on his own, in his time, begins to turn, like an Aristotle, the human "monster"; and, for the same reason, woman cannot exist either because castration, determination does not determine her, there is no way to close her in her own structural opening. And this is evident because everything has risen from the penis as phallus. And what if the "pussy" were raised as an opening and from there we generated the "transcendental deduction" of the human in its sexuation? And, if so, because it is obvious that it is so and it could not be otherwise for the Slovenians or for a certain feminism, there is only one gender: the masculine, as Žižek says in his current work: "that man is the only gender stricto sensu and that the woman is the first transgender figure".[232] She, the woman, is a certain moment in negativity. Lacan, faithful to his mathematizing formulas, wants to resolve what has been expressed everywhere in Europe for decades, and which Beauvoir herself affirmed very strongly (a great reader of Sade), but within his own thought and in his clinic. And he does, for psychoanalytic and patriarchal reasons, like Sade, make it all fall back on the masculine phallus and its fear of castration and oedipification (this is a pillar in psychoanalysis), the only gender; and the feminine remains as if outside of it and as well as a certain outside, just more of the masculine itself (I always prefer to speak of masculine and feminine so as not to make it fall on the man and the woman (for example, a woman can also have a masculine function). As he puts it in his sexuation formulas: the feminine as a not-whole, with respect to a masculine whole. Žižek is finer and Hegelianizes the Lacanian formulas. Lacan in *Seminar 18: From a Discourse that was not Semblant* (1971), says: "the woman is not-all",[233] but in relation to the phallus, to the masculine (always seen as a determination or the formula does not hold). Here is the patriarchal itself operating within Lacan and Žižek. The masculine through his phallus and essentially through his "penis" gives the total finishing unit, but always charged and in need of his outside for the same phallus that he is; and she the feminine articulates as a function in negativity of that masculine (I don't want to go into that this is also changing by itself and if, for example, the clitoris is another totality and is elevated to the category of phallus; and if the penis has passive non-phallic functions but of welcoming the other like the pussy, etc.). Lacan says that the feminine no longer has anything to do with the logic of the binary or its opposite, but rather as the supplementary: "... supplementary to what is designated as jouissance by the phallic function".[234] It is precisely that the feminine is not all in the phallic function; it does not exist phallically but as the open itself that operates together with the phallus, but Lacan has to clarify: "it does not mean that [the woman] is not at all. It's not true that she's not all there. She's fully there. But there is something else".[235] And that more is all the radical differential that constitutes the relationship and at the same time does not allow it: it is, once again, the Real happening as a failure that keeps us alive in this world, in the very tension between the human within itself, of some with Others, of WeOthers with everything. Here Lacan, the Slovenian school and especially Žižek play to be able to think, as far as possible, in a structural ontological way what happens in the human today; a Kantian, sadistic trace lives in the Slovene.

It is the exit from the Symbolic to the Real to find the human from the symbolic formulas, in this Miller is right in his criticism of Lacan, and in this the Real operates as an outside that does not exist as a framework of non-existence for the sexual relationship, be it for the woman who operates in the Symbolic itself, because of itself the Real is nothing substantial (it is a non-substantial Rock). It is possible that it is not about formulas, but about art, literature, cinema, etc., the ways of expression of the human. And it's most likely as simple as having sex.

In the sexual relationship there is the failure that we live daily, because the Real of it cannot be symbolized in any way (not even by formulas), because among other things what is named as masculine and feminine has never happened, or maybe it happened at some idealized moment in European history and in some psychopathology manual or in a Sade text (which is the extreme idealization), but it doesn't happen anymore. At the height of the end of the 20th century in Europe, the Real, in its being in the Symbolic, operates as an error, problem, failure, interruption, etc. The sexual relationship between these apparent doubles: masculine and feminine (because the feminine is not, but operates as if it were and at the same time as what dynamizes) is the occurrence of the very impasse of the Real in the human and thus the human itself is constituted. Žižek points it out this way in his dialogue with Butler and Laclau: "… far from serving as an implicit symbolic norm that reality can never reach, sexual difference as real/impossible means precisely that said norm does not exist: sexual difference is that 'rock of impossibility' on which all 'formalization' of sexual difference is founded".[236]

And in this Miller does not know how to follow Lacan and the human vanishes not from the Real, but rather from Miller himself. He understands the Real in such a naturalized way outside of the Symbolic that he sees in the progress of science itself, as well as a Heideggerian radical anti-science, and in the global advent of Capitalism the vanishing of everything that happens today, from the cosmos to the human (and he is blind to see how his own thought is part of how Capitalism is). And that the why of Miller's childish game of associating the feminine with matter in these times and with its non-existence:

> Progressively, physics has had to give rise to the probabilistic uncertainty coming from economics, that is, to a set of notions that threaten the subject supposed knowledge. It has not been possible, either, to make the real and matter equivalent. With subatomic physics, the levels of matter multiply and, let's say, the La of matter, like the La of women, vanishes.[237]

It's not that Miller doesn't know what to do with the Real, he doesn't know what to do with sexuation, and in short, he doesn't know what to do with the feminine today (and neither with the human: trans, queer, etc.). But the feminine, using the expression that Hegel himself says in the *Phenomenology*, is like the bone that is the being of the spirit; she is his truth, she is the truth of the sexual relationship because it is the truth of the masculine; she in her being "nothing" of the masculine and in it of the sexual relationship is a not-all of the properly masculine: it is the very perforation of the masculine, it is the Real of him. That performative nothingness, that Real, Rock, bone, is not substantial in the empirical sense (like Miller, like Lacan-Heidegger, as a certain French thought like Deleuze, like Butler, and also all the feminism of the difference, etc.), but the feminine is what makes possible the very center of everything, of that everything. It is the human as a perforated double where the perforation, that is, the feminine, is called woman (it is what Ariadne is for Dionysus himself).[238] Zupančič puts it in a Hegelian way (and moves away a bit from her beloved Kant-Miller): "To be a woman is to be nothing".[239] And woman as perforation, for being not-everything, is like a woman's nothingness (Kant is present again), but that she is nothing because she functions as an operator, in the sense of Lacanian formulas:

> More precisely, to recognize its shape itself, its negativity, as its only positive content. To be a woman is to be nothing. And this is good, this should be the feminist slogan. Obviously, 'nothing' is not used as an adjective here, describing a worth, it is used in the strong sense of the noun.[240]

However, the same symbolic formula of the feminine, of the sexual relationship, carries within itself the Real symbolically inscribed in the Symbolic and in this I cannot help but see a bias that Butler and other current theories try not to generate. It is interesting that Lacan at the end of his life (he died in 1981) gives way to a certain negative psychoanalysis; just as a negative theology arises that is reformulated by Heidegger's *Ereignis*; and I see Lacan more in that Heideggerian register than in Badiou's *Événement* against what Zupančič thinks: "This 'something' goes by several different names – although we will limit ourselves to two: for Lacan it is 'the Real'; for Badiou 'the event'".[241]

However, what if man were that nothingness for being the phallic itself, and hence his impossibility of enjoying, and of being nothing in the feminine itself; and therefore, the feminine behaved as the only gender? However, Lacan faithful to his psychoanalytic and ontological idea of the problem of castration (the masculine) gives a status to the feminine in its being nothing totally radical (she avoids castration), in a certain way he is indicating that she is the only that can love from her own impossibility of the sexual relationship and its failure, because the failure of the masculine due to his own determined phallus will lead him to seek again and again to overcome the failure, the Hegelian infinite evil within the masculine, instead in the feminine its own failure to always be open (supplement); and being nothing in her enjoyment would lead her to love that other. And Lacan points it out this way:

> there is an enjoyment of her, of that she who does not exist and means nothing. There is a jouissance of hers of which perhaps she herself knows nothing, unless she feels it: she does know it. She knows it, of course, when it happens. It does not happen to all.[242]

It is likely that what we call love, following Lacan, could only happen to some women or, rather, to female functions within the relationship. But that always occurs at the height of the event, of the Real in history, and as a certain inexorable unconditionality. And that is what Lacan seems to be seeing in his own clinic over the years, but that the Slovenians in their conceptual rigidity tend to mummify, but the question remains open the other way around, that is, what if the woman was the only genre? And underneath is the problem of psychoanalysis and Freud and of the philosophy of the 19th century, the problem of the self, namely, understanding the human as formations of the self, where what has prevailed, I believe that this is formally false, a double of those selves that would be the masculine and the feminine.

And if Butler wants in these times (since her *Undoing Gender*, 2004) to undo gender, in general, it is interesting that Lacan in the 1970s of had to undo the feminine in a certain way, he never did it with the masculine, and then the Slovenians structured an ontology where the feminine vanishes in Lacanian formulas. And so we move in Zupančič and Žižek these days. They "nothingfy" women, but they cannot think without the anchor point, essentially Kantian, of the masculine. And in this Hegel always shows himself to us as the thinker of relationships where the anchors, like the self, are only collected and subsequent moments, they are "knots" in the relationships that allow us to build structures, but knots in the relationships of measure, relations that are, therefore, historical and never allow themselves to be completely essentialized.[243]

The important thing about Zupančič and Žižek and the Slovenians, although they are sometimes locked in a Kantian-Lacanian structuring of Hegel (and I say it again, Heideggerian, even if it bothers Žižek), is that they can rethink the human in dialogue with other disciplines and allow us to see that the human today has been updated, but they do so in Lacan's classic ontological formulations, but with a great twist that can partly express what is happening today with the human. And Žižek says it forthrightly and obstinately like this because he knows that it filters into his conception of the human: Kant, the self, the substantial, and I hope he realizes that Heidegger's *Ereignis* filters through (Lacan drinks from him):

> ... the fact that sexual difference cannot be translated into a set of symbolic oppositions in no way implies that it is 'real' in the sense of some pre-existing external substantial entity outside the scope of symbolization: precisely as real, sexual difference is absolutely internal to the Symbolic – it is its inherent point of failure.[244]

Zupančič is very clear, she debates against a certain Butler and her performative queer feminism, but at the same time she debates against Copjec and her Kantian-Lacanian differential feminism that drags her patriarchal "Thing in itself". And in her operates that friendship of the troika with Dolar and Žižek; and it is noticeable. Hegel and Lacan function almost as ontological formulas in both thinkers to account for the human and that leads to error, as I have pointed out, because the human is not expressed in any formula, but, in any case, it helps because it allows us to see the great discovery of the Slovenians, updating Lacan, for these times in which the human becomes unclassifiable. And if this was not the case, we would be constantly being considered perverse pathologists from a psychopathology manual, like Sade's characters, in a certain sense crazy as caricatures (like those four libertines in the *120 Days of Sodom*), but we are those monsters and the same category of perversion must be updated and expanded to all that is human, and that neurosis must be kept for a while in the trunk of analysts; it has been squeezed enough since Vienna in the 19th century to the whole world, just like Königsberg's self.

Zupančič clearly shows that the human does not move on its own in the masculine-feminine symbolization, but the important thing is that it adds from that structural operative negativity of Kant-Hegel in Lacan's own Real knot that the feminine is nothing; the old Lacanian language is always operating and that is one of the problems of the Slovenians, but they still try to update and think about those old Lacanian categories that, in turn, always go directly from Freud to indicate the human in its eminently sexual character (where Freud speaks of drive, Lacan speaks of the Real). And there is a negative mediation, Hegelian, in that primordial Real, Kantian-Heideggerian, which does not allow itself to be trapped, but which is always giving some symbolization of itself. And so from there the knowledge that "the woman does not exist" (*la femme n'existe pas*), but it does not exist, it is nothing because it is what disturbs the masculine gender itself and in that the Real is a fault within the Symbolic itself. And Žižek, finally, because he deals with the subject over and over again in his books (because historical development obviously crosses it), explains it in this way trying to work within Lacan's formulas, but in these times (already 50 years old). And you can't pretend, I suppose, that those formulas will be like this forever, they will have to be adjusted again or thrown away (it would be more boring and repetitive than to endure another day of Sade's days). In 2019, Žižek shows what he thinks and shows the convergence with his friend Butler:

> There is, then, one sex and its remainder or excess, this being the transcendental genesis of sexual difference, which could not be formulated anymore as M/F (merely symbolic opposition), but M/+, where + represents the excessive element that transforms the symbolic opposition into the real of the antagonism.[245]

Kant's influence on Žižek can be seen in that transcendental genesis and in that reformulation of the Lacanian formula his Hegelian side, and it is as if Žižek wanted to lend a hand to his friend Butler, today, and be able to structurally find the human with an ontology that can account for what biopolitics expresses in its analysis. In the main, Žižek stakes his thought on the Real and that is very un-Hegelian (we must move in dynamic relationships), although he shows that this Real disturbs the Symbolic itself in its symbolization when it tries to express sexuation because it becomes impossible; and that happens daily today with everything that happens with the human; and this I mean not only thinking about transsexuals or whoever; but as perverse we all are, because we are monsters that structure ourselves throughout history. Sade's problem is thinking that there is no history, he is very Kantian and thinks of the human being born spontaneously from a dead god, that is, reason. In a certain way, in Žižek there is a Schelling of the *Essence of Freedom* (1809) and of the *Ages of the World* (manuscripts between 1810 and 1833), a certain Real that operates as a Non-foundation (*Un-Grund*) and from there articulates the dialectical systems as far as possible and in dynamism; but from the total differential with the Real;[246] it is Schelling, and with it Heidegger and his Schelling lessons that are fundamental to expressing the *Ereignis*, the one behind Žižek's Hegel.[247] But the Slovenian hides it because Schelling, like Heidegger, in particular, is touched by a certain conservative and politically incorrect whiff for these times: arbitrariness, darkness and dogmatism, a Hegelian would say.

However, Butler, as a good Hegelian, says it flatly like this: "the self in Hegel is marked by a primary captivity in the Other, a captivity in which it is exposed to risk".[248] And to love you have to take risks Mr. Kant, Mr. Sade, Mr. Freud, Mr. Heidegger, Mr. Lacan, Mr. Žižek, Mr. Miller. It has been the story of a mistake not being able to find the human and always trying to express it in an archetypal scene and then from there make all kinds of erasures or inscriptions, so that it fits what we want it to fit; however, things are not like that and it still flees, escapes from the archetypal scene that is postulated for the model to be functional.

References

Apollinaire, G., "Introduction", in Marquis de Sade, *L'Oeuvre du Marquis de Sade*, Collection des Classiques Galants, Paris, 1909.

Aulagnier, P., "Renarques sur la féminité et ses avatars", in *Le Désir et la Perversion*, Seuil, Paris, 1967.

Barthes, R., *The Love Speech*, Paidós, Madrid, 2011.

Butler. J, Laclau, E. and Žižek, S., *Contingency, Hegemony, Universality. Contemporary Dialogues on the Left*, Buenos Aires, FCE, Buenos Aires, 2004.

Buñuel, L., *My Last Breath*, Plaza & Janes, Barcelona, 1982.

Butler, J. *Undoing Gender*, Paidós, Santiago de Chile, 2019.

Canguilhem, G., *The Normal and the Pathological*, Siglo XXI, Buenos Aires, 1971.

Charenton, Saint-Maurice and Leley, G., "Biographical Compendium", *Marquis de Sade. Selected Works*, CS Ediciones, Buenos Aires, 2005.

Copjec, J., *Sex and the Euthanasia of Reason. Essays on Love and Difference*, Paidós, Madrid, 2006.

Deleuze, G., *Presentation of Sacher-Masoch. The cold and the cruel*, Amorrortu, Buenos Aires, 2001.

Dor, J., *Structure and Perversions*, Gedisa, Barcelona, 1995.

Espinoza, R. "An 'excessive' reading of Hegel's Science of Logic: around 'the nodal line of measure relations'", in *Philosophica*, 30, 2007, pp. 89–102.

Espinoza, R., "Joker 'contra'...", in *Le Monde Diplomatique*, October 21, 2019: https://www.lemondediplomatique.cl/joker-contra-por-ricardo-espinoza-lolas

Fonseca, C. and Quintero, M.L., "Queer Theory: the deconstruction of peripheral sexualities", in *Revista Sociológica*, 24(69), 2009: https://www.scielo.org.mx/scielo.php?script=sci_arttext&pid=S0187-01732009000100003

Foucault, M., *The Abnormal*, FCE, Buenos Aires, 2000.

Freud, S., *The Standard Edition of the Complete Psychological Works of Sigmund Freud*, Volume VII, Vintage Books, London, 2001.

Hamza, A. and Ruda, F., "Interview with Alenka Zupančič: philosophy or psychoanalysis? Yes, Please!". *Crisis & Critique*, Volume 6, No. 1, 2019.

Klossowski, P., "Sade or the perverse philosopher", in Marqués de Sade, *Selected Works*, CS Ediciones, Buenos Aires, 2005.

Lacan, J.: https://www.youtube.com/watch?v=ai6zzNoVkJU

Lacan, J., *The Seminar of Jacques Lacan, Book XX, On Feminine Sexuality, The Limits of Love and Knowledge*. Translated with notes by Bruce Fink, W.W. Norton & Company, Inc., New York, 1988.

Lacan, J., *The Seminar of Jacques Lacan, Book XIV. The Logic of Phantasy*. Translated by Cormac Gallagher from unedited French manuscripts, Karnac, London, 2002.

Lacan, J., *The Seminar of Jacques Lacan, Book XVIII: On a Discourse that Might not be a Semblance*. Translated by Cormac Gallagher from unedited French manuscripts, Karnac, London, 2002.

Lacan J., "Lacan por Vincennes!", in *Lacanian Number 11*, EOL Publications, Buenos Aires, 2011.

Lacan, J., *The Seminar of Jacques Lacan, Book XIX*. Edited by Jacques-Alain Miller, translated by A.R. Price, Polity Press, Cambridge, 2018.

Little, M., *Psychotic Anxieties and Containment*, Jason Aronson Inc., London, 1990.

Little, M., *Account of my Analysis with Winnicott,* Editorial Place, Buenos Aires, 1995.

López Villegas, M., *Presence of the Marquis de Sade in the Cinematographic work of Luis Buñuel* (Doctoral Thesis), Universidad Complutense de Madrid, Madrid, 1997 (Thesis supervised by José Royo Jara).

Marquis de Sade, *120 days of Sodom*: file:///C:/Users/howlr/OneDrive/Escritorio/Las-120-Jornadas-de-Sodoma-Marques-de-Sade-pdf.pdf

Marty, E. and Miller, J.A., Interview on "Le Sexe del Modernes" (March 21, 2021): https://www.thelacanianreviews.com/eric-marty-and-jacques-alain-miller-interview-on-the-sex-of-moderns1/

Miller, J.A., https://wapol.org/es/articulos/Template.asp?intTipoPagina=4&intPublicacion=38&intEdicion=13&intArticulo=2468&intIdiomaArticulo=1

Miller, J.A., *The Real Experience in the Psychoanalytic Cure*, Paidós, Buenos Aires, 2004.

Miller, J.A., *The Experience of the Real in Psychoanalytic Treatment*, Paidós, Buenos Aires, 2011.

Nietzsche, F., *Thus spoke Zarathustra*, Alianza, Madrid, 2000.

Nietzsche, F., "The gay science", in *Complete Works.* Volume III. *Mature Works I*, Tecnos, Madrid, 2014.

Otto, W., *The Gods of Greece*, Siruela, Madrid, 2002.

Otto, W., *Dionysus*, Herder, Barcelona, 2017.

Pérez Turrent, T. and De La Colina, J., *Buñuel by Buñuel*, Plot Ediciones, Madrid, 1993.

Sacher-Masoch, L., *The Mother of God*, The Silver Bowl, Buenos Aires, 2010.

Schelling, F.W.J., *Philosophical Research on the Essence of Human Freedom and Related Objects*, Anthropos, Barcelona, 2004.

Tostain, R., "Essai apologétique de la structure perverse", in *La Sexualité dans les Institutions*, Payot, Paris, 1978.

Verardi Bocca, F., *Do Estado à Orgia. Essay on the End of the World*, CRV, Curitiba, 2020.

Žižek, S., *The Indivisible Remainder*, Godot, Buenos Aires, 2016.

Žižek, S., *Sex and the Failure of the Absolute*, Paidós, Barcelona, 2020.

Zola, É., "De la moralité en littérature", in *Emile Zola, Documents Litteraires*, Charpentier, Paris, 1881.

Zupančič, A., *Ethics of the Real. Kant and Lacan*, Verso, London, 2012.

8

The slaughterhouse bank ...
the untold story

If we think of Goya and two of his series of engravings: *The Caprices* (80 engravings from 1799) and *The Disasters of War* (82 engravings between 1810–1815) we can see, in the Spanish artist, a work both in form and in the composition, the technique and the logics that move him to express a savage criticism of the human in the very human of his time. In *Los Caprichos*, from the end of the Spanish 17th century, the caricature is fierce against the brotherly power that is expressed in the nobility (Duke of Blangis) and the clergy (the Bishop). Those deformed faces, like those of beasts, have already become an icon of human monstrosity, of which we are all parts; even Goya himself. The mixed technique of etching, aquatint and dry point to give certain retouches gives each image what Sade was looking for in the precision of the *120 Days of Sodom* in the days of November of the first class of passions, namely high precision descriptive visual for that gaze of the Spanish bourgeois of the 18th and 19th centuries. And in this, the engravings function as a mirror of that unconscious that does not want to be seen at all. Being images that in themselves have a certain meaning (but always open) and, at the same time, the series has a meaning in itself (which is not the same as each image), it allows a certain freedom of movement for the viewer, which is impossible in Sade's reader; instead, Goya allows and gives freedom to stay in each one or see some or try to understand the whole: those grotesque whims of the human (such as Bacon's heads, Van Gogh's sunflowers, Lucien Freud's bodies). It's like saying, those passions of a society and a bourgeoisie that is exhausted; and in which we are not different from animality. It is essential to realize that these whims have a certain erotic, but embedded in the materiality of the finitude of the human; a human who in his power becomes apelike for Goya. The series was a scandal in the artist's life, which is quite obvious; as I have pointed out, the elite do not seek to be reflected in these types of snapshots of their practices and ways of life. And in this we see how Goya and the Sades are articulated in their aesthetic-political, ultimately human, work. And in this Foucault is right when he says:

> Through Goya and Sade, the western world has acquired the possibility of going beyond reason with violence, and of rediscovering the tragic experience above the promises of the dialectic. After Sade and Goya, and since then, unreason belongs to what is decisive, for the modern world, in every work;[249]

DOI: 10.4324/9781003370116-9

although Sade's unreason carries a lot of reason within itself (the "sadistic" aspect of his work is the excess of rationality).

And in *The Disasters of War* he is really cruel in his images; all the more so than Sade himself, because he achieves with drawing what the literary stroke can never achieve; the richness of the stroke does not go for the construction of an image, even if it is very precise and of "high resolution" in writing, because of itself it cannot find the image if it seeks to represent it (and a good image does not seek to represent it either), but the line does allow us to open, evoke, insinuate, provoke with a description that not only shows horror before our eyes, but does so by sculpting our own heart with its line; and that is done writing with blood (the writings of Genet, Celine, Foster Wallace). The Spanish War of Independence that is splattered with blood is what these images indicate, which are a visual expression of that blood that constitutes the life of the Spaniards at the beginning of the 19th century. It is a war that is not idealized or romantic, it is what it is in its harshness; there are no heroes, but there are people suffering, torn to pieces, mutilated, dead (Picasso was always influenced by Goya and this is clear in his *Guernica* and you can see how he is inspired by engraving No. 30 "Havoc of war"). And, also, the series generated a scandal and the engravings were not shown in those times of war, because those images also expressed the absolutist government that ruled; and the horror of that very rule by means of allegorical figures of animals (Goya was never neutral, like no great). He did not use aquatint because in the middle of the war everything was scarce and it was difficult to have the materials; he primarily used etching technique and mixed with burnisher, gouache and drypoint. Goya was a great social and human critic, all too human; but he was not a moralist like Sade; he places himself in a position in the midst of pain, where he is one more who suffers. Goya is like a precursor of the contemporary. He is closest to Georg Büchner, Friedrich Nietzsche, Friedrich Wilhelm Murnau, Franz Kafka, James Joyce, Camille Claudel, Béla Bartók, Bertolt Brecht, Carl Dreyer, Jean Cocteau, Melanie Klein, Karen Blixen, Orson Welles, Man Ray, Pier Paolo Pasolini, Luis Buñuel, Sarah Kofman, Ana Mendieta, Federico Fellini, Samuel Beckett, Margarite Duras, Sarah Kane, Chris Marker, Monique Wittig, György Ligeti, Gloria Anzaldúa, Mark Fisher, Hélène Cixous, Marina Abramovic, Paul B. Preciado, Nick Cave, PJ Harvey, many others. And each of these humans do not allow themselves to be classified in philosophical taxonomy, let alone psychoanalytic (Sade would not know what to do with them in his rational rigid binary scheme of "good and bad"). I'd say they're all perverse.

Freud, a long time ago, as I have pointed out from the beginning of this Book, almost created a typification of the human that moves between neurosis, perversion and psychosis. And this categorization survives and has been modulated for more than a century, but it does not want to disappear (Miller loves it and many analysts from different psychoanalytic schools and even beyond psychoanalysis), it takes hold, and even fights with other more rigid taxonomies and biologists like the psychiatric ones. And in those we have lived and they have wanted to determine us again and again. In addition, this neurosis almost operates as the reference system, the system of homogenization and sameness for the human (a quite complex and dynamic system). For Freud, as I have already said, psychoanalysis was at stake in neurosis and he made it very clear in 1913 to all his disciples and it has nothing to do with psychosis:

> If the patient does not suffer from hysteria or obsessional neurosis, but of para-phrenia, he will not be able to keep his promise of cure, and thus has particularly serious reasons to avoid misdiagnosis. In a trial treatment of a few weeks, you will often perceive suspicious signs that may determine you not to continue with the attempt.[250]

And what about perversion and psychosis in psychoanalysis? The other categories such as perversion, which always has a bad reputation (Sade dixit), and psychosis are like deformations of neurosis (and not treatable); I would say that they are like borderline cases of neurosis. The pervert is moving the neurotic internally and the psychotic is throwing him out of himself. And we have those German "words" of Freud, which Lacan liked to use so much in his Parisian *Seminars*, as expressions of the essence of each of these so-called personality structures: *Verdrängung* is the same for neurosis, *Verleugnung* for perversion and *Verwerfung* for psychosis.

Furthermore, it is very interesting how Freud works with these words when all of them indicate movement (not only forms of negation); furthermore, a type of movement as movement (the particle *"ver-"* wants to show that a movement that functions as a push, now to remove, now to reinforce) with a certain typicality of its own that specifies it in each of these categories. In *Verdrängung* (which translates as "repression") there is a vertical movement of subjectivity, a push that seeks to move downwards (it hides, covers up, "throws dirt on top" of something we do not want to name); what is typical of the neurotic (obvious in the hysterical and the obsessive: the two types of typical humans that are treated by analysts) and which makes it impossible for us to live is displaced: life itself, the Real (the neurotic lives trapped in the Labyrinth of the symbolic). In *Verleugnung* (which is generally translated as "denial") it is the horizontal movement that constitutes us, we push ourselves into the plane of immanence of the Symbolic of ourselves and we do not want to assume the castration that is imposed on us, it is radically denied; and in it we transgress; typical of the perverse. An attempt is made to disprove the Name of the Father, which is why it could be said that it operates from the Real to the Symbolic, that is why it removes the Law. And, finally, in *Verwerfung* (which is usually translated as "rejection") is the movement that pushes us "outside" of ourselves; we throw ourselves out of the Symbolic into the Real in order to be able to radically assume that impossible that pierces us; it is a rejection of what structures us and throws us radically (perhaps in madness we merge with the Real itself and stop suffering). This is explained very well by a psychotic analyst like Margaret Little, who we have seen was analyzed by Winnicott, in her great book *Transference Neurosis*

& *Transference Psychosis* (1981): "The transference delusion hides a state in the patient which he both needs and fears to reach. In it subject and object, all feeling, thought, and movement are experienced as the same thing".[251] And, furthermore, one can be an analyst while being psychotic;[252] and this is worth noting, even with some irony. Because there is no problem with psychosis or with perversion as neurotics point out (if it is not invalidating, the same as neurosis itself); it is like a bullying of neurotics against those different from themselves. And if it were not so? What if the categories themselves are exhausted? Nor is neurosis only neurosis? If Oedipus is later than it appears and never structures as it should, why can't it? What if before castration we are fused in some way? What if the self is a one-sided fiction of the WeOthers? The complex child analyst Melanie Klein, also beloved by Deleuze, pointed out cautiously but very surely in 1928 (her work with young children is fundamental), a long time ago, almost 100 years and Freud was alive (and therefore it was difficult to talk with the living founder of psychoanalysis), that:

> ... I wish above all to point out that they do not, in my opinion, they do not contradict the statements of Professor Freud. I think that the essential point in the additional considerations which I have advanced is that I date these processes earlier and that the different phases (especially in the initial stages) merge more freely in one another than was hitherto supposed (...) The early stages of the Oedipal conflict are so largely dominated by the pregenital phases of development that the genital phase, when it begins to be active, is at first heavily shrouded and only later, between the third and fifth years of life, become clearly recognizable.[253]

And it is clear that the patriarchy of natural representation has prevailed for more than a century and has wanted to homogenize the human;[254] and that is why castration and Oedipus and the prevailing taxonomies as if they were themselves part of a Sade scheme: *The 120 years of Sodom*.

We already know that Freud created the term in 1896 and he says it this way and also defines what Psychoanalysis is in terms of neurosis:

> As regards the second class of major neuroses, hysteria and obsessional neurosis, the solution of the aetiological problem is of surprising simplicity and uniformity. I owe my results to a new method of psycho-analysis, Josef Breuer's exploratory procedure; it is a little intricate, but it is irreplaceable, so fertile has it shown to be in throwing light upon the obscure paths of unconscious ideation.[255]

And Freud's self-analysis (as a result of the death of his father) is from 1897.[256] It is like the founding gesture of Psychoanalysis, Freud's own analysis (as there is always a horizon of transcendence at the beginning of something and here Freud is part of this discipline in his own flesh, like Lenin with the October Revolution).

But not even Freud's self-analysis is a self-analysis of Freud (self-analysis is not immediate for itself; that would be a psychotization of Freud himself). The self is articulated from another self (Freud from his Father), as Hegel would say in the *Phenomenology* of 1807. In self-analysis, it is Freud's father who is operating in him as the new founder of a new religion. And so, it remained, psychoanalysis, on the one hand, patriarchal and, on the other, condemned to the solipsism of the self. And from Freud's self-analysis to the foundational book of psychoanalysis of 1899 it is only one step (which was later given the 1900 edition date): *The interpretation of dreams*. "However, it moves" (*Eppur si mouve*) and as Hegel says:

> Self-consciousness only reaches its satisfaction in another self-consciousness (...) It is a self-consciousness for a self-consciousness. And that is the only way it is, in reality, because only in this way does the unity of itself become for it in its other being (...) Self-consciousness is in and for itself inasmuch as and because it is in itself and for itself for another self-consciousness.[257]

And Nietzsche says it succinctly and uniquely in the Poem "Sils-Maria" from *The Gay Science*:

> Here I was, waiting, waiting — but waiting for nothing, / Beyond good and evil, enjoying / Already the light, and in the shade, all just play, / All lake, all noon, all time without goal. / And suddenly, friend! One became Two — / — And Zarathustra passed by my side...[258]

It is a movement between one and the other that constitutes us: "In the same boat". Therefore, the human was not a mere monolithic self in and of itself: coordinating support of all things (Descartes), transcendental subject that allows us to know and operate practically (Kant) or radical freedom that forges the world (Fichte), but constitutively we are movement that moves structurally and radically and I would add, once again from Hegel (and Hölderlin), that it moves because there is an object (*Gegenstand*) that constitutes it as movement (the "object relations" of Klein and Winnicott). Something that opposes it: himself as Other of himself; any other, things, humans, the world, etc. The word for conscience in German and used by Hegel is *Bewusstsein* (*The Phenomenology of the spirit* is not understood, without its internal truth called "Science of the experience of consciousness", *Wissenschaft der Erfahrung des Bewussteins*); and the German thinker uses it, pre-Freud, in a dynamic temporal sense. It is as if we were a movement, a life (*sein*) that we constitute ourselves from our past (*wusst*), but transitively with the world, with things, with the other (*be*), with WeOthers as the Other. That is conscience for Hegel and it indicates to us that internally we are torn, because life is a constant failure (there is no possible recognition); the characteristic of conscience is despair (*Verweifung*, to remain in doubt, not being able to get out of it) we do not know what to do and totally and brutally finite, being it, our conscience (life) since the death of some with

Others in the bank of slaughterhouse (*Schlachtbank*) of history (so he says in the Introduction to the *Philosophy Lectures on History* of 1824).[259] Hegel is more radical than Sade, since there is no archetypal scene or visual construction for it (much less as a game to provoke the bourgeois on duty); and let us not forget that the end of the *Phenomenology* is shocking when it points to the calvary (*Schädelstätte*) of the absolute spirit as the very expression of the history of humanity viewed from its own unity.[260] For this reason, neurosis as the first analogue of the late 19th century, in the Victorian era, is really short and does not express the human, but a simple caricature of immediacy. And if in these times perversion, if we go beyond Sade (and his idealization) and his infantilized fiction of his provocative writings, we can see what Hegel indicated to us, even before 1807. In *Glauben und Wissen* of 1802 he ends by saying against Kant, Jacobi and Fichte (all three were alive) and at the beginning of a new century that:

> The most diaphanous, unfounded and individual of the dogmatic philosophers as of the natural religions has to disappear. Only from this hardness can and must resurrect the supreme totality in all its seriousness and from its deepest foundation, at the same time encompassing everything and in its figure of the most radiant freedom.[261]

Hegel is clear about it so that a certain freedom is given, one in life, in how human we are, must radically assume the pain of our existence. And everything immediate, as a symbolic construction of homogenization, must disappear (not even Euclidean geometry holds up, much less to show what is human). Be it on a critical level, as a fideist, as a voluntarist, it is impossible to continue thinking about the human. Hegel does not want anything more to do with that "Thing in itself" that is said in multiple ways and does not stop trapping us in a fantasy that drags us along for centuries. And that reappears again and again, as in Lacan's Real and from there it finds and does not find the human at the end of the 20th century and that continues to this day with Miller and Žižek in the lead (although the Slovenian fiercely combating the French but carrying on his shoulders a heavy load, like *Zarathustra's camel*: the Real).

The Freudian categories that Lacan carries within himself in his first teachings, that of the Symbolic, are transgressed by the perverse Lacan himself at the end of his life, especially after *May 68*, and in this Lacan himself becomes a parricide of himself and of Freud. Lacan has been great as a thinker. And that Lacanian gesture is forgotten by Miller himself and by many analysts. And he is scared of what can happen and in fact is happening in clinic today, and I would add in philosophy, in discourses about the human:

> This translates the extension of the category of madness to all speaking beings who suffer from of the same lack of knowledge regarding sexuality. This aphorism points to what the so-called clinical structures share: neurosis, psychosis,

perversion. And, of course, it shakes, it agitates the difference between neurosis and psychosis that was, until now, the basis of psychoanalytic diagnosis, an inexhaustible theme of teachings.[262]

And that difference is shaken from the very limit between them, that limit is perverted. And that is why everything falters today in the analysis, because the human does not stop recreating its own history and does not want to carry within itself anything natural, substantial or immediate that articulates it and tells it what it has to be, do and wait: even less to love. Žižek explains it this way:

> there is another, more radical and authentically Hegelian way of understanding the dislocation of sexuality: what if balanced 'natural' sexuality is a human myth, a retroactive projection? What if this image of nature is the ultimate human myth, the ultimate 'invented tradition'?[263]

That invented nature is part of that immediacy that always appears to us as a remainder in the very development of our history, but it is a remainder, as Schelling would say, it is a beginning, as Hegel would say, never the origin of anything. And that is why the performative to understand the human in its sexuality is not that the cultural is opposed to the biological natural, but that the biological itself is placed by the history of the human at the same level of its event. In this Butler and Žižek join hands in their Hegelian unity. And we can also understand the contempt that Miller feels for Butler explicitly in the middle of 2021 (and incidentally for Žižek without naming him):

> I think of Foucault's phrase, which you quote on page 389 [referring to Éric Marty and his book *Le sexe des Modernes*], in which he trusts his hope of producing 'real effects in our present history'. Well, this Judith Butler did just that. I say: hats off! And even, why not: 'Well dug, old mole!'.[264]

Miller's hatred for Butler is visceral; he can't hide it. In Butler, and his henchmen, Miller sees that Real in disorder and destruction of everything human (to that Sade of *120 Days of Sodom*, to Buñuel of *The Golden Age*):

> And the intellectual universe of the genre seems Hobbesian to me, if I may say so. As if, once the Name-of-the-Father was eliminated, once the Leviathan was stripped naked and dispersed, the only social bond that would remain was the fight to the universal death.[265]

And if it were the opposite, and we see the human with a certain Žižek (a less Kantian-Schelligian one) and the Slovenians, with a certain more Hegelian Butler, we would realize that the monstrous springs from the beginning in quite accidental ways and from those random forms, the mortal sexed human is fulfilled in that impossible thing that is to be with the Other, but it generates socio-historical fabrics, a WeOthers, with all its complexity, but it happens. And it is unavoidable. The (she) thinker Pedro DiPietro says it brilliantly like this:

> It teaches us, in this way, that trans is neither a deviation that emerges from those more established continents that are called man or woman, nor an accident within them. The deconstructivist contribution brings us closer to a new materialism that does not deny the concreteness of each individuated body and that, at the same time, disputes the ultra-individualistic notions that emerge from the paradigm, such as the fusion of all personal expression of gender with a sense of omnipotence.[266]

It is about another materiality that must be seen in the light of one with Others (from that unity with the Mother to that unity of WeOthers). And there the functions operate: feminine as well as masculine, but functions, after all. And in these functions there is a differential that is articulated with the other without being anything concrete (from love to the struggle for life or death).

In the feminine, in the feminine position, which can be of a man, a woman or whatever, Žižek, faithful to his thinking and provoking, but with the philosophical nuance (with and against Zupančič and all the Feminism of Equality as well as that of Difference-essence) tells us that the feminine is: "less than nothing".[267] Žižek, like Hegel in his *Science of Logic*, starts running the system through the being and not through the nothing of the "Doctrine of Being", but it's common knowledge this is arbitrary, but it is so because Hegel is European and sees the being as the free; and from there the movement is shown at its beginning (Hegel cannot start from nothing, because he is not Oriental, hence his arbitrariness). Žižek does the same operation as Hegel and the woman ends up as that "less than nothing" with respect to being a man. Here Žižek plays the game of showing that nothingness is still something "substantial" within the formulation of Lacan and Zupančič, in the most Kantian style. And the attempt is to deconstruct that nothingness, insofar as what it carries is an ethical non-position within a positive totalitarian masculine (it is the same Hegelian gesture of treating nothingness as "less than nothing" and the system of Science working from its Eurocentrism). So if we go beyond the nihilistic Christian European ontology, and we go beyond that *Creatio ex nihilo* so dear to the West and we go to the Greeks and their physis (to the Amerindians and their Abya Yala), who were not Christians, and we rethink their materialism, like that of Democritus, we realize that it is never a question of "nothing" of things (because formally they are not even things), but of "less than nothing", that is, a certain wave in the middle of the sea of life, a position in contingency without ontological support. Therefore, if the feminine is that; if it is something, it is merely "less than nothing" because it operates as a void: "... the distinction between nothing and void. Nothingness is localized, as when we say 'there is nothing here', while the void is a dimension without limits".[268] And here lies that non-being of the feminine;

because that contingency of its being, beyond nihilism, Christianity, of the European capitalist, the feminine is that perforation. The feminine operates with that perforation of the system itself that makes the system itself possible. And it makes it possible by disturbing it, moving it, tearing it apart, exasperating it. It is, as I say, the very perversion of consciousness that is at stake in human sexuation in the midst of life. The feminine thus operates as the trans par excellence.

And if the feminine is something like that, it is why it can, as Lacan says, love. And the French thinker writes it in a simple and remarkable way: "así si la satisficiera en la exigencia del amor, el goce que se tiene de una mujer la divide convirtiendo su soledad en su pareja, mientras que la unión queda en el umbral".[269] The feminine as "less than nothing", or differential within the very interior of the human is what structures the human and tears it apart internally, it is its dynamism. It is not about things, or formulas, or dialectics, or performatives, but rather it is about a dynamic human structure that pierces us and updates itself at the level of its history. The ancient Greeks thought of the human from that *deinon* and with it they were able to give a certain plasticity to what we are, perhaps that current Queer term opens much more of itself, and expresses in another way what is perverse and transgressive. And it updates that multiple monster that we are and that operates in that shell of a "feminine-masculine", namely, what the term Queer indicates:

> Queer reflects the subversive and transgressive nature of a woman who detaches herself from the custom of subordinate femininity; of a masculine woman; of an effeminate man or with a sensitivity contrary to the dominant typology; of a person dressed in clothing of the opposite gender, etc.[270]

From Dionysus to Butler passing through Bowie, it seems that we have dressed in clothes that are opposed to what the measurement relationship at the level of that hegemonic and homogeneous time allowed. Today that rule that determines us as if fallen from heaven and which operates as the new Father is Capitalism. And before it we rebel, because among other things it makes us sick. We can no longer stand those patterned dresses that are put on the citizen so that he becomes a neurotic and an operator of the Labyrinth of Capitalism. Mark Fischer said it before his suicide very clearly and in front of everyone in *The Guardian*:

> Depression is the shadow side of entrepreneurial culture, what happens when magical voluntarism confronts limited opportunities (…) It's high time that the blame was placed elsewhere. We need to reverse the privatisation of stress and recognise that mental health is a political issue.[271]

What is at stake in the human, in the sexual relationship, in love, in WeOthers, etc., is the way we are today, fight after fight, pushing beyond the rigidity of capitalizing on the market in a badly infinite way of a neurosis that is at the extreme. The revolution, if there is one, is yet to come; and that is what is at stake today. Today Sade has become a French "public good", a brand that capitalizes on the world market; the one who was detained by the French State because he wrote "perversions", and was half crazy, becomes a "national treasure" in 2017: the *120 Days of Sodom* will be bought by the French State for millions of euros and right now (2021) it is looking for patrons to help it in this "great feat", namely, that the manuscript be kept in the National Library. A story like others, the perverse became good business for many neurotic monsters and also enhances the French identity that these days is really diluted.

In these times of the Labyrinth of Capitalism we are left to risk loving in the multiple differences with each other; and in that love, in so many fused monsters, to pervert what is imposed on us as another normalization that seeks to capitalize us as merchandise and thus recognize us as successful. Let's not be afraid to love, because, even if we go crazy, the same love will heal us over and over again in a painful and, also, jovial way; and heals us when we sail "In the same boat"...

Three simple untold stories of monsters:
The one about madness...

For me, D.W. did not *represent* my mother. In my transference delusion, he *was* my mother.[272]

The one of all who are at the border...

Borders are designed to define places that are safe and those that are not, to distinguish the *us* (we) of *them* (they). A border is a dividing line, a thin line along a steep edge. A border territory is a vague and undefined place created by the emotional residue of an unnatural border. It is in a constant state of transition. Its inhabitants are the forbidden and the *banned*. *The pierced ones* live there: the cross-eyed, the perverse, the *queer*, the problematic, the street pimps, the mulattoes, the mixed-race, the half-dead; in short, those who cross, who go over or go through the confines of the 'normal'.[273]

The one about love...

> ANNE
> No, I don't want to
> GEORGES
> Who turned on the tap?
> ANNE
> You did!
> GEORGES
> Can you tell?
> ANNE
> No, I can't. Do you want to

to hurt me? Don't bother me!
Georges looks at her sharply.
GEORGES
Don't you think it would be better
to fetch Dr.?
ANNE
No!
She picks up her coffee cup, as if to show that nothing is wrong,
and drinks it. When she wants to refill her cup
she doesn't know how to do it and makes a mess. She realises
this and bursts into tears.

References

Anzaldúa, G., *Borderlands/La Frontera*, Captain Swing Books, Madrid, 2016.

Anzieu, D., *Freud's Self-analysis and the Discovery of Psychoanalysis*, Siglo XXI, Madrid, 1988.

DiPietro, P., "Neither humans, nor animals, nor monsters: The decolonization of the transgender body", in *Eidos*, No. 34, 2020, pp. 254–291.

Fisher, M., "Why mental health is a political issue", in *The Guardian*, Monday, July 16, 2012: https://www.theguardian.com/commentisfree/2012/jul/16/mental-health-political-issue

Fonseca, C. and Quintero, M.L., "Queer Theory: the deconstruction of peripheral sexualities", in *Revista Sociológica*, Volume 24. No. 69, 2009: https://www.scielo.org.mx/scielo.php?script=sci_arttext&pid=S0187-01732009000100003

Foucault, M., *History of Madness III*, FCE, Bogotá, 1993.

Freud, S., *The Standard Edition of the Complete Psychological Works of Sigmund Freud*, Volume III, Vintage Books, London, 2001.

Freud, S., *The Standard Edition of the Complete Psychological Works of Sigmund Freud*, Volume XII, Vintage Books, London, 2001.

Hegel, G.W.F., *Vorlesung über die Geschichte der Philosophie*. Teil I. In Werke 18, Suhrkamp, Frankfurt am Main, 1995.

Hegel, G.W.F., *Phenomenology of Spirit*, FCE, Mexico City, 1966.

Hegel, G.W.F., *Faith and Knowledge*, Nueva librería, Madrid, 2000.

Klein, M., "Early stages of the oedipal conflict", in *Int. J. Psychoanal.*, No. 9, 1928: pp. 167–180.

Lacan, J., "El atolondradicho" in *Ornicar?, No. 1*, Paidós Biblioteca Freudiana, Buenos Aires, 1984.

Little, M., *Transference Neurosis & Transference Psychosis*, Jason Aroson, New York, 1981.

Little, M., *Account of My Analysis with Winnicott*, Editorial Place, Buenos Aires, 1995.

Marty, E. and Miller, J-A., Interview on "Le Sexe del Modernes" (March 21, 2021): https://www.thelacanianreviews.com/eric-marty-and-jacques-alain-miller-interview-on-the-sex-of-moderns1/.

Miller, J-A., : https://wapol.org/es/articulos/Template.asp?intTipoPagina=4&intPublicacion=38&intEdicion=13&intArticulo=2468&intIdiomaArticulo=1.

Nietzsche, F., "Autumn 1885–Autumn 1886", in *Posthumous Fragments. Volume IV (1885–1889)*, Tecnos, Madrid, 2008.

Nietzsche, F., "The gay science", in *Complete Works. Volume III. Maturity Works I*, Tecnos, Madrid, 2014.

Žižek, S., *Less Than Nothing. Hegel and the Shadow of Dialectical Materialism*, Akal, Madrid, 2015.

Žižek, S., *Absolute Recoil*, Akal Madrid, 2016.

Žižek, S., *Sex and the Failure of the Absolute*, Paidós, Barcelona, 2020.

Afterword

Jorge Nico Reitter

Why did he ask me? I wondered the same thing, honey. I felt a bit like Socrates when the oracle tells him that he is the wisest and he doesn't understand why him. Well, not because I felt the wisest, but the other way around, because I know that Ricardo could have asked whoever he wanted for the epilogue, but he asked me, a South American psychoanalyst far removed from the world of philosophy. Ricardo is the author, Ricardo Espinoza Lolas. Do you know him? He is a philosopher and a Chilean. I was walking through Plaza de Mayo, stopping at those towering palm trees that I never get tired of looking at, when I received a message asking me to do the epilogue of a book that would be called *Sade Reloaded.* The truth is that I said yes because I like Ricardo very much, I didn't think much about it. Besides, what was I going to think about a book I hadn't read? Like so many times in life, it was an act of faith. Faith in his book, and that I could say something. We barely spoke a few times, we never met in person, nor did we share a dinner or a wine, but with Ricardo we understand each other, as if we had known each other forever. We were both born in a humble middle class and we both grew up next to South American oceans, that must mean something.

What is the book about? The book is a tumult, an orgy, a disproportionate and apparently chaotic *collage.* It has something outrageous in both senses of the word, of acting without taking into account the law (the forum), and of being excessively large and intense. It is a monstrous book that talks about monsters, and that changes the meaning of many words, for example the word monster. In a procession, preceded by a chariot pulled by two leopards which carries Dionysos and Ariadne, dancing ecstatically, as in a great pride march, and surrounded by their maenads, Hegel parades together with Žižek, Butler and Lacan, Kubrick and the Marquis de Sade, Nietzsche with Preciado, Goya with Winnicott, Deleuze and Anzaldúa, and Oscar Wilde, and Mark Fischer, and Melanie Klein, Lenin, Silvia Plath, all to the beat of *Space Oddity*, sung by David himself in chorus with Ricardo. Even I am part of the procession, and very glad to have been invited. Don't laugh, love, I'm really invited, I'll show you later. As Ricardo says, we monsters transfer ourselves to each other.

The book tries to *think about* something that it defines as "the human", or rather rethink it. Not the eternal human, but the human that is always historical, always

DOI: 10.4324/9781003370116-10

mutating, in transit, "up to the times". *To think*, not to pray, as is the style in so many psychoanalytic parishes; and I guess in the philosophical too. It states that new times demand new categories. It is life pushing thought against all dogmatism. Where I, the psychoanalyst, say *subject*, Ricardo, the philosopher, says *the human*. I like it, although I think I will continue to say *subject*. The strength of tradition, which is not only that of custom, but that of a genealogy.

At some point he says that the human is about the experience of being in the same boat. He also says it about the analyst, because in the book there is a lot of dialogue with psychoanalysis. That the patient and the analyst are in the same boat. Do you remember that the other day I told you that something changed in my way of being with patients when I realized, really, that the analysand and I had a *unique opportunity*? Well, that is realizing that we are in the same boat, on the same journey. The essential thing is to understand that it is not only a unique opportunity for the analysand, but also for the analyst. That's the only way it makes sense. Ricardo bets, like me, on a certain psychoanalysis, or a certain post-psychoanalysis, I don't know how to call it, in which patient and analyst sail in the same boat, over the sea of sex and death, like Dionysos and Ariadne. Let me read you a passage that I loved:

> Nietzsche tells us about the boat of Dionysos and Ariadne where they sail over death (which can be seen literally in many ancient Greek objects). That boat is life in the midst of death (empty and meaningless), of life with Others, of love, of the struggle for life or death, of sexual intercourse, of the child-mother bond, of transference, of breaking with the natural representation that has built us as neurotics at the service of the Symbolic: the Capitalism of the contract par excellence that is the Law of the Father that regulates us.

A Dionysian psychoanalysis, as true psychoanalysis always was. I get the impression that Ricardo does not see, or does not give importance to, the Dionysian side of Freud, the one who was willing to move the infernal powers, he only sees the bourgeois Freud (which he also was). Like me, he wants nothing to do with the bourgeois psychoanalyst. Well, the *bourgeois psychoanalyst* is my way of naming it, he doesn't call him that, but I think he would agree. I'm not boring you, am I? Come on, pour me another drink. I'd kiss you right now, but no, I still want to talk to you about the book. Thus, chatting with you, ideas come to mind: your smile inspires me. I refrain from kissing you, but it's not hard for me, I like to tighten the rope while you look at me like that. But I'm not really boring you, am I?

Sade bores me. It bores and excites me, but in the long run he bores me. If the book is about Sade? Yes and no. Sade as the epitome of perversion. You know that I don't like *at all* the word perversion and its use among my colleagues. I already told you what that word made me suffer, they even told me that as a pervert I couldn't even be an analyst. You understand me, sweetheart, they also made you feel sick, a sinner, against nature. Only that Ricardo wants to make something else out of perversion, and neurosis, and psychosis. The pervert, in his book, is the monster, and we are all the monster, even the bourgeois analyst, even if he doesn't want to find out. The perverse of this book is the Freudian polymorphous perverse, but not as an evolutionary moment, but as a revelation of the *deinon* that inhabits us all. No, darling, I didn't know what *deinon* meant either, but I loved the word: it's the terrifying, the terrible, the violent. The anzald and the fright, Quignard dixit. Ricardo puts it in a beautiful musical metaphor: "a certain tense chord of meaning that ranges from the marvelous to the terrifying", and compares it to Turner's palette. I think of the famous Tristan chord. The *deinon* is the human itself, and the monstrous, and the perverse, but the perverse à la Espinoza Lolas.

The book could have been called *Salvation through perversion*, but the perversion Ricardo speaks of is not that of the bourgeois psychoanalysts and their fear of everything *deinon*, everything Dionysian; nor that of Sade, but that of the monster that we all are, that of the queer. I like the word queer, nothing to do with the word perversion. Queer is a word that sexual and gender dissidence appropriated, perversion was thrown in. I agree with Ricardo when he says that the Queer category (he puts it that way, with capital letters) tries to overcome the perversion category of psychoanalysis. The queer, or cuir, as we sometimes write it here, is not the recycled perverse, it is something else. It is the rejection of the speeches and devices that invented the perverse. I read you something:

> The ancient Greeks thought of the human from that *deinon* and with this they were able to give a certain plasticity to what we are, perhaps that current term Queer opens much more of itself, and expresses in another way what is perverse and transgressive. And it updates that multiple monster that we are and that operates in that shell of a 'feminine-masculine', namely, what the term Queer indicates.

And by expressing it in another way, it says something else, it has very other effects. That is why so much psychoanalysis is reluctant to talk about what is queer and perhaps that is one of the reasons why Ricardo asked me to do the epilogue... I almost said to you an epitaph. Of course, the epitaph of a certain psychoanalysis that I prefer to forget.

You're so smart, darling! That is the question that hits the mark! What would perversion save us from? From neurosis. But from neurosis "à la Espinoza Lolas". I mean, the sense that he gives to "neurosis", which is not the sense in which I use it. The meaning he gives it, however, is not arbitrary, I understand what he means and in fact I share the spirit of what he says. At some point he speaks of neurosis as "that construction of the normal that does not resist itself". I find that way of putting it beautiful, except that I could add (I am a psychoanalyst, not a philosopher) that the symptom always resists. It even resists the desire for normalization of the neurotic himself, who comes to analysis terrified of his own abnormality, who asks that the analysis normalize him, homogenize him. But if an analysis works (it doesn't always happen), what I understand as a true analysis, one ends up enjoying the abnormality itself, the only enjoyment that is worthwhile. I guess that what I call "the own abnormality" is what Ricardo would call perversion as a way out of neurosis. Of course, the neurotic's longing for normalization is not the key point, the burning issue is the psychoanalyst's own longing for normalization, what Ferenczi called, long before Lacan, the analyst's resistances. Resistance to the monstrous, to the *deinon*. The bourgeois psychoanalyst is the one who, instead of honoring the deinon, the Dionysian, fears it. So, when Ricardo talks about neurosis, he refers to something that he defines in a very nice and precise way: "the idealized paradise of neurosis", which a certain psychoanalysis constructs. Neurosis as an ideal of normality and homogenization for all that is human. The ideal of a world of normal, cis, heterosexual and genital everyone: what the great Kosofsky Sedgwick calls the genocidal project of the West. A world where you and I would have no place, sweetheart, nor any of those who come dancing and singing in the Dionysian march of this book. Yes, a desperately boring world, which fortunately has no chance of being realized. But beware, wanting to do it does a lot of damage, as you and I know. Come on, pour me more wine. Ricardo speaks of a "bullying of neurotics against those who are different from themselves". I presume that he is referring in particular to the bullying of the bourgeois psychoanalyst, who "as a good omnipresent obsessive neurotic thinks he is Superman and seeks to 'listen' to the other under his own patriarchal and capitalist neurotic structuring" and who does not listen to the other "because the singularity of the another does not happen to him". Are we familiar with that bullying! But luckily, and because of so many fights, and because we are in the right time, we, the monsters that transfer to each other, learned to hit back, right? Between WeOthers, as Ricardo would write.

Look at this sentence: "perversion helps to break the a-historical categorical rigidity of a certain analysis and a certain philosophy; let us always keep in mind the monster Preciado and his speech". I think that in this sentence, perversion is (happily) very far from the psychoanalytic concept, that bastard concept that I would throw away in the same trunk of psychoanalysts in which Ricardo wants to keep the neurosis-normality. In this phrase "perversion" is synonymous with the LGBTQ+ liberation movement, of all the voices that have been saying enough, we are here, we exist, we are not going to shut up. Although it is not mentioned so many times, I feel that the Preciado monster and his intervention before the bourgeois psychoanalysts fly over the entire book and the idea of the monster that we all are. The monster thing is also against Aristotle and the many Aristotelians, but I'll explain that to you another day.

I read you a sentence that I understand goes to the core of what the book seeks. He says that if we rethink the human keeping up with the times "what we are is understood in another way and our enjoyment opens as a Yes in the midst of the No of the Labyrinth of Capitalism that intends to imprison us under categories that are absolutely exhausted". A big Yes to Dionysos and Ariadne. The phrase, and it immediately evoked one of the most beautiful *yesses* I know, let me read it to you:

… Or that abysmal torrent O and the sea the crimson sea sometimes like fire and the glorious sunsets and the fig trees in the gardens of the Alameda yes

and all those strange alleys and the houses in pink and blue and yellow and the rose gardens and the jasmines and the geraniums and the prickly pears and the Gibraltar of my childhood when I was a flower of the mountain yes when I put a rose in my hair like Andalusian girls did or will I wear a red one yes and how he kissed me together to the Moorish wall and I thought it would be the same for him as anyone else and then I asked him with my eyes to ask me again yes and then he asked me if I wanted yes to say yes my flower of the mountain and at first I held him in my arms yes and I pressed him against me so that he could feel my breasts all perfume yes and his heart seemed out of control and yes I said yes I want Yes.

What a symphonic ending! Did you recognize it? It is the end of Joyce's *Ulysses*, another monster. You didn't know him! What happiness to have been the one who made you meet him!

In the book there is also a long and deep debate about Hegel, about the different Hegels, Žižek's and Butler's, especially, but, in those debates, I listened like someone who is having dinner for the first time at the house of his new boyfriend and he does not understand what the new political family is talking about, although he understands that something important is being said.

Well, I won't talk to you anymore, without realizing it, now it's late. Do you remember the *Children's Scenes* we heard the other day? Do you remember that the last one was like something apart; as if, instead of being 13 scenes, Schumann had written 12 plus an epilogue? Wait until we put it on. It is so simple and perfect. Always by Argerich, when you've heard it performed by her you don't want to hear any other version, all the others seem clumsy or lying. Do you know what this scene is called? *The poet speaks.* I thought of playing with that title for the epilogue that Ricardo asked me for and to call it *The psychoanalyst speaks.* After all, you can't expect me to get involved in the philosophical debate, but as a psychoanalyst, and especially as a queer mutant psychoanalyst, I could say something.

Well, I'll shut up, I can no longer resist tightening the rope, at this point in the night your beauty wins, I surrender happily to my defeat. Come, sit here, by my side, let's call on Eros again. And again and again.

Notes

1 "This whole life is not contained in love in the same way as it is in this sum of many particular and isolated feelings; in love, life is present as a duplicate of itself and as a single and unified self." Hegel, GWF, "Love". (Nohl, pp. 378–382) https://www.marxists.org/reference/archive/hegel/works/love/index.htm

2 Shelley, M., *Frankenstein or the Modern Prometheus*, The Project Gutenberg eBook of Frankenstein.

3 The verb "analyse" already appears in "Preliminary communication (1893)", p. 7 in "The mechanism of hysterical phenomena", *The Standard Edition of the Complete Psychological Works of Sigmund Freud*, Volume III, Vintage Books, London, 2001. Freud used the expression "psychical analysis" in his first work on "The Neuro-psychoses of Defense" (1893–1899) of the same Volume III p. 47; in that same article he also used "psychological analysis" (pp. 53, 59, 60) and the verb "to hypnotize" appears on p. 3 "On the psychical mechanism of hysterical phenomena: preliminary communication" (1893). The term "psychoanalysis" was coined later, in his work "Heredity and the Aetiology of the Neuroses" (1896), Volume III, p.151. The case of "Mrs. Emmy von N. (40 years old, from Livonia) (Freud)", in *The Standard Edition of the Complete Psychological Works of Sigmund Freud*, Volume II, *Studies on Hysteria*, Vintage Books, London, states on p. 7: "...A highly complicated case of hysteria was analysed in this way, and the symptoms, which sprang from separate causes, were separately removed."

4 See, Freud, S., "The Neuro-psychoses of defence (1896)", in *The Standard Edition of the Complete Psychological Works of Sigmund Freud*, Volume III. p. 272.

5 Freud, S., "Sexuality in the aetiology of neuroses", in *The Standard Edition of the Complete Psychological Works of Sigmund Freud*, Volume III.

6 "In our country, as in a large part of the world, the word *hysteria* is used to refer to the most diverse phenomena, attitudes, or forms of behavior (...) And, of course, in the psychoanalytic field: 'This woman is textbook hysterical'. 'This is a hysterical conversion', 'That is a hysterical character' (...) We see hysteria escaping from the field of medical repression to suddenly find itself trapped in that of religious repression". Mayer, H., *Hysteria*, Paidós, Buenos Aires, 1990, pp. 13, 15. It even became a European social phenomenon, especially in the bourgeoisie. And it is important to keep this in mind at the beginnings of psychoanalysis. And to observe how Freud behaves towards the matter and its seriousness. Let's not forget that even the first electric vibrator was invented in the late 1880s, by English doctor Joseph Mortimer Granville (he considered the use given to his invention was immoral, it was designed to relieve muscle pain). And the contraption was used to relieve symptoms of hysteria; in order to, on the one hand, stop the doctor from "working" so much with his pelvic massages in women or to achieve hysterical paroxysms (the doctor produced orgasms

in his patients to relieve their "illness") and, on the other hand, to enable the woman to pleasure herself through this object (which was much simpler, you just needed the money).

7 See, Freud, S., "Observation of a severe case of hemi-anesthesia in a hysterical male (1896)", in *The Standard Edition of the Complete Psychological Works of Sigmund Freud*, Volume I, Vintage Books, London pp. 25–27.

8 Ibid., p. 25.

9 See, Michelet, J, in *The Witch of the Middle Ages*. In chapter VI "The Covenant" the woman, now a witch, lives her sexuality in truth and not repressed. And Satan speaks to her: "You were mine from birth through your inborn wickedness, through those devilish charms of yours. I was your lover, your husband. Your own has shut his door against you: I will not shut mine. I welcome you to my domains, my free prairies, my woods." p. 88.

10 See, Lacan J., *Jacques Lacan Seminar. Book 23: The Sinthome*, Paidós, Buenos Aires, 2006. This Seminar is between 1975 and 1976. The very old Lacan defines obsessive neurosis as "the beginning of consciousness". Lacan, J., *Jacques Lacan Seminar. Book 24: L'insu que sait de l'une-bévue s'aile à mourre*, (unpublished). This Seminar is between 1976 and 1977. The Class is from 17 May 1977.

11 See, Freud, S., "Three essays on sexual theory. I. The sexual aberrations", in *The Standard Edition of the Complete Psychological Works of Sigmund Freud*, Volume VII (1901–1905), Vintage Books, London, p. 135.

12 See, Marx, K., *Elementos Fundamentales para la crítica de la economía política (Grundrisse) 1857–1858*. Volume 2, Siglo XXI, Mexico, 1997.

13 See, Espinoza, R., *Capitalism and Business. Towards a Revolution of WeOthers*, Libros Pascal, Santiago, 2018.

14 *The Sinthome: The Seminar of Jacques Lacan, Book XXIII, 1975–1976*. Ed. J-A. Miller, translated by A.R. Price. Polity Press, Cambridge, 2016, p. 21.

15 Freud, S., "Three essays on sexuality", in *The Standard Edition of the Complete Psychological Works of Sigmund Freud*, Volume VII. Vintage Books, London, 2001, p. 136.

16 Ibid., p. 124.

17 See Saiegh, R.: https://www.youtube.com/watch?v=dtOhhUm8Z2g (Madrid, January 25, 2014).

18 Little is known about Freud as a philosophy reader, but we do know he read Schopenhauer and liked it (among other things because he realized the radical articulation between human and sexuality). See, Schopenhauer; A., *The World as Will and Representation*, Volume I, Dover Publications, Inc., New York, 1966. And, Schopenhauer, A., *The World as Will and Representation*, Volume II, Dover Publications Inc., New York, 1966. It is a book from 1819 and a second edition corrected and enlarged in 1844; and a third edition in 1859 (Schopenhauer died in 1860). This book owes enormously to Schelling's less well-known book *Philosophical Investigations into the Essence of Human Freedom* of 1809. Schopenhauer always hid how much he owes Schelling as a philosopher himself, and, moreover, as he used him against his mortal enemy: Hegel. And it is Schelling who works on the unconscious operation of the will and hence his radical freedom.

19 Schelling, J.W.F., *Philosophical Investigations into the Essence of Human Freedom*, State University of New York Press, Albany, 2006. In this book, Schelling criticizes Hegel's *Phenomenology of Spirit* of 1807; he attempts to rethink his *System of Transcendental Idealism* of 1800 (which Hegel demolishes in his *Phenomenology*) and in it he proposes no longer a principle of identity, but a disintegration (*Un-Grund*) as an opening that delivers of itself what there is. It is the Unconscious inside and from its drive, that Schelling sees it operate from desire. It is interesting to show that

Böhme's influence on Schelling's thought was so great (especially with his idea of non-foundation, or an abysmal foundation that is the "basis" of the difference that constitutes God in itself) that the malicious Schopenhauer thought the writing on freedom was a copy of a writing by the "Shoemaker Philosopher". We quote a note found in the Introductory Study of the *Investigations*. It is a comment by A. Leyte and V. Rühle: "[…] Schopenhauer should not have felt very influenced by Schelling's work. In this regard, X. Tilliete collects in his work on Schelling of 1970, p. 538 "…texts from Schopenhauer's Naxhlass in which the author of the treatise on freedom is not presented as original. Indeed, according to Schopenhauer, Schelling's writing is a 'version' of J. Böhme's Mysterium Magnum", Leyte and Cortés, op. cit., p. 62. But if we read between the lines of Schopenhauer's writings, we cannot resist seeing in him a certain influence from Schelling (even from his "archenemy" Hegel).

20 See, Nicolás Román, S., "Entre el amor y la torutura: *Cleansed* de Sarah Kane", University of Almería: https://webs.ucm.es/info/especulo/numero44/cleansed.html

21 Hegel, G.W.F., *Phenomenology of Spirit*, p. 187 https://www.marxists.org/reference/archive/hegel/works/ph/phba.htm

22 Sierz, A., *In-Yer-Face Theatre. British Drama Today*, Faber and Faber, London, 2001.

23 ibid., p. 241.

24 Kritzer, A.H., *Political Theater in Post-Thatcher Britain. New Writing: 1995–2005*, Palgrave Macmillan, Basingstoke, 2008, p. 25.

25 It is a critic of *The Guardian* that can be found in: Vieites, M.F., "Dramaturgies of pain and barbarism in the face of 'spectacle'", in *First Act II*, 2002, No. 293, p. 36.

26 See, *Skin* played by Ewen Bremner and Marcia Rose. Produced by Tapson/Steel Films for British Screen and Channel 4 Films, it was filmed in September 1995 and directed by Vincent O'Connell. The script was written in the summer by Sarah Kane, *Skin*: https://www.youtube.com/watch?v=G2ZjplLullc

27 "Es NATURAL pensar que…". Hegel, G.W.F., "Introducción", en *Fenomenología del espíritu*, op. cit., p. 51.

28 "El ser es lo inmediato indeterminado". Hegel, G.W.F., "Sección Primera. Determinidad", en *Ciencia de la lógica. 1. La lógica objetiva. El ser (1812). 2. La doctrina de la esencia (1813)*, Abada, Madrid, 2010, p. 225.

29 "The definition with which any science makes an absolute beginning can-not contain anything other than the precise and correct expression of what is imagined to be the accepted and familiar subject matter and aim of the science." Hegel, G.W.F., *Science of Logic*: https://www.marxists.org/reference/archive/hegel/works/hl/hlintro.htm p.50

30 Kane, S., *Cleansed*, Methuen Random House, London, 1998, p. 25 https://kupdf.net/download/sarah-kane-cleansed-2000-pdf_58a3c01e6454a7df31b1e9cf_pdf

31 Barthes, R., *El discurso amoroso*, Paidós, Madrid, 2011, 397.

32 "Hegel wrote that the only thing we can learn from history is that we learn nothing from history, so I doubt the epidemic will make us any wiser". S. Žižek, *Pandemic. COVID-19 Shakes the World*, OR Books New York and London, 2020, p. 3.

33 Hegel's text, never quoted by anyone; is at the base of Marx and his *18th Brumaire*, Benjamin, Žižek and so many thinkers of the 20th and 21st centuries; it is the famous text on repetition (*Wiederholung*) that mentions what is typical of history; and the important thing about the text is that it shows not only that we do not learn anything from history, but, even, that we do it in a more botched, farcical, stupid way, etc.; history repeats itself and what was contingent then becomes necessary: "Durch die Wiederholung Wird das, was im Anfang nur als zufällig und möglich erschien, zu einem Wirklichen und Bestätigten". "Rom vom zweiten Punischen Kriege bis zum Kaisertum", in *Werke 12, Vorlesungen über die Philosophie der Geschichte* (3. Teil, 2. Absch.: ", ad fin. [1830]), Frankfurt/M, Suhrkamp, 1970, p. 380. "By repetition that which at first appeared merely a matter of chance and contingency, becomes a real

and ratified existence". G.W.F. Hegel, *Philosophy of History*, Dover Publications Inc., Mineola, 2004, p. 313.

34 Lenin, V.I., "Where to begin?", in *Complete Works.* Volume 5 p. 13.

35 See, Espinoza, R., *NosOtros: Manual to Dissolve Capitalism*, Morata, Madrid, 2019.

36 *The Seminar of Jacques Lacan, Book XIV. The Logic of Phantasy.* Translated by Cormac Gallagher from unedited French manuscripts, 2002, Karnac, London, p. 167.

37 (p. 253) *The Seminar of Jacques Lacan, Book XIV. The Logic of Phantasy.* Translated by Cormac Gallagher from unedited French manuscripts, 2002, Karnac, London, p. 253.

38 "… the beating fantasy and other analogous perverse fixations would also only be precipitates of the Oedipus complex, scars, so to say, left behind after the process has ended, just as the notorious 'sense of inferiority' corresponds to a narcissistic scar of the same sort". Freud, S., "'A child is beaten'. A contribution to the study of the origin of sexual perversions (1919)", in *The Standard Edition of the Complete Psychological Works of Sigmund Freud*, Volume XVII, Vintage Books, London, 2001, p. 193.

39 "Se trata mucho más de una supresión que se ha de pensarse como un *Aufhebung.* La ecuación de los sujetos, … se deshace en el instante mismo en que encuentra su estatuto. No es que el pivote no sea conservado; simplemente, lo que se enunciaba en términos de ecuación se enuncia en términos de coincidencia y de encuentro. A quién hoy preguntase qué que son una coincidencia y un encuentro, el nudo lo esclarecería: se trata del anudamiento borromeo de una determinación real (el sujeto), de una determinación imaginaria (el individuo), de una determinación simbólica (el significante)" Milner, J.C., *La obra clara. Lacan, la ciencia, la filosofía*, Manantial, Buenos Aires, 1996, p. 150. Milner resolves the knot in the Hegelian way, because otherwise it doesn't hold and it would be Kantianism itself, that is, Miller dixit.

40 And she also brings the categorizations of Foucault, Derrida, Deleuze, Beauvoir, Wittig, among others. And Butler's beloved Hegel is always present in what is most typical of her thinking, which sometimes certain studies on the American philosopher try to hide, but it's impossible. Let's not forget that she received the Adorno Award in 2012 (the same that Habermas received in 1980, Derrida in 2001, etc.).

41 The article was published as: "Sexual indifference and lesbian representation", in *Theater Journal*, Volume 40, No. 2 (May, 1988), pp. 155–177. And in Italian, as a book, with the title: *Differenza e Indifferenza Sexy. Per l'elaborazione di tm pensiero lesbico,* Festro Strumenti, Florence, 1989.

42 De Lauretis, T., "*Differences. Stages of a Path through Feminism*", Hours and Hours, Madrid, 2000, p. 91.

43 For two examples: Jorge Nico Reitter and Fabrice Bourlez. The first, from Argentina, published a very important work entitled: *Oedipus Gay: Heteronormativity and Psychoanalysis* (Second Edition), Letra Viva, Buenos Aires, 2019. And the second from France published: *Queer psychanalyse. Clinique mineur et déconstructions du genre*, Ed. Hermann, Paris, 2018. They are two really valuable works due to the current relevance of the subject and because of the need to rethink psychoanalysis from within itself, that is, the clinic. Reitter is very clear about how he arrives at his book and his position as an analyst: "Theoretical production in psychoanalysis does not usually arise from pure and disinterested science (if any science does): it includes the subject and his desire. This book is the journey, the product and the testimony of a sustained and intense subjective work (and a painful mourning) to resolve issues that no psychoanalysis could resolve. Therefore, although most of what it says is transferable to other forms of sexual diversity, it is especially focused on the gay issue". Reitter, J.N., *Oedipus Gay: Heteronormativity and Psychoanalysis*, op. cit., p. 11.

44 Butler, J., *Bodies that Matter*, p. 236: https://warwick.ac.uk/fac/arts/english/currentstudents/postgraduate/masters/modules/femlit/bodies-that-matter.pdf.

45 See, Espinoza, R., *Nietzsche: Pagan Ideology*, Akal, Madrid, 2024.

46 "…In effect, let us try to put an order, a measure, into what is involved in the sexual act in so far as it has a relation with the function of repetition. Well then, it leaps to the eye, not that it is not known, since the Oedipus complex is known from the beginning, but that people are not able to recognise what that means, namely, that the product of repetition, in the sexual act qua act, namely, in so far as we participate in it as subjected to what is signifying in it, has its impact, in other words, in the fact that the subject that we are is opaque, that it has an unconscious" (pp. 130–131). *The Seminar of Jacques Lacan, Book XIV. The Logic of Phantasy*. Translated by Cormac Gallagher from unedited French manuscripts, 2002, Karnac, London.

47 Sade later published another version: *The New Justina or the Misfortunes of the Virtue* in 1797.

48 Marquis de Sade, "The misfortunes of virtue", p. 4: https://altexploit.files.wordpress.com/2017/07/4322115-marquis-de-sade-justine-in-english-translation.pdf

49 "El desencadenamiento de las pasiones está en juego y el desencadenamiento de las pasiones es el bien, que jamás puede estar subordinado a la fría utilidad de las leyes y al cual las están hechas para servir. El desencadenamiento de las pasiones es el único bien, -esto es lo que tenía que decir-. Desde el momento en que la razón ya no es divina, no hay Dios", Bataille. G., "Sade y la moral", in *Marqués de Sade. Obras Selectas*, C. S. Ediciones, Buenos Aires, 2005, p. 14.

50 Deleuze, G., *The Desert Island and Other Texts*, pp. 254–255: https://monoskop.org/File:Deleuze_Gilles_Desert_Islands_and_Other_Texts_1953-1974.pdf

51 Nietzsche, F., *So Spoke Zarathustra*: https://www.logoslibrary.org/nietzsche/zarathustra/56.html.

52 See Little, M., *Psychotic Anxieties and Containment. A Personal Record of an Analysis with Winnicott*, Jason Aronson Inc., London, 2000.

53 Winnicott, D.W., "The psychology of madness", in *Psychoanalytic Explorations*, H. Karnac (Books) Ltd, London, 1989, p. 125.

54 Preciado, Paul B., *Yo soy el monstruo que os habla*, Anagram, Barcelona, 2020, p. 104.

55 Klein, M., "A contribution to the psychogenesis of manic-depressive states", *Int. J. Psychoanal.* 170(16) (1935): pp. 145–174 at p. 170.

56 Winnicott, D.W., "The psychology of madness", in *Psychoanalytic Explorations*, H. Karnac (Books), London, 1989, p. 122.

57 Bosch painted *The Ship of Fools* between 1503 and 1504; it is a late work of the great master. And you can see that it is inspired by the German satirical book *Ship of Fools* by Sebastian Brant published in Basel in 1494. And both the book and the painting are allegorical and exemplary of that time. The foolish, the crazy are humans who have strayed away from the straight path that God's law imposes and whoever expresses it among humans, some king in power. It's a work that could be used as a normalizer of the perverse and which indicates to neurotics that if they do not follow that normative path, they will become the worst. Just as Rubin remembered about lesbians. The painting could be updated and called today *The Ship of the Queer*. Once again art and the artist at the service of normalization.

58 Kant, I., "The transcendental logic", in *Critique of Pure Reason*: http://files.libertyfund.org/files/1442/0330_Bk.pdf

59 Butler, J. "Melancholy Gender / Refused Identification", p. 5: https://web-facstaff.sas.upenn.edu/~cavitch/pdf-library/Butler_MelancholyGender.pdf.

60 Reitter, J.N., *Oedipus Gay*, op. cit., p. 21.

61 Nietzsche, F., "Beyond Good and Evil", in *Friedrich Nietzsche. Complete Works*. Volume IV. *Work of Maturity II*, op. cit., p. 437.

62 The myth of Ariadne is complex and has several variants. However, it can be understood in a triple moment of manifestation and always hand in hand with the god

Dionysus. Ariadne is Labyrinth, she is Lament and she is Dance. These are the three manifestations of Ariadne. The one in the labyrinth is the one left behind after she betrays Crete and its values and runs away with the hero Theseus who has killed, with her help, his half-brother Minotaur; and then she is abandoned by Theseus on the island of Naxos on their way to Athens. And in that mortal lament, from the top of the highest mountain on the island, she is reborn together with the god Dionysus in the very act of dancing. And from there everything that did not make sense or was mere emptiness blossoms and asserts itself despite the very finitude of all things.

63 "Oh, wretched race of a day, children of chance and misery, why do ye compel me to say to you what it were most expedient for you not to hear? What is best of all is for ever beyond your reach: not to be born, not to *be*, to be *nothing*. The second best for you, however, is soon to die". Nietzsche, F., *The Birth of Tragedy*, p. 34: https://www.gutenberg.org/files/51356/51356-h/51356-h.htm#THE_BIRTH_OF_TRAGEDY

64 "Perhaps truth is a woman who has reasons for not revealing her reasons?... Perhaps her name, to use a Greek word is Baubo?—Oh these Greeks, they understood the art of living! For this it is needful to halt bravely at the surface, at the fold, at the skin, to worship appearance, and to believe in forms, tones, words, and the whole Olympus of appearance! These Greeks were superficial—from profundity...". p. 77. Nietzsche, F. *Nietzsche contra Wagner*: https://www.gutenberg.org/files/25012/25012-pdf.pdf

65 Preciado, Paul B., *I Am the Monster that Speaks to You*, op. cit., p. 105.

66 Freud, S., "The uncanny", in *The Standard Edition of the Complete Psychological Works of Sigmund Freud*, Volume XVII, Vintage Books, London, 2001, pp. 245, 247. Heidegger uses the German term to translate the famous *to deinon* from Sophocles' *Antigone* (in doing this he removes all Dionysian tension from the term). About *to deinon* I will discuss in the section "Dionysus, the old Queer god". Heidegger ontologizes not only the Greek but the German; where Freud sees movement (and this is typical of him), a repetition that occurs in us, Heidegger sees what is typical of human beings (and therefore not dynamic), a human being elevated above the usual-familiar insofar as humans are articulated with logos. "Logos as gathering, as human self-gathering to fittingness, first transposes Being-human into its essence and thus sets it into the un-canny, inasmuch as at-homeness is ruled by the seeming of the customary, the usual and the trite". Heidegger, M., *Introduction to Metaphysics* p. 180: http://dhspriory.org/kenny/PhilTexts/Heidegger/IntroductionMetaphysics.pdf.

67 It is the virtual, in social networks, in that reality that we call Virtual Reality that... "simply generalizes this procedure of offering a product deprived of its substance: it provides reality itself deprived of its substance, of the hard resistant kernel of the Real – just as decaffeinated coffee smells and tastes like real coffee without being real coffee...". Žižek, S., *Welcome to the Desert of the Real*, p. 11: http://www.rebels-library.org/files/zizek_welcome.pdf.

68 "At this point we must widen the range a little. We succeeded in explaining the painful disorder of melancholia by supposing That (in those suffering from it) an object which was lost has been set up again inside the ego – that is, that an object-cathexis has been replaced by an identification. At that time, however, we did not appreciate the full significance of this process and did not know how common and how typical it is. Since then we have come to understand that this kind of substitution has a great share in determining the form taken by the ego and that it makes an essential contribution towards building up what is called its 'character'". Freud, S. (1923), "The Ego and the Id". *The Standard Edition of the Complete Psychological Works of Sigmund Freud*, Volume XIX, Vintage Books. 2001, p. 28.

69 Hegel, G.W.F., "First program of a system of German idealism", p. 22: https://philarchive.org/archive/FEROSP-4.

70 Cixous, H. and Derrida, J., *Lengua por venir / Langue to come. Barcelona Seminar*, Icaria Editorial, Barcelona, 2004, p. 100.
71 "If I had a little patience and if I wanted my improntus to continue, I would tell them that the revolutionary aspiration has only one chance to culminate, always in the discourse of the Master (death). This is what experience has robbed us of. What you aspire to as a revolutionary is a Master. You will have it". *The Seminar of Jacques Lacan XVI: From an Other to the Other*, 2002, translated by Cormac Gallagher from unedited French manuscripts, London, Karnac.
72 Butler, J., *The Force of Non-violence*, Paidós, Santiago de Chile, 2020, p. 231.
73 See Rose, J., *Why War?: Psychoanalysis, Politics and the Return to Melanie Klein*, Wiley-Blackwell, New Jersey, 1993.
74 See, Abram, J., *The Language of Winnicott*, Karnac, 1996; Ogden T., *Reclaiming Unlived Life*, Routledge, London, 2016.
75 Sacher-Masoch, L., *The Venus of the Skins*, Alianza, Madrid, 1973, p. 91.
76 It is in this *Seminar* that Lacan rebukes young people and points out that this revolution is changing one master for another; the slave will be, like a good "masochist", love par excellence. You can read the old analyst between the lines and it is almost a Seminar that deals with perversion and the ways of masochism (not forgetting, obviously, the sadistic oppressor); namely against Foucault, Derrida, Barthes, and all the young revolutionaries. Because they who were the ones who suffered from the power of the institution by rebelling will now be worse than the executioners. Basically, following Freud, sadomasochism of the master and the slave operates in revolution. And that is why Lacan recalls Sacher-Masoch 's *Venus in Furs*, that is, Wanda, the cruel lady, is a poor victim of the slave Severin: "Let's say that, in a way, as far as he wants it, the masochist is the real master. He is the master of the real game. Of course, he can fail. There is even every possibility that he fails, because he needs nothing less than the Other. When the eternal Father is no longer there to play this role, there is no one. If they turn to a woman, of course, to Wanda, there is no chance, the poor thing does not understand anything. But no matter how much he fails, the masochist enjoys anyway, so it can be said that he is the master of the real game". *The Seminar of Jacques Lacan XVI: From an Other to the Other*, 2002, translated by Cormac Gallagher from unedited French manuscripts, London, Karnac. And it goes without saying that Lacan's attitude is repeated today with Miller.
77 Benjamin, W., "Kapitalismus als Religion", in *Gesammelte Schriften*, Rolf Tiedermann-Hermann Schweppenhäuser, Frankfurt, 1985. ("Capitalism as religion", in Benjamin, W., *Works. Book VI. Fragments of Miscellaneous Content. Autobiographical Writings*, Abada, Madrid, pp. 127–135).
78 See, Espinoza, R., *Hegel and the New Logics of the World and the State*, Akal, Madrid, 2016.
79 See, Espinoza, R., "Auditory images", in *NosOtros. Manual to Dissolve Capitalism*, Morata, Madrid, 2019, pp. 212–237. The articulation of the image with the sound, and of the forms of sensations with each other, is essential to understand not only current art, but the human itself beyond poor caricature determinations of our sensations. "That articulation that can be seen explicitly masterfully in Richard Wagner and his *Tristan und Isolde* (written between 1857 and 1859 and premiered in Munich on June 10, 1865) at the end of its Third Act, when Tristan 'hears the light' before the arrival of his imminent death; and before his Iseult (his Other). And so, at that moment, the meanings articulate with each other and overlap (in fact, they always were) with each other: 'Wie, hör ich das Licht? / Die Leuchte, ha! / Die Leuchte verlisch / Zu ihr! Zu ihr!'; this that seems impossible: to hear the light! (or see the sound! or touch the painting in front of you with your eyes!, etc.), an apparent chaos of sensations and senses, a

disorder in the analysis we make of what we feel, sometimes. Some philosophers have thought of it explicitly, such as Zubiri in his *Sentient Intelligence* (1980) or Deleuze in his *Francis Bacon. Logic of Sensation* (1981), in art, in its theory, for example, with the brilliant Donald Kuspit in his text *Arte Digital y Videoarte*", ibid., p. 232.

80 Reynolds, S., *Like a Lightning Strike*, Caja Negra, Buenos Aires, 2017, p. 110.

81 Büchner G., "Woyzeck", in *Complete Works Georg Büchner*, Trotta, Madrid, 1992, p. 199.

82 Valéry, P., *The Fixed Idea*, Viewer, Madrid, 1988, p. 40.

83 Nietzsche, F., "Human, all too human", in *Friedrich Nietzsche. Complete works. Volume III. Mature Works I*, Tecnos, Madrid, 2017, p. 272.

84 Reynolds, S., *Like a Lightning Strike*, op. cit, p. 122.

85 "I am sad / I feel that the future is hopeless and that things cannot improve / I am bored and dissatisfied with everything". See, Kane, S., https://www.tdterror.com/up-loads/1/6/1/7/16174818/4.48_psychosis.pdf.

86 "You are not *Hispanic India black spanish* / *nor gabacha, you are mestizo, mulatto,* half-caste / caught in the fire crossing between the sides / while you carry the five races on your back / without knowing which side to turn to, which one to flee from". Anzaldúa, G., *Borderlands / La Frontera*, Captain Swing Books, Madrid, 2016, p. 261.

87 Ibid., p. 36.

88 Let us not forget Marx, who repeats Hegel. "Hegel says somewhere that all the great events and characters of universal history appear, as it were, twice. But he forgot to add: once as a tragedy and the other as a farce". K. Marx, *18 Luis Bonaparte Brumaire*, CS Ediciones, Buenos Aires, 1999, p. 10. Written by Marx in December 1851–March 1852. Published with his signature, as the first number of *Die Revolution* magazine in 1852, in New York (Seg. Ed. 1869, and Ter. Ed. 1885 by Engels).

89 See, Espinoza, R., *Capitalism and Business. Towards a Revolution of WeOthers*, Libros Pascal, Santiago, 2018.

90 Space can be understood from three structures that relate the points that constitute it: topology (next-to), affinity (in direction-toward) and metric (at distance-from). It is known that the topology (next to) can be, although it is not necessary, also affine (direction) and can lead, not necessarily, to a metric (distance), however, with respect to topology, not all topology is continuous, it is also discontinuous and discrete. And to understand the human today we can no longer understand it from a continuous topological geometry. "It is not necessary that every topological space -that being next to- be always continuous. No way. Let us call this character continuity to express a little the generic idea, within which different types of what we call continuity, discontinuity, discretion are inscribed". Zubiri, X., *Espacio. Weather. Matter* (new edition), Alliance, Madrid, 2008, p. 47. And also, space is not only continuous (with its respective variants), but can also be connected, compact, separable, dimensional. "Well, as I say, some points next to others. The a-join is a spatial conjunction that is either continuous or discontinuous, or discrete, connected or unconnected, compact or non-compact, separable or not, in different dimensions". ibid., p. 53.

91 See, Espinoza, R., *NosOtros... "despite" Capitalism and the Pandemic*, in El Salto Diario, October 23, 2020: https://www.elsaltodiario.com/el-rumor-de-las -crowds/us-capitalism-pandemic

92 The Etna Volcano, thanks to Hölderlin, is a metaphor for madness, for that psychosis that launches us into the Real itself; that madness of fusion through death, a certain death to what was in Ariadne's Labyrinth. The madness of "Etna" in which Nietzsche himself ended up sunk, but with the great difference that Nietzsche never wanted to jump into the void, he was a Dionysian, a dancer, etc. Nietzsche was very influenced from a young age by Hölderlin, by his poems and mythical-literary narratives. And

in Hölderlin's *The Death of Empedocles* (published only 1846; when Hölderlin was totally insane) there is one of the model bases for *Thus Spoke Zarathustra* and for the returning update of the myth of Ariadne and Dionysos, from the Lament not of Naxos but of Etna itself. "Empedocles, induced by his sensibility and his philosophy long ago to hate culture, to despise any well-defined occupation, any interest directed towards differentiated objects, mortal enemy of all one-sided existence, and therefore dissatisfied, unstable, suffering, even in really beautiful conditions, simply because they are particular conditions and they only satisfy him fully felt in harmony with everything that lives, simply because he cannot, with an omnipresent heart, love them and inhabit them, fervid as a god, free and extensive as a god, simply because, as soon as his heart and his thoughts embrace what exists, he is bound by the law of succession". Hölderlin, F., *Empedocles*, Hyperion, Madrid, 2008, p. 25. The beginning of *Empedocles* (Frankfurt Plan text of 1797) is to see Hölderlin and his madness. And it's like that impossible fusion articulation that Klein shows in month-old children with respect to their mother. And that then drags, like that of a living dead, because the child does not exist.

93 Ibid., p. 256.
94 "... my conviction that patriarchy, or gender relationship based on inequality, is the most archaic and permanent political structure of humanity". Segato, E., *The War against Women*, Prometeo, Libros/Lom, Santiago de Chile, 2020, p. 17.
95 Preciado, Paul B., *I Am the Monster that Speaks to You*, op. cit., p. 18–19.
96 Hegel, G.W.F., *Faith and Knowledge*, New Library, Madrid, 2000.
97 Žižek, S., *Sex and the Failure of the Absolute*, Paidós, Barcelona, 2020, p. 155.
98 See, Espinoza, R., "Dionysus, the Queer god", in *Eidos*, No. 34, 2020, pp. 292–321.
99 Espinoza, R., *Nietzsche: Pagan Ideology*, Akal, Madrid, 2024.
100 "Nature is either 'less than nothing' or simply another 'Monster' of the Labyrinth of Modernity; and it has to be 'less than nothing' because it cannot respond to anything that has to do with nothing, that is, with the metaphysical-theological nature of medieval and modern Europe. Espinoza, R., "'Nature'... another monster from the Labyrinth of Modernity that persecutes us...", in *Periferia Magazine. Christianity Postmodernity Globalization*, No. 8, 2021, pp. 50–63.
101 DiPietro, P., "Neither human, nor animal, nor monster: The decolonization of the transgender body", in *Eidos*, No. 34, 2020, p. 255.
102 "γνώσετ αι δὲ τὸν Διὸς Διόνυσον, ὅσπ ἔφυκεν _ ἐν τέλει θεός, δεινότ ατος, ἀνθρώ ποισι δ᾽ ἤπ ιώτ ατος". Euripides, *The Bacchae*, pp. 859–860.
103 Schelling, F.W.J., *Philosophie de la Revelation. Livre II*, PUF, Paris, 1991, p. 349.
104 And therefore we should rethink that poem by Hölderlin entitled *The Only One* (1801–1803); where the great German poet generates a synthesis between paganism (Dionysos) and Christianity (Jesus) via the mythical figure of Hercules, as the masculine giant of force that realizes and tames the primitive of the myth. See, Hölderlin, F., "Der Einzige" (two versions), *in Hölderlin Werke. Auswahl in zwei Bänden*, Deutsche Verlag-Anstalt, Stuttgart Berlin Leipzig, 1930, pp. 256–263. Hölderlin, F., "The only one" (two versions), in *Hölderlin. Complete Poetry. Bilingual edition*, Editions 29, Barcelona, 1977, pp. 385–395.
105 Otto, W., *Dionysus*, Herder, Barcelona, 2017, pp. 196–197.
106 Ibid., p. 193.
107 "Sexuality is not simply the content of the unconscious, understood as a container of repressed thoughts. relationship ... between sex and the unaware is not that between a content and its container. Or that between some primary, raw being, and repression (and other operations) performed on it. unconscious ... is a thought process, and it is, sexualized from within, so to say. unconscious ... is not sexual because of the dirty

thoughts it may contain or hide, but because of how it works". Ruda, F. and Hamza, A., "Interview with Alenka Zupančič: Philosophy or psychoanalysis? Yes, please!", *Crisis & Critique*, Volume 6, No. 1, 2019, p. 440.

108 Espinoza, R., "Dionysos, the Queer god", in *Eidos*, No. 34, 2020, p. 319. And this is well explained in my book *Ariadne. A Queer Interpretation* (Herder, 2023).

109 See Žižek: https://www.youtube.com/watch?v=HPWY8YXS_JA.

110 See Dollar: https://www.youtube.com/watch?v=C42F29T6bXQ.

111 See Zupančič: https://www.youtube.com/watch?v=9sybd4W3Xw4&t=262s.

112 See Kobe: https://www.youtube.com/watch?v=MtMjdebXYPY.

113 See, Butler, J., *Subjects of Desire. Hegelian Reflections in Twentieth-century France*, Amorrortu, Buenos Aires, 2012.

114 Hegel, G.W.F., "The first program of the system of German idealism", in, *Escritos de Juventud*, FCE, México, 1998, p. 219.

115 See, Espinoza, R., "Zizek's thought is possible today", in *Res Publica*, Volume 23. No. 3, 2020, pp. 331–340.

116 See some books that talk about Hegel, Žižek, S.: *The Sublime Object of Ideology, The Prickly Subject, Parallax Vision, The Fragile Absolute, The Most Sublime of Hysterics, Event, Less Than Nothing, Absolute Backlash, Sex and the Failure of the Absolute, Hegel in a Wired Brain* (as of the date of this text, there is still no translation of this book), etc. And not to mention that, in most of his books, which are many, Hegel is always present in some way, for example, when he talks about Lacan, about Marx, about violence, about sex, about politics today, about the COVID-19 pandemic, etc.

117 "In this context, the reading of Hegel that Žižek has proposed in *Less than Nothing* takes on some of the creative traits of a remix rather than an interpretation". Ripalda, J.M., "El punto", in Espinoza, R., and Barroso, O., *Žižek Reloaded. Politics of the Radical*, Akal, Madrid, 2018, p. 289.

118 On the death of Hegel, you can see this great video from the Círculo de Bellas Artes de Madrid (2020) where Félix Duque together with the doctor Juan Antonio Vargas show us the true cause of his death and why cholera was said. This was organized by Valerio Rocco. See: https://www.youtube.com/watch?v=pKSu6BP_0_U&t=2905s.

119 Spinoza, B., *Ethics Demonstrated According to the Geometric Order*, Editorial Trotta, Madrid, 2000, p. 81.

120 Lenin in his *Notebooks* of 1914 makes a great analysis of Hegel's *Science of Logic*. Hegel's analysis is so brilliant, when Lenin carries out the experience of reading him directly (without Plejanov), that a materialist Hegel has come from there until now, which has survived beyond the European philosophical Schools. And that also gave Lenin the vision of how to carry out a Revolution that would be successful and that would not end like all others, that is, in a resounding failure and in a great pool of blood of so many innocents, as was, for example, the Commune of Paris (March 18, 1871 to May 28, 1871). Lenin himself began to dance in the snow after his Revolution lasted a day longer than the Parisian one.

121 Lacan's Hegel was always Kojève. And from there he worked on it, which is why, among other things, Miller can't stand Žižek. Žižek's Hegel is not that of Kojève, which psychoanalysts have made Lacan their own, but, let us not forget, that when Žižek went to Paris 8 to do his doctorate with Miller he was already a Doctor of Philosophy. And his doctorate from Slovenia was on a materialist Hegel based on the *Science of Logic* to rethink psychoanalysis. Žižek's 1981 Thesis in Ljubljana is called: *The Possibilities of a Hegel's Materialist Turn in Psychoanalytic Theory*. Žižek, S., *Možnosti 'materialističnega obrata Hegla v psihoanalitični teoriji*, doktorska lecture, Ljubljana 1981.

122 Hegel, G.W.F., *Science of Logic. Volume II, Solar Editions*, 6th ed., Buenos Aires, 1993, pp. 559–560.

123 Hegel, G.W.F., *Encyclopedia of the Philosophical Sciences in Compendium*, Alliance, Madrid, 1997, pp. 117–118.

124 Lenin, V.I., *Complete Works. Volume XLII. Philosophical Notebooks*, Akal/Popular Culture Editions, Madrid/Mexico, sa, p. 99.

125 Naturally, the work devoted to such a study, such an interpretation, and such a propaganda of Hegel's dialectic is extremely difficult, and doubtless the first attempts in this direction will be accompanied by errors. But only those who do nothing are not wrong. Based on the way in which Marx applied Hegel's dialectic, conceived in a materialist way, we can and should develop this dialectic in all its aspects, publish fragments of Hegel's main works in the magazine, interpret them in a materialist way, commenting on them with examples of the application of dialectics by Marx and also with examples of dialectics applied to the field of economic and political relations, examples that contemporary history, especially the current imperialist war and revolution, offer us in an extraordinarily abundant quantity. The group of editors and collaborators of *Pod Znameniem Marxizma* magazine, in my opinion, should constitute something like a "society of materialist friends of the Hegelian dialectic". Lenin, V.I., *On the Meaning of Militant Materialism*, in *Marxists Internet Archive*, January 1, 2001. Corrected, January 25, 2013 (original text published in *Pod Znameniem Marxizma*, No. 3, March p. 192.

126 Some of Žižek's books on Lenin (or edited by Žižek): *Repeat Lenin, Lenin Reactivated. Towards a Politics of Truth, Uncharted Territories. Lenin after October, Lenin 2017*, etc.

127 Zupančič, A., *What is Sex?* The MIT Press, Cambridge, MA, 201, p. 150.

128 See: "Interview with Ricardo Espinoza Lolas: Hegel, the most materialistic of all", by María Luiza De Castro Muniz; Andrés Echeverría, Andrés Osório, Martín Aulestia, Omar Bonilla, Rafael Polo Bonilla, in *Social Sciences Magazine*, Volume 1. No. 42 (2020): Bolivar Echeverría. https://revistadigital.uce.edu.ec/index.php/CSOCIALES/article/view/2772.

129 Žižek likes Lenin's attitude, he never backs down and keeps going. "So if I say Lenin, I don't mean the Lenin of *State and Revolution*; I am referring more to that totally desperate Lenin who asked himself: 'My God, can we achieve it?' [referring to the book *What to Do?*], Espinoza, R. and Barroso, O., "Interview with Slavoj Žižek, or 'Do you want to be Slavoj Žižek?'", in *Žižek Reloaded. Politics of the Radical*, op. cit., p. 356.

130 Zupančič evidences this materialism of Hegel in the light of Mladen Dolar. She quotes and paraphrases it like this: "As Mladen Dollar has pointed out: direct opposition to a long (Aristotelian) tradition, aligning truth with the rule of non-contradiction, Hegel took a very different step with the first of his 'habilitation theses' (which served as the basis of his PhD defense in August 1801) when he said: 'Contradictio it regulates veri, non contradictio falsi'— Contradiction es the rule of truth, non- contradiction of the false". Dollar, M., *Fenomenologija duha I, Društvo whoa theoretically I Psychoanalysis*, Ljubljana, 1990, p. 20.

131 Žižek, S., *Less Than Nothing. Hegel and the Shadow of Dialectical Materialism*, Akal, Madrid, 2015, p. 7.

132 See some books written by Zupančič, A., *Ethics of the Real: Kant and Lacan,* Verso, London-New York, 1995; *The Shortest Shadow. Nietzsche's Philosophy of the Two*, The MIT Press, Cambridge, MA, 2003; *The Odd One In. On Comedy*, The MIT Press, Cambridge, MA, 2008.

133 Hegel, G.W.F., *Wissenschaft der Logik. Erster Teil. Die Objective Logik. Ernest Band. Die Lehre vom Sein* (1832), Hamburg, Felix Meiner Verlag, 1985, p. 68. Hegel, G.W.F., *Science of Llogic I. Objective* Logic, 1 Being (1812) // 2. The Doctrine of Essence (1813), Abada, Madrid, 2011, p. 225.

134 Hegel, G.W.F., *Science of Logic I. Objective Logic, 1 Being (1812) // 2. The Doctrine of Essence (1813)*, Abada, Madrid, 2011, p. 225.

135 Hegel, G.W.F., "Die Lehre vom Wesen", in *Wissenschaft der Logik. Ernest Band. Die objektive Logik (1812–1813)*, Felix Meiner Verlag, Hamburg, 1978, p. 241.

136 "Being is immediate. Insofar as knowledge wants to know what is true, what being is in and for itself, it does not stand still for what is immediate and its determinations, but rather goes through it from part to part. with the presupposition that behind this being there is still something other than being itself, and that this background constitutes the truth of being. This knowledge is mediate knowledge". Hegel, G.W.F., *Science of Logic I. Objective Logic, 1 Being (1812) // 2. The Doctrine of Essence (1813)*, op. cit., p. 437.

137 Interview with Paul B. Preciado, by Jesús Carrillo. At https://www.scielo. br / scielo. php?script = sci_arttext&pid =S0104-83332007000100016.

138 Žižek, S., *Absolute Backlash*, op. cit., p. 215.

139 "Der Begriff zeigt yeah obenhin betractet, als die Einheit des Seyns und Wesens. Das Wesen ist die erste Negation des Seyns, das dadurch zum Schein geworde ist, der Begriff ist die zweyte, oder die Negation dieser Negation; also das wiederhergestellte Seyn, aber als die unendliche Vermittlung und Negativität desselben in sich selbst". Hegel, G.W.F., *Wissenschaft der Logik. Zweiter Band. Die Subjective Logik (1816)*, Felix Meiner Verlag, Hamburg, 1981, p. 29.

140 Butler, J., *The Disputed Gender*, Paidós, Barcelona, 2007, p. 48.

141 See, Espinoza, R., "Introduction. A possible history from the beginning", *Hegel and the New Logics of the World and the State*, Akal, Madrid, 2016, pp. 31–62.

142 Butler, J., *Bodies that Matter. On the Material and Discursive Limits of 'Sex'*, Paidós, Buenos Aires, 2002, p. 19.

143 Hegel, G.W.F., *Wissenschaft der Logik. Zweiter Band. Die Subjective Logik (1816)*, Felix Meiner Verlag, 1981, p. 11. "On this side, we must see for now the concept, in short, as the third with respect to being and essence, to the immediate and to reflection. To that extent, being and essence are the moments of his becoming, while he is the foundation and truth of those, being the identity in which they have fallen, and in which they are contained". Hegel, G.W.F., *Science of Logic. Volume II: Subjective Logic. 3. The Doctrine of the Concept (1816)*, Abada, Madrid, 2016, p. 125.

144 Hegel, G.W.F., *Wissenschaft right Logik. Zweiter Band. Die Subjective Logik (1816)*, op. cit., p. 33.

145 Hegel, G.W.F., *Science of Logic. Volume II: Subjective Logic. 3. The Doctrine of the Concept (1816)*, op. cit., p. 151.

146 Butler, J. *Bodies that Matter*, Op. cit., p. 278.

147 Hegel, G.W.F., *Wissenschaft der Logik. Zweiter Band. Die Subjective Logik (1816)*, op. cit., p. 12. "... the concept is the truth of the substance; and since the determined mode of relation proper to substance is necessity, freedom appears as the truth of necessity and as the mode of relation of the concept". Hegel, G.W.F., *Science of Logic. Volume II: Subjective Logic. 3. The Doctrine of Concept (1816)*, op. cit., p. 126.

148 Spinoza, B., *Ethics Demonstrated According to the Geometric Order*, Editorial Trotta, Madrid, 2000, pp. 61–62.

149 Zubiri, X., *About Man*, Alianza, Madrid, 2007, p. 466.

150 Butler, J., *Psychic Mechanisms of Power*, Cátedra, Valencia, 2015, p. 151.

151 Beauvoir, S., *The Second Sex*, Aguilar, Madrid, 1981, p. 247.

152 "We are just three friends who got together and that's it. There you have your Stalinist KGB-style troika again – you know, the communists were always organized as a troika, to liquidate people or whatever. It is strictly a troika with Alenka Zupančič, Mladen Dollar and me". Žižek, S. and Daly, G., *Conversations with Žižek*, Polity Press, Cambridge, 2004, p. 37 (translation of Camarena and Aguilar).

153 Zupančič, A., *What is Sex?* op. cit., p. 123.

154 Gómez Camarena, C. and Aguilar Alcalá, S., "Coffee without milk, School without a concept: features, operations and readings in the Slovenian School", in *Res Publica*, Volume 23. No. 3, 2020, p. 314.

155 See, the *Sentient Intelligence Trilogy of the Spanish Thinker*. 1. Zubiri, X., *Intelligence and Reality*, Alliance, Madrid, 1980. 2. Zubiri, X., *Intelligence and Logos*, Alliance, Madrid, 1982. And 3. Zubiri, X., *Intelligence and Reason*, Alliance, Madrid, 1983.

156 For example, this is seen in Lacan's criticism of Foucault from Heidegger's ontology in 1967 (and the category of Rejection psychosis is articulated as Rejection of being and that expresses the ontic of Foucault and his denial of the human as humanity): "In fact, being is so thoroughly excluded from everything that may be at stake, in order to enter into this explanation, I could say, that to take up one of my familiar formulae - that of Verwerfung - it is indeed something of this order that is at stake. If something is articulated in our day, which can be called the end of a humanism - which does not of course date from yesterday or the day before, nor from the moment when M Michel Foucault articulates it, nor myself, which is something that has been settled for a long time - it is very precisely from the fact that the dimension is opened up to us which allows us to discover how there operates - in accordance with the formula that I have given of it - this Verwerfung, this rejection of being". *The Seminar of Jacques Lacan, Book XIV. The Logic of Phantasy*. Translated by Cormac Gallagher from unedited French manuscripts, 2002, Karnac, London, p. 71.

157 In France there is something very interesting and worth noting, it is like an over-coding of one author over another, of a certain parasitic nature. For example, how many times are we chatting about Hegel with a Frenchman (or someone "trained" in France) and it happens that it was not Hegel, but Kojève, and the same thing happens with Marx, it was Althusser, and with Nietzsche, it was Deleuze. And in Lacan's case, it was Miller. Interestingly, this has always been the case in the history of thought: Thomists still think they know Aristotle, etc.

158 Zupančič, A., *Etihcs of the Real. Kant and Lacan*, op. cit., p. 22.

159 *The Sinthome: The Seminar of Jacques Lacan, Book XXIII, 1975-1976*. Ed. J-A. Miller, Translated by A.R. Price. Polity Press, 2016, Cambridge, p. 142.

160 Foucault, M., *Histoire de la sexualité 1, La volonté de savoir*, Gallimard, Paris, 1976, p. 120.

161 Ibid.

162 Miller, J-A. https://wapol.org/es/articulos/Template.asp?intTipoPagina=4&intPublica cion=38&intEdicion=13&intArticulo=2468&intIdiomaArticulo=1.

163 See, The Žižek Course at Birkbeck titled: "Is Surplus-Value Marx's Name For Surplus- Enjoyment?". Žižek, S., https://backdoorbroadcasting.net/2016/04/slavoj-zizek-masterclass-2-surplus-value-surplus-enjoyment-surplus-knowledge/.

164 See, Zizek, S., https://www.youtube.com/watch?v=REky3bRQfkc.

165 Miller, J-A., https://wapol.org/es/articulos/Template.asp?intTipoPagina=4&intPublica cion=38&intEdicion=13&intArticulo=2468&intIdiomaArticulo=1.

166 Little, M., *Account of my Analysis with Winnicott*, Editorial Place, Buenos Aires, 1995, pp. 21–22.

167 Miller, J-A., https://wapol.org/es/articulos/Template.asp?intTipoPagina=4&intPublica cion=38&intEdicion=13&intArticulo=2468&intIdiomaArticulo=1

168 Zupančič, A., *Ethics of the Real*, op. cit., p. 235.

169 Badiou, A., *Logics of the Worlds. The Being and the Event 2*, Manantial, Buenos Aires, 2008, p. 590.

170 Reading *Seminar XI Lacan's Four Fundamental Concepts of Psychoanalysis: The Paris Seminars in English*. Suny Series, *Psychoanalysis & Culture*, 1995, Richard Feldsteing Editor, Maire Jaanus (Series Editor), Bruce Fink. State University of New York Press, Albany, p. 17.

171 Hegel, G.W.F., *Writings of Youth*, op. cit., p. 220.

172 Žižek, S., "Taking sides: A self-interview", *Metastases of Enjoyment: Six Essays on Women and Causality*, Verso, London, 1994, p. 199.

173 "The best symptom of being lies is the almost zero difference between his saying and his saying or between his act and the mere fact of uttering it. From where a representation of the world history of philosophy arises. German idealism inaugurates a history of philosophy, a history that can be declined according to Slavoj Žižek in 6 stages. First, Greek prehistory, important but prehistoric. Second, a critical birth, with Kant. Later, two idealistic insistences: Fichte and Schelling. Fourth, a definitive dialectical matrix, in quotes, in Hegel. In a fifth moment, a creative repetition in Lacan of Hegel. And sixthly, a creative repetition of the creative repetition of Hegel by Lacan, namely Žižek", Badiou, A., "La méthode de Slavoj Žižek" preface to the French edition of: Žižek, S., *Moins que rien. Hegel et l'ombre du matérialisme dialectique*, Fayard, Paris, 2015, pp. 16–17.

174 *The Seminar of Jacques Lacan, Book XX, On Feminine Sexuality, the limits of Love and Knowledge*, Translated with notes by Bruce Fink. W.W. Norton & Company, Inc. 1998, New York.

175 Žižek, S., "Why 'Ljubljana School' remains faithful to philosophy", in Espinoza, R., *The Slovenian School*, Akal (in press).

176 Miller, J-A.: https://wapol.org/es/articulos/Template.asp?intTipoPagina=4&intPublica cion=38&intEdicion=13&intArticulo=2468&intIdiomaArticulo=1.

177 Žižek, S., *Less than Nothing*, op. cit., p. 627.

178 Hamza, A. and Ruda, F., "Interview with Alenka Zupančič: Philosophy or psychoanalysis? Yes, please!", op. cit., p. 438.

179 Let's look at two very early examples by Melanie Klein, one from Berlin (1923) and the other from London (1926). In both she already distances herself from Freud (and makes important corrections to his theory) and his patriarchal and closed hegemony over the subject and his Oedipus; finally, the objects appear and finally the mother is seen and from there something that founds Oedipus. And thanks to the fact that Klein had an experiential treatment of young children: "... we see that *identification* is a preliminary stage not only of the formation of symbols, but at the same time, of the evolution of language and of sublimation. The latter occurs through the formation of symbols; libidinal fantasies are fixed in a symbolic-sexual way on objects, activities and special interests". Klein, M., "Infant analysis", in *Love, Guilt, and Reparation*, op. cit., p. 104. "... for a long time the child does not consciously elaborate the interpretations. But I have been able to prove that this elaboration is really established afterwards. For example, children begin to distinguish between the 'imagined' mother and the real mother, and between the wooden doll and her brother as a live baby. So they firmly insist that they wanted to do this or that damage only to the toy baby; They say of course they love the royal baby". Klein, M., "Psychological principles of child analysis", in *Love, Guilt, and Reparation*, op. cit., p. 158.

180 Klein, M., "Early states of oedipal conflict", in *Love, Guilt, and Reparation*, op. cit., p. 214.

181 See, Miller, J-A., *The Experience of the Real in Psychoanalytic Treatment*, Paidós, Barcelona, 2011.

182 Canguilhem, G., *The Normal and the Pathological*, Siglo XXI, Buenos Aires, 1971, p. 231.

183 Miller, J-A., *The Experience of the Real in Psychoanalytic Treatment*, Paidós, Buenos Aires, 2011, p. 198. And Miller continues: "there was here and there a literature that sought to establish a community of readers in the non-sense, which was transmitted according to certain channels. And Lacan calls it into question, asking reasons for this literature for what characterizes it: 'Is it possible for the coastline to constitute a discourse that is characterized by not coming from the semblant?'. Not because this avant-garde literature is made of the coastline can it claim to prove anything other than the fracture of which it is itself an effect. As for the break itself, it cannot produce it, only a discourse is capable of doing so". It is a *Seminary* from 1998–1999.

184 Lacan J., "Lacan por Vincennes!", in *Lacanian Number 11*, EOL Publications, Buenos Aires, 2011, p. 7

185 Little, M., *Account of my Analysis with Winnicott*, op. cit., pp. 63–64.

186 See, https://www.youtube.com/watch?v=ai6zzNoVkJU.

187 Miller, J-A., https://wapol.org/es/articulos/Template.asp?intTipoPagina=4&intPublica cion=38&intEdicion=13&intArticulo=2468&intIdiomaArticulo=1.

188 See, Espinoza, R., "Joker 'contra'…", in *Le Monde Diplomatique*, October 21, 2019. https://www.lemondediplomatique.cl/joker-contra-por-ricardo-espinoza-lolas.html.

189 See, Dor, J., *Structure and Perversions*, Gedisa, Barcelona, 1995 (the French original is from 1987, six years after Lacan's death and, therefore, from the end of the 20th century).

190 ibid., p. 170.

191 Fonseca, C. and Quintero, M.L., "Queer Theory: the deconstruction of peripheral sexualities", in *Revista Sociológica*, Volume 24. No. 69, 2009. See: http://www.scielo.org. mx/scielo.php?script=sci_arttext&pid=S018701732009000100003.

192 Butler. J, Laclau, E. and Žižek, S., *Contingency, Hegemony, Universality. Contemporary Dialogues on the Left*, Buenos Aires, FCE, Buenos Aires, 2004, p. 148.

193 Copjec, J., *Sex and the Euthanasia of Reason. Essays on Love and Difference*, Op. cit., p. 33.

194 Miller, J-A., https://wapol.org/es/articulos/TemplateImpresion.asp?intPublicacion=38 &intEdicion=13&intIdiomaPublicacion=1&intArticulo=2468&intIdiomaArticulo=1.

195 Marty, E. and Miller, J-A., Interview on "Le Sexe del Modernes" (March 21, 2020): https://psicoanalisislacaniano.com/2021/03/30/jam-interview-sexo-de-los-modernos-eric-marty-1-20210321/?fbclid=IwAR1kYdOOz1fR8SMk5EUoXFXHmxf zbm-OMfZdyHOO4lx6-SE-hCieAbyNuxo.

196 Nietzsche, F., "The gay science", in *Complete Works. Volume III. Mature Works I*, Tecnos, Madrid, 2014, p. 802.

197 Nietzsche, F., "On reading and writing", in *Thus Spoke Zarathustra*, Alianza, Madrid, 2000, p. 74.

198 Foucault, M., *The Abnormal*, FCE, Buenos Aires, 2000, p. 49.

199 Deleuze, G., *Presentation of Sacher-Masoch. The Cold and the Cruel*, Amorrortu, Buenos Aires, 2001, p. 20.

200 Sacher-Masoch, L., *The Mother of God*, The Silver Bowl, Buenos Aires, 2010, p. 92.

201 ibid., p. 160.

202 Brazilian philosopher Francisco Verardi Bocca is one of the great scholars of Sade in Ibero-America and his reading is really novel, since he understands it from a materialist conception that is at the height of the knowledge of the time and shows a decadent State and in it the passions are the only thing that the human being can perform as a materialistic affirmation of life. See, the excellent book: Verardi Bocca, F., *Do Estado à Orgia. Essay on the End of the World*, CRV, Curitiba, 2020.

203 Klossowski, P., "Sade or the perverse philosopher", in *Marquis de Sade, Selected Works*, CS Ediciones, Buenos Aires, 2005, p. 376.

204 Zola, É., "De la moralité en littérature", in *Emile Zola, Documents litteraires*, Charpentier, Paris, 1881.

205 Ibid. p. 24.

206 "M. le docteur Duehren published in 1904… a manuscript by the Marquis de Sade containing one of his most audacious works. 11 s'agit des 120 jours de Sodome ou l'Ecole du liberlinage, manuscrit qu'on avait pris au marquis à la Bastille et dont il ressentit très vivement la disparition". Apollinaire, G., "Introduction", in *Marquis de Sade, L'Oeuvre du Marquis de Sade*, op. cit. p. 23.

207 "In the conception of investment, pathological points of view have been replaced by anthropological ones. This change is due to Iwan Bloch (1902-03)". Freud, S., "Three

essays on sexual theory", in *Complete Works. Sigmund Freud.* Volume 7, Amorrortu, Buenos Aires, p. 127.

208 Freud, S., "Fragment of analysis of a case of hysteria" 1905 (1901)", in *The Standard Edition of the Complete Psychological Works of Sigmund Freud*, Volume VII. Vintage Books, London, 2001 p. 136. And Freud adds a very complimentary note: "These remarks upon the sexual perversions had been written some years before the appearance of Bloch's excellent book (*Beiträge zur Ätiologie der Psychopathia sexualis*, 1902 and 1903)". Ibid., p. 51.

209 Apollinaire, G., "Introduction", in *Marquis de Sade, L'Oeuvre du Marquis de Sade*, op. cit., p. 61.

210 See, the excellent doctoral study by: López Villegas, M., *Presencia del Marqués de Sade in the cinematographic work of Luis Buñuel* (Doctoral Thesis), Universidad Complutense de Madrid, Madrid, 1997 (Thesis supervised by José Royo Jara).

211 Pérez Turrent, T., De La Colina, J., *Buñuel by Buñuel*, Plot Ediciones, Madrid, 1993, pp. 28–29.

212 "The influence he exerted on me was undoubtedly considerable. About The Golden Age, in which Sade's quotes were obvious, Maurice Heine wrote an article against me, stating that the Divine Marquis would be very upset. Indeed, he had attacked all religions, not limiting himself, like me, only to Christianity. I answered that my purpose was not to respect the thought of a dead author, but to make a film". Buñuel, L., *My Last Breath*, Plaza & Janés, Barcelona, 1982, p. 212.

213 "Days before July 14, 1789 and for having tried to revolt the people of the Saint-Antonie neighborhood, shouting through the window of his room that he wanted to slaughter the prisoners, he was taken out of the fortress and transported to the residence of the religious of Charenton-Saint-Maurice". Leley, G., "Biographical compendium", *Marquis de Sade. Selected Works*, Op. cit., p. 373.

214 Ibid., p. 31.

215 Marquis de Sade, *120 Days of Sodom*, p. 319. See: file:///C:/Users/howlr/OneDrive/Escritorio/Las-120-Jornadas-de-Sodoma-Marques-de-Sade-pdf.pdf.

216 Ibid.

217 *The Seminar of Jacques Lacan, Book XX, On Feminine Sexuality, the Limits of Love and Knowledge*, Translated with notes by Bruce Fink. W.W. Norton & Company, Inc. 1998, New York.

218 Tostain, R., "Essai apologétique de la structure perverse", in *La Sexualité dans les Institutions*, Payot, Paris, 1978, p. 33. And let's not forget that *Vers le pere* is the name of a book that is already a classic by Emiel-Maurice Guerry (a famous Catholic priest) 1891–1969.

219 Aulagnier, P., "Renarques sur la féminité et ses avatars", in *Le Désir et la Perversion*, Seuil, Paris, 1967, p. 79.

220 Ibid.

221 "Verse", Zizek, S.: https://www.youtube.com/watch?v=REky3bRQfkc.

222 *The Seminar of Jacques Lacan, Book XX, On Feminine Sexuality, the Limits of Love and Knowledge*, Translated with notes by Bruce Fink. W.W. Norton & Company, Inc. 1998, New York.

223 Miller, J-A., *The Real Experience in the Psychoanalytic Cure*, op. cit., p. 31.

224 Žižek, S., *Sex and the Failure of the Absolute*, op. cit., p. 402.

225 *The Seminar of Jacques Lacan, Book XIV. The Logic of Phantasy.* Translated by Cormac Gallagher from unedited French manuscripts, 2002, Karnac, London pp. 166–167.

226 "It can be said that the sexual act still drags with it, and will drag for a long time, that kind of bizarre effect, of discordance, of something that cannot be fixed and that is called guilt. I do not believe, like all the writings of the elevated spirits that surround us, that it is titled the morbid universe of fault, as if it were from then on conjured;

it is one of my friends who has written it, I always prefer to quote people I love. All this does not settle the question; having to deal with it for a long time yet, it would be enough to approach this universe around its faults which is a question of considering its status; the flaws are perhaps essential flaws in the structure of the sexual act". *The Seminar of Jacques Lacan, Book XIV. The Logic of Phantasy*. Translated by Cormac Gallagher from unedited French manuscripts, 2002, Karnac, London.

227 "The sexual act clearly presents itself as a signifier, firstly, and as a signifier which repeats something. Because it is the first thing that was introduced to it in psycho-analysis. It repeats what? The Oedipal scene, of course!. It is curious that it is neces-sary to recall these things which constitute the very soul of what I proposed to you to see in analytic experience". *The Seminar of Jacques Lacan, Book XIV. The Logic of Phantasy*. Translated by Cormac Gallagher from unedited French manuscripts, 2002, Karnac, London, p. 129.

228 Klossowsk, P., "Sade or the wicked philosopher", in *Marquis de Sade. Selected Works*, op. cit., p. 380.

229 "Lacan…or Worse". *The Seminar of Jacques Lacan, Book, XIX*. Edited by Jacques-Alain Miller, translated by A.R. Price, Polity Press, 2018, Cambridge, p. 14.

230 "Lacan…or Worse". The Seminar of Jacques Lacan, Book, XIX. Edited by Jacques-Alain Miller, translated by A.R. Price, Polity Press, 2018, Cambridge, p. 26.

231 Otto, W., *The Gods of Greece*, Siruela, Madrid, 2002, p. 8.

232 Žižek, S., *Sex and the Failure of the Absolute*, op. cit., p. 164.

233 *The Seminar of Jacques Lacan XVIII: On a Discourse that Might not be a Semblance*, translated by Cormac Gallagher from unedited French manuscripts, 2002, Karnac, London.

234 *The Seminar of Jacques Lacan, Book XX, On Feminine Sexuality, the limits of Love and Knowledge*, Translated with notes by Bruce Fink. W.W. Norton & Company, Inc. 1998, New York.

235 *The Seminar of Jacques Lacan, Book XX, On Feminine Sexuality, the Limits of Love and Knowledge*, Translated with notes by Bruce Fink. W.W. Norton & Company, Inc. 1998, New York.

236 Butler, J., Laclau, E. and Žižek, S., *Contingency, Hegemony, Universality. Contempo-rary Dialogues on the Left*, Op. cit., p. 308.

237 Miller, J-A., https://wapol.org/es/articulos/Template.asp?intTipoPagina=4&intPublica cion=38&intEdicion=13&intArticulo=2468&intIdiomaArticulo=1.

238 "Dionysus is always surrounded by women. The nurse becomes a beloved, whose beauty her gaze hangs in intoxicated fascination. Her perfect image is called Ariadne". Otto, W., *Dionysus*, op. cit., p. 193.

239 Ruda, F. and Hamza, A., "Interview with Alenka Zupančič: Philosophy or psychoa-nalysis? Yes, Please!", op. cit., pp. 434–453.

240 ibid p. 448.

241 Zupančič, A., *Ethics of the Real. Kant and Lacan*, op. cit., p. 235.

242 *The Seminar of Jacques Lacan, Book XX, On Feminine Sexuality, the Limits of Love and Knowledge*, Translated with notes by Bruce Fink. W.W. Norton & Company, Inc. 1998, New York, p. 93. I deal with this in detail in my book *Ariadna. A Queer interpre-tation* (Herder, 2023), in which I show everything that is happening with the feminine in these times, from the sexual to the political construction. A feminine as an expres-sion of the human and prior to the man-woman dichotomy.

243 See, Espinoza, R. "Una lectura 'desmesurada' de la ciencia de la lógica de Hegel: en torno a 'la línea nodal de relaciones de medida", in *Philosophica*, Volume 30, 2007, pp. 89–102.

244 Butler, J., Laclau, E. and Žižek, S., *Contingency, Hegemony, Universality. Contempo-rary Dialogues on the Left*, FCE, Buenos Aires, 2004, p. 131.

245 Žižek, S., *Sex and the Failure of the Absolute*, op. cit., pp. 156–157.

246 See, Schelling, F.W.J., *Philosophical Research on the Essence of Human Freedom and Related Objects*, Anthropos, Barcelona, 2004.

247 See, Žižek, S., *The Indivisible Remainder*, Godot, Buenos Aires, 2016.

248 Butler, J., *Undoing Gender*, Paidós, Santiago de Chile, 2019, p. 213.

249 Foucault, M., *History of Madness III*, Fondo de Cultura Económica, Bogotá, 1993, p. 148.

250 Freud's complete text is priceless; I copy the complete text, because it is obvious that after more than a hundred years it's still a dogma for many analysts: "There are also diagnostic reasons for beginning the treatment with a trial period of this sort lasting for one or two weeks. Often enough, when one sees a neurosis with hysterical or obsessional symptoms, which is not excessively marked and has not been in existence for long - just the type of case, that is, that one would regard as suitable for treatment - one has to reckon with the possibility that it may be a preliminary stage of what is known as dementia praecox ('schizophrenia', in Bleuler's terminology; 'paraphrenia', as I have proposed to call it), and that sooner or later it will show a well-marked picture of that affection. I do not agree that it is always possible to make the distinction easily. I am aware that there are psychiatrists who hesitate less often in their differential diagnosis, but I have become convinced that just as often they make mistakes. To make mistakes, moreover, is of far greater moment for the psycho-analyst than it is for the for the clinical psychiatrist, as he is called. For the latter is not attempting to do anything that will be of use, whichever kind of case it may be. He merely runs the risk of making a theoretical mistake, and his diagnosis is of no more than academic interest. Where the psycho-analyst is concerned, however, if the case is un-favourable he has committed a practical error; he has been responsible for wasted expenditure and has discredited his method of treatment". Freud, S., "On Beginning of Treatment (Further recommendations on the technique of psychoanalysis, I) (1913)", in *The Standard Edition of the Complete Psychological Works of Sigmund Freud*, Volume XII, Vintage Books, London, 2001, p. 124.

251 Little, M., *Transference Neurosis & Transference Psychosis*, op. cit., p. 84.

252 "Except for the ending, which is about Winnicott as a teacher, Part I was written from the point of view of the patient, a borderline psychotic. It contains few references to the practical and theoretical considerations that concern the analyst". Margaret Little refers to her Book: *An Account of My Analysis with Winnicott*, op. cit., p. 79.

253 Klein, M., "Early Stages of the Oedipal Conflict", *Int. J. Psychoanal.*, 9 (1928): pp. 167–180.

254 Generally gay and lesbian studies theorists violently reject the entire supposedly phallocentric approach to psychoanalysis, and I think with good reason. How could they not reject an approach that says they are sick, that they have not reached mature and genital sexuality, that leaves them on the side of perversion or of the "unhappy" solutions of the Oedipus complex? In my opinion, they are very right in their rejection, and at the same time there is much truth in the Freudian position of the phallus as the organizer of sexual jouissance. The issue is how to free phallic phase theorizing from the ballast that makes it heteronormative. Reitter, J.N., *Oedipus Gay*, op. cit., p. 31. It is this question of Reitter's that I attempt to answer in this book.

255 Freud, S., "Heredity and eetiology of the neuroses (1896)", in *The Standard Edition of the Complete Psychological Works of Sigmund Freud*, Volume III, Vintage Books, London, 2001, p. 151.

256 See, Anzieu, D., *Freud's Self-analysis and the Discovery of Psychoanalysis*, Siglo XXI, Madrid, 1988.

257 Hegel, G.W.F., *Phenomenology of Spirit*, op. cit., pp. 112–113.

258 Nietzsche, F., "The gay science", in *Complete Works. Volume III. Maturity Works I*, op. cit., p. 903.

259 "Aber ouch indemnity wir die Geschichte als diese Schlachtbank betrachten, auf welchem das Glück right Völker, die Weisheit right Staaten und die Tugend right Individual zum Opfer gebracht worden, so entsteht dem Gedanken notwendig auch die Frage, wem, welchem Endzwecke diese ungeheuersten Opfer gebracht worden sind ["But even insofar as we regard history as the executioner's bench on which the happiness of peoples, the wisdom of states and the virtue of individuals have been sacrificed, so *the question necessarily also arises in thought: for whom, for what goal has this immense sacrifice been offered?*] Hegel, G.W.F., *Vorlesung über die Geschichte der Philosophie, Teil I. In Werke 18*, Suhrkamp, Frankfurt am Main, 1995, p. 80.

260 "The goal, the absolute knowledge or the spirit that knows itself as a spirit has as its path the memory of the spirits as they are in themselves and how they carry out the organization of their kingdom. its conservation seen from the side of its free being there, which manifests itself in the form of the contingent, is history, but seen from the side of its conceptual organization it is the science of knowledge that manifests itself, one and the other together, the history conceived, form the memory and the ordeal of the absolute spirit, the reality, the truth and the certainty of its throne, without which the absolute spirit would be lifeless solitude; only (...) *from the chalice of this realm of spirits overflows for him its infinity*". Hegel, G.W.F., *Phenomenology of Spirit*, FCE, Mexico City, 1966, p. 473.

261 Hegel, G.W.F., *Faith and Knowledge*, New Library, Madrid, 2000.

262 Miller, J-A., https://wapol.org/es/articulos/Template.asp?intTipoPagina=4&intPublicacion=38&intEdicion=13&intArticulo=2468&intIdiomaArticulo=1.

263 Žižek, S., *Absolute Backlash*, Akal Madrid, 2016, pp. 212–213.

264 See,   file:///C:/Users/howlr/OneDrive/Escritorio/Jacques-Alain%20Miller%20-%20 2021-03-21%20Interview%20sobre%20Le%20Sexe%20des%20Modernes%20-%20 2da%20Delivery.pdf.

265 Miller, J-A., https://wapol.org/es/articulos/Template.asp?intTipoPagina=4&intPublicacion=38&intEdicion=13&int Articulo=2468&intIdiomaArticulo=1.

266 DiPietro, P., "Neither humans, nor animals, nor monsters: The decolonization of the transgender body", in *Eidos*, No. 34, 2020, p. 257.

267 Žižek, S., *Sex and the Failure of the Absolute*, op. cit., p. 169.

268 Žižek, S., *Less than Nothing*, op. cit., pp. 61–62.

269 Lacan, J.; "El atolondradicho" in *Ornicar?* No. 1, Paidós Biblioteca Freudiana, Buenos Aires, 1984, p. 37.

270 Fonseca, C. and Quintero, M.L., "Queer Theory: the deconstruction of peripheral sexualities", in *Revista Sociológica*, Volume 24. No. 69, 2009. See: http://www.scielo.org.mx/scielo.php?script=sci_arttext&pid=S018701732009000100003.

271 Fisher, M., "Why mental health is a political issue", *The Guardian*, Monday, July 16, 2012. See: https://www.theguardian.com/commentisfree/2012/jul/16/mental-health-political-issue.

272 Little, M., *Account of my Analysis with Winnicott*, op. cit., p. 91.

273 Anzaldúa, G., *Borderlands/La Frontera*, op. cit., p. 42.

Index

For Product Safety Concerns and Information please contact our EU
representative GPSR@taylorandfrancis.com
Taylor & Francis Verlag GmbH, Kaufingerstraße 24, 80331 München, Germany

www.ingramcontent.com/pod-product-compliance
Lightning Source LLC
Chambersburg PA
CBHW050611280326
41932CB00016B/3003

9 781032 440392